TEXTUAL SOURCES FOR THE STUDY OF RELIGION
edited by John R. Hinnells

Sikhism

TEXTUAL SOURCES FOR THE STUDY OF RELIGION

Zoroastrianism ed. Mary Boyce
Judaism ed. Philip Alexander

Further titles are in preparation

TEXTUAL SOURCES FOR THE STUDY OF
Sikhism

translated and edited
by W. H. McLeod

Manchester
University Press

Copyright © W. H. McLEOD 1984

Published by MANCHESTER UNIVERSITY PRESS
Oxford Road, Manchester M13 9PL, U.K.
51 Washington Street, Dover, N.H. 03820, U.S.A.

British Library cataloguing in publication data

Sikhism – (Textual sources for the study of religion)
  1. Sikhism – Sacred books
 I. McLeod, W. H.   II. Series
  294.6'82   BL2017.A4

ISBN 0–7190–1063–2
ISBN 0–7190–1076–4 Pbk

Photoset in Plantin by
Northern Phototypesetting Co., Bolton
Printed in Great Britain by
Bell & Bain Ltd., Glasgow

294.6
+355m

243167

CONTENTS

GENERAL INTRODUCTION

This series is planned to meet a fundamental need in the study of religions, namely that for new, reliable translations of major texts. The first systematic attempt to provide such translations was the monumental *Sacred Books of the East* in the nineteenth century. These were pioneering volumes but, naturally, are now somewhat out of date. Since linguistic studies have advanced and more materials have come to light it is important to make some of these findings of twentieth-century scholarship available to students. Books in this series are written by specialists in the respective textual traditions, so that students can work on the secure foundation of authoritative translations of major literary sources.

But it is not only that linguistic and textual studies have advanced in the twentieth century. There has also been a broadening of the perspective within which religions are studied. The nineteenth-century focus was largely on scriptural traditions and the 'official' theological writings of the great thinkers within each tradition. Religious studies should, obviously, include such materials; but this series also reflects more recent scholarly trends in that it is concerned with a much wider range of literature, with liturgy and legend, folklore and faith, mysticism and modern thought, political issues, poetry and popular writings. However important scriptural texts are in a number of religions, even the most authoritative writings have been interpreted and elucidated; their thoughts have been developed and adapted. Texts are part of living, changing religions, and the anthologies in this series seek to encapsulate something of the rich variety to be found in each tradition. Thus editors are concerned with the textual sources for studying daily religious life as exemplified in worship or in law as well as with tracing the great movements of thought. The translations are accompanied by generous annotation, glosses and explanations, thus providing valuable aids to understanding the especial character of each religion.

Books in this series are intended primarily for students in higher education in universities and colleges, but it is hoped that they will be of interest also for schools and for members of some, at least, of the religious communities with whose traditions they are concerned.

John R. Hinnells

ACKNOWLEDGEMENTS

A NOTE ON FORMAT

This work owes its existence to John Hinnells. I am grateful to him for the invitation to prepare these translations and for the tactful guidance which carried them through the editing process.

For assistance with problems of translation I should like to express my gratitude to Professor Harbans Singh, Maharaj Bir Singh, Professor Narinder Singh Duggal, Principal Parkash Singh, and Dr Surjit Singh Hans. In thanking them I must also free them from all responsibility for the actual selection of material, for any errors which remain in the translations, and for all that has been added as introduction and annotation.

Kevin Cunningham is entitled to the same grateful thanks and the same disclaimer. I thank him sincerely for having bestowed on chapters 3 and 5 the eye of a friendly yet critical poet.

For faultless typing under trying circumstances I thank Irene Marshall and Flora Kirby.

And as always I thank my wife Margaret for her patience and support.

W.H.M.
University of Otago, Dunedin

Because most of the text of the Adi Granth is metrical it was originally intended that the Adi Granth translations included in this volume should be set in the format used for English poetry or hymns. The same also applied to the selections from the Dasam Granth and from the works of Bhai Gurdas and Bhai Nand Lal. This, however, posed a problem. If these works were to be set in display the actual quantity would have to be significantly reduced. A prose format, on the other hand, would accommodate a larger and more representative selection but would obscure the metrical nature of the originals.

The dilemma was a real one because an attempt had been made to produce translations which scanned and which (it was hoped) would thereby communicate a clearer impression of the nature of Sikh scripture. The solution was to adopt the actual style of the originals. Whenever the Adi Granth is recorded in manuscript form or set in letterpress the text of each hymn runs through to the right-hand margin without taking a new line for each line of the hymn. The end of each hymn line is marked by the insertion of two vertical strokes (*do dande*). It is a convention which supplies a useful model, one which has accordingly been adopted in this volume. Translations of hymns and poems have been set in a prose format, with the end of each line indicated by a *do dande* symbol.

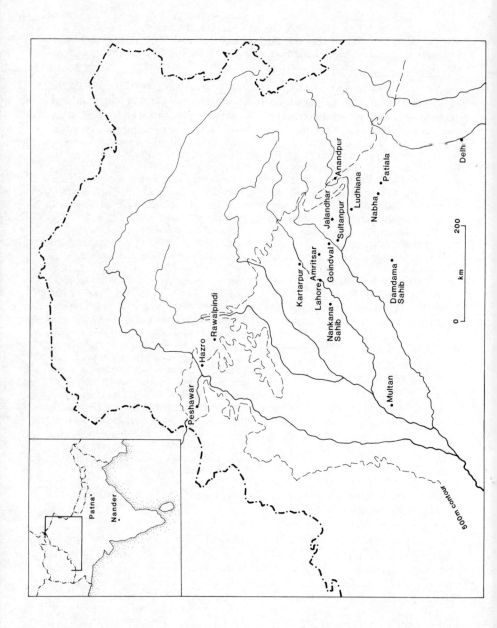

Delhi

Patiala

Nabha

Ludhiana

Anandpur

Jalandhar

Sultanpur

Goindval

Amritsar

Lahore

Kartarpur

Nankana
Sahib

Damdama
Sahib

Multan

Rawalpindi

Hazro

Peshawar

Patna

Nander

500m contour

0   km   200

1 THE LITERATURE OF THE SIKHS

1.1 A SURVEY OF SIKH LITERATURE

Sikh literature, like the faith which it expresses, begins with Guru Nanak. The first Guru of the Sikhs lived from 1469 until 1539, and it can be assumed that the community of his followers (the Panth) was drawn together during the early decades of the sixteenth century. To these followers Guru Nanak imparted his message of deliverance through religious songs of simple clarity and a notable beauty. The beginnings of the Sikh faith are intimately associated with these songs and although they were not definitively recorded until the first decade of the seventeenth century there is an obvious logic in regarding them as the founding contribution to Sikh literature.   *[1*

The pattern of devotion and instruction adopted by Guru Nanak was imitated by his immediate successors, with the result that a substantial quantity of distinctively Sikh hymns soon emerged. It was, however, a growth which posed increasingly serious problems of access and authenticity. The first attempt to record a single collection of approved works was evidently made during the period of the third Guru, Amar Das (1552–74).[1] This collection remained in the possession of the Guru's elder son, unavailable for consultation or circulation, and as the years passed an uncertain situation began to develop. How were authentic and approved compositions to be recognised? It was a serious problem because the leadership of the Panth had become a disputed issue and one of the rival claimants was issuing hymns which purported to be within the legitimate tradition. Ordinary Sikhs were confused, unable to distinguish between the authentic and the spurious.   *[2*

The problem thus confronting the early Panth was eventually solved by the fifth Guru, Arjan (1581–1606). A group of anxious Sikhs had approached him and had represented before him the serious problem caused by the increasing circulation of his rival's compositions. The need, they respectfully suggested, was for an authorised version, for a scripture bearing the Guru's imprimatur which could be safely trusted by simple believers. Guru Arjan accepted the suggestion and instructed his disciple Bhai Gurdas to prepare such a work (2.2.4). The collection, compiled under the Guru's supervision and completed in 1604, is now variously known as the Adi Granth, the Granth Sahib, or the Guru Granth Sahib (1.2).   *[3*

The decision was an important one for at least two major reasons. The responsibility which Guru Arjan entrusted to Bhai Gurdas produced a reliable version of some fundamental texts while providing the Panth with an enduring answer to a crucial question. By commissioning a careful compilation of the works of the first five Gurus at a comparatively early date he ensured the preservation of an authentic text. At the same time he prepared the way for a permanent answer to the question of ultimate authority within the Panth. For the first two centuries of the Panth's existence this need was served by the succession of ten personal Gurus, beginning with Guru Nanak and concluding with the death of Guru Gobind Singh in 1708. According to tradition the last of the personal Gurus decreed that after his death the authority of the Guru should pass to the corporate community (the Guru Panth) and the sacred scripture (the Guru Granth) (2.2.8 [23–4]). During the eighteenth century the first aspect of this doctrine was well suited to existing circumstances. Subsequently, however, it has been the scriptural authority which has proved to be particularly effective. [4

Because all orthodox Sikhs regard it as the eternal Guru the Adi Granth must occupy a position of primacy in any discussion of Sikh texts. It is 'the manifest body of the Guru' (4.4.3 [4]) and as such receives honour due to the Guru alone. In theory it shares this status and authority with a second scripture. In practice it stands supreme for the reverence it attracts and the attention it receives. [5

The second scripture is the Dasam Granth, a substantial collection associated with Guru Gobind Singh (1.3). Although it too bears the title of Guru most of it is seldom read. This can be explained partly by the difficult nature of its language and partly by the considerable attention which it devotes to tales from Hindu tradition. The latter feature has produced chronic controversy and largely accounts for the ambivalent attitude towards the Dasam Granth which still prevails within the Panth. There are, however, passages from it which command the highest respect and some of these are prominently incorporated in the daily devotional offices of the Panth. All such passages are attributed to Guru Gobind Singh (1.3 [3–4]). [6

A third rung in the scriptural hierarchy is occupied by the compositions of Bhai Gurdas and Bhai Nand Lal, two distinguished poets from the days of the Gurus (1.4). Bhai Gurdas's active life extended from the period of the third Guru to that of the sixth, and Nand Lal belonged to the entourage of Guru Gobind Singh. Although their works do not rank in terms of sanctity with the two Granths, they share with them a particular distinction. Apart from the contents of the Adi Granth and the Dasam Granth they are the only compositions traditionally approved for recitation in gurdwaras (4.5 [10]). [7

This distinction is an important one and its existence arguably confers on these four collections the status of a Sikh canon. There are, however, two other varieties of early materials which occupy positions of substantial influence in the religious tradition of the Sikhs. These are the janam-sakhis (1.5) and the rahit-namas (1.6). The janam-sakhis are hagiographic accounts of the life of the first Guru, most of them anthologies of narrative anecdotes and the remainder exegesis with a narrative structure. Ever since they first appeared (probably in the late sixteenth century) the janam-sakhis have enjoyed a widespread popularity in the Panth and although their period of sustained growth has long since ceased they continue to exercise a strong influence on popular beliefs.   [8

The rahit-namas record the Panth's distinctive code of conduct, the pattern of prescribed behaviour known as the Rahit which tradition ascribes to Guru Gobind Singh (4.2). Were it possible to demonstrate that any particular rahit-nama derived from the Guru himself it would obviously assume the status of a canonical text, for the Rahit is a feature of fundamental importance to the life of the Panth. Unfortunately no single text possesses such credentials. Although the earliest of them claim to record the actual words of the tenth Guru, none can offer an assured text. In spite of this difficulty the rahit-namas retain a considerable significance. A modern 'authorised' version, the *Sikh Rahit Maryada* (4.5), has won widespread acceptance within the Panth as an accurate statement of the Guru's intention.   [9

Occupying a lower rank in the hierarchy we find a succession of historical works, commencing in the early eighteenth century and continuing to appear intermittently into the twentieth (1.7). The earlier of these histories extend the janam-sakhi style to the later Gurus (particularly Guru Gobind Singh) and shift the emphasis from devotional to militant piety. Eventually they develop into more general histories of the Panth but without shedding their characteristic stress on heroism and destiny. This approach has produced works which properly belong to the specifically religious tradition of the Sikhs, defiantly expressing the sense of militant destiny which became so prominent within the Panth during the eighteenth century and effectively transmitting this same spirit to later generations. The influence of this vigorous, self-confident historiography is still vibrantly alive today.   [10

Finally there is the range of theological literature which, having begun to appear within the Panth a century ago, continues to the present day without significant change in style or doctrinal emphasis. Most of the books, pamphlets and newspapers which initiated and decisively moulded this tradition appeared under the auspices of the Singh Sabha movement or from individuals closely associated with it (1.9). The Singh Sabha was a reformist movement which emerged in the Punjab during the late nineteenth century in response to the challenge of Western culture and the evidence of serious Sikh decline. Literature was its principal weapon and the tradition which it so successfully established remains strongly dominant among the writers and intellectuals of the Panth. Marxism has been a rival, yet never to the point of seriously challenging the ascendancy of the Singh Sabha tradition. The reason for its success can be easily identified. The approach initiated by the Singh Sabha reformers represents a congenial marriage between the traditional and the modernist, one which has proved to be unusually lasting.   [11

1.2 THE ADI GRANTH (GURU GRANTH SAHIB)

For orthodox Sikhs the Granth Sahib is the Guru, and having witnessed the treatment bestowed on the sacred scripture one can scarcely fail to be impressed by the profound reverence which it commands (4.5 [9]). This reverence is expressed in many different ways. In a public gurdwara (and in many private gurdwaras) the sacred volume sits under a canopy. One must bow when entering its presence and sit at a level lower than its lectern. When not in use it must be draped and whenever it is opened it should be protected by waving a whisk over it. If ever a copy has to be moved it should be borne on the head, and if it is to be transported through a public place advance notice must be given of its approach. All Sikh rituals are conducted in the presence of a copy and devout Sikhs are expected to read a passage at least once a day. They are also expected to work their way progressively through its entire contents, and on special occasions an unbroken reading (*akhand path*) may be organised (4.5 [11]). [1

Three recensions of the Adi Granth exist, two of them accepted as authentic. A private family living in Kartarpur (Jalandhar District) possess a manuscript which is believed to be the original copy inscribed by Bhai Gurdas. At some stage during the late seventeenth century compositions by Guru Tegh Bahadur were added, producing what is known as the Damdama version. A third recension, the so-called Banno version, also supplements the Kartarpur text but in a manner which the Panth has long regarded as unacceptable. The standard authorised version is the Damdama text. The Banno text, stigmatised as spurious, is strictly proscribed.[2] [2

The differences which distinguish the three versions are important as textual problems, but none of them affects the structure of the Adi Granth. Guru Arjan's scripture is a remarkably systematic collection. A regular pattern is plainly evident throughout the volume and very few exceptions to this pattern can be found. In the case of the modern printed editions regularity is carried to the extent of maintaining a standard pagination. All editions have a total of 1,430 pages, and all correspond exactly in terms of the material printed on individual pages. The complete volume may be divided into the following primary categories: [3

Introductory section	pp. 1–13
The ragas	pp. 14–1353
Miscellaneous works pp. 1353–1430	

The introductory section records the following compositions:

1. The *Japji* of Guru Nanak, preceded by the *Mul Mantra* and ending with a stanza by Guru Angad (5.1.1). This work, which is regarded as an epitome of the teachings of Guru Nanak, is customarily recited by devout Sikhs shortly after rising in the morning. [4

2. *Sodar*. A collection of nine hymns, four of which are by Guru Nanak, three by Guru Ram Das, and two by Guru Arjan. The collection takes its name from the first word of the first hymn (a variant version of stanza 27 of *Japji*). The nine hymns together constitute the greater portion of *Sodar Rahiras*, a

selection which is customarily sung at sunset (5.2).   [5
  3. *Sohila*, or *Kirtan Sohila*. A collection of five hymns, three of them by Guru
Nanak and one each by Guru Ram Das and Guru Arjan (5.3). This selection is
customarily sung immediately before retiring at night and also at funerals.   [6

All the hymns which constitute *Sodar* and *Sohila* are subsequently repeated
under their appropriate ragas (including the one which has already appeared as
a stanza of *Japji*). Their appearance at the beginning of the Adi Granth
indicates that they had already acquired a distinctive devotional or liturgical
function by the time the original volume was compiled in 1603–04.   [7
  The ragas constitute by far the greater portion of the Adi Granth and it is
here that we find the characteristic pattern of division and subdivision. The
primary division is by raga or metre. First comes *Siri Ragu*, followed by *Majh*.
Next comes *Gauri*, then *Asa*, and so on through a total of thirty-one different
ragas. Within each of these ragas there is a secondary division according to the
length and nature of the composition. First come the hymns with four stanzas,
followed by those with eight. At the conclusion of this secondary progression
comes the *bhagat bani* (3.1.6). This comprises the works of various religious
poets (notably Kabir, Namdev, and Ravidas) which were evidently included in
the Adi Granth because the beliefs which they express correspond to those of
the Gurus. Yet another subdivision occurs within each of the secondary
categories. First come the works of Guru Nanak, followed by those of each
succeeding Guru in turn. At first sight it appears to be an exceedingly
complicated pattern. It is in fact a relatively simple one and it sustains an almost
flawless consistency throughout the entire raga section.   [8
  At the conclusion of the collection comes the brief epilogue, which comprises
a series of miscellaneous works. Prominent among these are selections of
couplets attributed to the Sufi teacher Sheikh Farid and to Kabir. The entire
work ends with fifty-seven couplets by Guru Tegh Bahadur, two brief
compositions by Guru Arjan (5.2. 8–9), and a cryptic description of the ragas
entitled *Rag-mala*.[3]   [9
  A final point to be noted with regard to the Adi Granth concerns its language.
Different authors produced distinctive linguistic emphases, but in general
terms the language of the Adi Granth can be described as Sadhukari or Sant
Bhasa. This language, closely akin to both modern Punjabi and modern Hindi,
was widely used by the religious poets of northern India during the fifteenth and
sixteenth centuries.[4] The entire collection is recorded in Gurmukhi, the script
used for modern Punjabi. As a result of its association with the Gurus and the
sacred scripture Gurmukhi acquired a considerable sanctity within the Panth.
Apart from modern works in English virtually all Sikh literature (regardless of
language) is recorded in the Gurmukhi script.   [10

1.3 THE DASAM GRANTH

Considerable mystery still surrounds the origin of the Dasam Granth, both in terms of its individual components and also the manner in which they were brought together as a single collection. Even its name involves uncertainty. *Dasam* means 'tenth' and is generally understood to indicate that the contents of the scripture are the work of the tenth Guru, Gobind Singh. There is, however, an alternative theory which claims that the extant collection is so named because it constitutes the tenth part of a much larger corpus, most of it lost during disturbances which occurred during the period of Guru Gobind Singh. [1

Although the Dasam Granth is commonly confused with the Adi Granth the two scriptures are in fact completely separate. There is no overlap in terms of content and the general tenor of the two collections differs considerably. The Adi Granth consistently stresses its patently religious message of liberation through meditation on the divine Name. In contrast the Dasam Granth is more varied in content, much of its interest focusing on legends from the Hindu Puranas and on anecdotes which appear to have little do do with religious belief. [2

The contents of the Dasam Granth can be divided into four groups. First, there are two works which may be regarded as autobiographical, or at least as biographical. Both concern Guru Gobind Singh himself. In the *Bachitar Natak* or 'Wondrous Drama' (3.2.3) the Guru describes his lineage, his previous incarnation as an ascetic in the Himalayas, the call from God to take human birth, and the early battles which he waged against neighbouring rajas in the Shivalik Hills. The *Zafar-nama* is a letter written in Persian which the Guru defiantly addressed to the Mughal emperor Aurangzeb. [3

A second cluster consists of four devotional compositions, also attributed to the tenth Guru, which dramatically express the militant piety so characteristic of his belief and example. These are the *Jap* (5.1.2), *Akal Ustat* (3.2.2, 5.1.3), *Gian Prabodh*, and *Shabad Hazare*. The *Jap* should not be confused with Guru Nanak's *Japji*, a mistake which easily arises from the similarity of their names and the fact that both are included in the early-morning devotional office. Together with *Akal Ustat* the *Jap* remains a work of considerable influence. [4

Two miscellaneous works constitute a third group. These are the *Savayye* or 'Panegyrics', and the *Shastar Nam-mala*, or 'Inventory of Weapons'. [5

Fourthly there is the substantial portion which includes legendary narratives and numerous popular anecdotes. Prominent among these are stories about the god Krishna and cautionary tales concerning the wiles of women. This fourth section contains the vast bulk of the Dasam Granth, covering in all a total of 1,185 pages in the current printed edition. The three remaining sections together occupy 237 pages. [6

The Dasam Granth has attracted little scholarly attention, with the result that the many problems which it raises still remain unanswered. The traditional answer to the question of authorship is that the entire collection is the work of Guru Gobind Singh himself. A more cautious view restricts his contribution to the first three sections, attributing the remainder to poets of his entourage; and a rigorous interpretation holds that nothing except the *Zafar-nama* can be safely attached to the Guru. None of these theories has yet been adequately researched. The question, like so many others, remains open. [7

An obvious reason for the comparative neglect of the Dasam Granth is its dominant language. Most of its contents are in Braj, the language of what is now eastern Uttar Pradesh. Although Braj was extensively used in the devotional literature of the period, it raises serious problems of understanding in the Punjab of today. This alone, however, cannot explain its neglect. As we have already noted there are certain portions of the Dasam Granth which continue to receive devout attention and most of these are in Braj. This attention concentrates almost exclusively on the first three groups described above, a feature which suggests that the nature of the fourth group constitutes a second reason for the neglect. It is in fact a divided response which the Dasam Granth receives. Whereas the collection as a whole ranks well below the Adi Granth in importance and usage a few of its constituents remain popular and influential. These include the *Jap*, *Bachitra Natak*, *Akal Ustat*, portions of the *Savayye*, *Chandi ki Var*, and the *Zafar-nama*. [8

1.4 BHAI GURDAS AND BHAI NAND LAL

Gurdas Bhalla, born in the mid-sixteenth century, was in some way related to the third Guru, Amar Das, and remained closely associated with the line of Gurus until his death *c.* 1633. During this period he served the Panth as a missionary, steward, and personal emissary of the Gurus; and as we have already seen he was chosen by Guru Arjan to act as scribe and amanuensis during the compiling of the Adi Granth (1.1 [3]). His enduring contribution, however, was as a poet and theologian. Apart from the Gurus themselves he was the first and greatest theologian to emerge within the Panth and it is fitting that his works should collectively be known as 'the key to the Guru Granth Sahib'. As a result of his reputation for piety and scholarship the respectful title of 'Bhai' (Brother) is invariably attached to his name. [1

The works of Bhai Gurdas consist of a series of thirty-nine lengthy poems called *vars* (3.3.1) and a collection of 556 briefer works known as *kabitts*. The latter are verses in Braj and are seldom read. The *vars*, however, are in Punjabi and are thus much more accessible. Although their poetic quality varies several are of a high order and as a whole they include material of considerable interest. Some of them are narrative works which relate episodes from the lives of the earlier Gurus or incidents which occurred during the author's own time. Many more can be classified as doctrinal or exegetical. As such they considerably extend our understanding of the Gurus' teachings. [2

Nand Lal Goya is a different kind of poet and although he is traditionally ranked with Bhai Gurdas in terms of formal status his works have been less influential. Once again language can be identified as a major reason for neglect. The authentic works of Nand Lal are all in Persian, a feature which has always restricted their circulation to a comparatively small elite. Punjabi translations exist,[5] but because Persian poetry stresses such mellifluous devices as assonance and consonance it is supremely difficult to translate satisfactorily.   /3

The interests which dominate the poetry of Nand Lal may also have contributed to their limited circulation. Although he was closely associated with Guru Gobind Singh his works lack the militant spirit of the period and it is perhaps for this reason that they were not included in the Dasam Granth. His approach is much more akin to the spirit of the Adi Granth, repeatedly emphasising meditation on the divine Name as the infallible means of deliverance. The most prominent of his compositions are his *Divan* and *Zindagi-nama*, both of them works of considerable length (3.3.2). The *Divan* is a collection of 61 *ghazals* (odes) and the *Zindagi-nama* a series of 510 couplets. Nand Lal adopted 'Goya' ('one who speaks') as a pen-name. After the death of Guru Gobind Singh he retired to Multan and died there in 1712.   /4

1.5 THE JANAM-SAKHIS

It is natural that Nanak, first of the Gurus and founder of the Panth, should have attracted a particularly devout response from successive generations of Sikhs. This reverence is strikingly embodied in the janam-sakhis, hagiographic accounts of the Guru's life which stress the divine quality of his calling and the many wonders which he performed.   /1

It is not known when the first janam-sakhi was recorded, but a well developed tradition certainly existed during the lifetime of Bhai Gurdas and finds poetic expression in his first *var* (3.3.1 [1]). During the course of the seventeenth century the janam-sakhis expanded and diversified. Their growth slackened during the eighteenth century, but a significant contribution appeared in 1823 when Santokh Singh completed his *Nanak Prakas*. A further period of growth took place when lithography was introduced during the latter half of the nineteenth century and by the beginning of the twentieth a substantial corpus of janam-sakhi stories had entered circulation. They retain a considerable popularity to the present day.   /2

Most of the janam-sakhis are collections of anecdotes concerning the life of Guru Nanak, loosely organised into a rough chronological sequence. Two periods which receive particular interest and attention are his childhood in the village of Talvandi and his travels beyond the Punjab. Various kinds of stories appear in anecdotal form (*sakhi*). Some are simple wonder stories, others point a moral. Many of them incorporate quotations from his works, the narrative component serving as a scene-setting device for a particular hymn or series of couplets. In some instances exegetical supplements may be added, with the result that narrative recedes still further as theological concerns advance.   [3

During the course of the late sixteenth and seventeenth centuries several distinct janam-sakhi traditions emerged. These traditions differ from each other in terms of their varying selections of anecdotes, their conflicting chronologies, and their diverse interests. The more important are the *Puratan* tradition, the *Bala* tradition, the *Miharban* tradition, a collection called the *Adi Sakhis*, and a late tradition known as *Mahima Prakas* ('The Light of Glory'). This latter tradition comprises two distinct works, a prose janam-sakhi entitled *Mahima Prakas Varatak* and the versified *Mahima Prakas Kavita*. Of these various collections the *Miharban* tradition leans strongly towards discourse and exegesis, the remainder towards narrative. An eighteenth-century work which draws from several different traditions and thus combines a variety of styles is the so-called *B40 Janam-sakhi*.[6] The various traditions are linked by overlapping choices of anecdotes, but the differences which distinguish them are substantial, and even within a particular tradition considerable variety can occur.   [4

The anecdotal form of the janam-sakhi seems plainly to be modelled on earlier Sufi examples which were still widely current among the Muslims of the Punjab. Several of the actual anecdotes, duly amended to fit their new context, have also been borrowed from Sufi sources. Others have been taken from the Hindu epics and Puranas, or from the Nath yogi tradition. In a few instances there appears to be an authentic incident behind a particular story. Other material which is native to the Sikh tradition has been developed out of suggestive references in the works of Guru Nanak, or from a complete hymn which serves as a framework for a discourse.   [5

The enduring popularity of the janam-sakhis is easily explained. They represent a vigorous and attractive prose style, one which lends itself to oral circulation and to presentation in brief instalments. It is a style admirably suited to its purpose and although the janam-sakhis have never been accepted as sacred scripture they occupy a position of continuing influence in the life and beliefs of the Panth.[7]   [6

1.6 THE RAHIT-NAMAS

From the earliest days of the Sikh Panth all who venerate the Gurus have been expected to live in a manner consonant with their faith. As the Panth developed certain features were spelt out in greater detail, notably those which related to the devotional discipline expected of devout Sikhs. There is, however, a substantial difference between the limited range which can be observed during the period covered by the first nine Gurus and the substantial lists of injunctions which are to be encountered during the eighteenth and nineteenth centuries. A significant change took place under the direction of the tenth Guru and during the tumultuous decades which followed his death in 1708.   [1

The code of conduct which emerged from this period is known as the Rahit (4.2) and the manuals which eventually appear as a means of promulgating it are known as rahit-namas (4.3–5). The crucial event in the development of the Rahit was the inauguration of the Khalsa order by Guru Gobind Singh in 1699 (2.2.8 [3], 4.1). Although many of the details are obscure there can be no doubt that this critically important occasion included an initiation ceremony and the issuing of a code of conduct to all who accepted initiation into the ranks of the Khalsa. It is evident that this code was subsequently augmented, but the inauguration ceremony conducted in 1699 has always been perceived as the key event in the emergence of a formal Rahit. Certain features such as the 'Five K's' are well known (4.5 [43]). Others are more obscure.   [2

Although the Guru did not write a rahit-nama himself there are several such manuals which claim to have been prepared at his command and to record his actual words. In no instance is it possible to establish such claims as authentic. The earliest extant rahit-nama appears to be a version which dates from the middle of the eighteenth century. This is the *Chaupa Singh Rahit-nama* (4.3), allegedly the work of a personal servant of Guru Gobind Singh. The next in sequence is probably the anonymous treatise known as the *Prem Sumarag*, a work which carries us into the nineteenth century. Other prominent examples include two brief rahit-namas attributed to Nand Lal (the *Tanakhah-nama* and *Prasan-uttar*) (4.4.1–2). Although their date is uncertain it would be very difficult to establish a firm connection with Nand Lal Goya. A similar rahit-nama is attributed to a certain Prahlad Singh (4.4.3). He too claims to have personally received his instructions from Guru Gobind Singh. Two other manuals following this style bear the names of Desa Singh and Daya Singh, both of them lodging the same claims to authenticity. A collection of injunctions which can probably be located towards the middle of the nineteenth century is the *Sau Sakhian*.   [3

As this catalogue indicates there were several different rahit-namas in existence by the latter half of the nineteenth century. It was during this period that the Singh Sabha reformist movement emerged within the Panth and one of its major objectives eventually became the compiling of a satisfactory rahit-nama, one which would accurately represent the Panth's understanding of the intention of Guru Gobind Singh. It proved to be a lengthy quest, but one which eventually achieved a notable success. A manual issued in 1915 having failed in its intention, another attempt was initiated in 1931. After a draft version had been speedily prepared a series of delays postponed its appearance until 1950. It was finally issued in that year under the title *Sikh Rahit Maryada* (4.5), a comparatively brief compendium which seems clearly to have answered the need for an agreed statement of the Rahit.   [4

1.7 THE GUR-BILAS TRADITION AND LATER HISTORICAL WORKS

During the course of the Guru period the nature and policy of the Panth underwent a radical change. The early Gurus had been religious teachers preaching the message of the divine Name and attracting little or no attention from the Mughal authorities of the time. Guru Arjan, however, died in their custody and his son Guru Hargobind adopted a more militant posture (2.2.5). This new policy receded after Hargobind's death in 1644, but it revived as a result of the execution of Guru Tegh Bahadur in 1675 and reached a climax under Guru Gobind Singh. In 1699 it was given institutional form in the Khalsa order and has remained a powerful impulse within the Panth ever since.   [1

The eighteenth century provided conditions congenial to an aggressively militant spirit and for Sikhs this is the heroic period of the Panth's history. Although the Panth was hard pressed by the Mughals during the early decades of the century Mughal authority soon crumbled and by the middle of the century warrior bands of Sikhs (the so-called *misls*) were bidding for control of the Punjab. The century eventually came to a triumphant conclusion with the unification of the *misls* under Ranjit Singh and his recognition as Maharaja of the Punjab.   [2

As the form and dominant philosophy of the Panth changed so too did its religious perceptions and the literature which gave them expression. The janam-sakhis continued to retain a considerable measure of their earlier popularity, but during the eighteenth and early nineteenth century a new approach to the lives of the Gurus appeared. This was the *gur-bilas* or 'splendour of the Guru' style, a treatment which exalted the courage of the Gurus and lauded their skill in battle. Inevitably its exponents concentrated their attentions on the two great warrior Gurus, on Guru Hargobind and pre-eminently on Guru Gobind Singh.   [3

Like the janam-sakhis the *gur-bilas* literature is far more important as a testimony to the beliefs of writers and their contemporary circumstances than to the actual lives of the Gurus. In a sense the tradition is an extension of the janam-sakhi impulse and style, both forms being clear expressions of devotion to the Guru. It was, however, a very different kind of piety which produced the *gur-bilas* and it was one which shifted the focus from the first Guru to the tenth. A more obvious antecedent is *Bachitar Natak*, the account of Guru Gobind Singh's early life which appears in the Dasam Granth[8] (1.3 [3]). Destiny is stressed, both the destiny which brought the tenth Guru into the world to restore righteousness and also the promise of the Panth's ultimate triumph. The means whereby these ends are to be achieved is the sword, for only thus can the power of evil be destroyed.   [4

The first example of the *gur-bilas* style to appear was *Gur Sobha* or 'Radiance of the Guru', a narrative poem attributed to a writer called

Sainapati. This work, which is variously dated 1711 and 1745, is significant in that it provides a rare testimony to the beliefs and traditions current within the Panth during the early eighteenth century. A notable example is the stress laid on the paramount importance of both the Khalsa and the Word (the sacred scripture) as joint heirs to the Guru's authority following the death of the last of the personal Gurus (2.2.8 [23–4]). Three other products of the *gur-bilas* tradition which also deserve to be noted are Sukha Singh's *Gur-bilas Dasvin Patsahi* (1971), Koer Singh's *Gur-bilas Patsahi 10*, and *Gur-bilas Chhevin Patsahi*, attributed to a poet called Sohan. Although the latter two claim to be eighteenth-century works it has been shown that both belong to the mid-nineteenth century.[9]   [5

Towards the middle of the nineteenth century a further development took place in this heroic tradition. In 1841, between the death of Maharaja Ranjit Singh and British conquest of the Punjab, Ratan Singh Bhangu completed his *Prachin Panth Prakas*.[10] Although Ratan Singh retains the same emphasis on destiny and struggle his focus is clearly on the Khalsa. The Khalsa, he maintains, was created to rule, and all who acknowledge its discipline must be prepared to assert that right (4.1 [2]). For Ratan Singh this was no mere doctrine. The Punjab of 1841 was slipping into the confusion which was soon to lead to the Anglo-Sikh wars. Once again the Khalsa was to be tested.   [6

Three years after Ratan Singh had completed *Prachin Panth Prakas* another major work was brought to its conclusion. This was Santokh Singh's *Gur Pratap Suray*, popularly known as the *Suraj Prakas*. The *Suraj Prakas* marked a reversion to earlier forms and interests, although this did nothing to deprive the work of its enormous and continuing influence. Santokh Singh's earlier work, the *Nanak Prakas*, is strictly a janam-sakhi, distinguished from its predecessors only by the fact that it is expressed in verse. In the *Suraj Prakas* he extends the janam-sakhi style to Guru Nanak's successors. Although the author was by no means immune from later developments this vast poem follows seventeenth-century conventions rather than the Khalsa model devised by Ratan Singh Bhangu.   [7

The Khalsa emphasis had, however, come to stay and a successor to Ratan Singh soon appeared. This was Gian Singh who in 1880 issued his *Panth Prakas*. Between 1891 and 1919 he published his substantial *Tavarikh Guru Khalsa* or 'History of the Guru Khalsa', a lengthy work which is still extensively consulted. In form and approach *Tavarikh Guru Khalsa* appears to be a popular history of the Panth. It is indeed this, but like its predecessors it is much more. Sikh belief is intimately connected with the history of the Panth and the relating of that history inevitably incorporates a substantial doctrinal content. This is most conspicuously present in the reverential presentation of the lives of the Gurus, the prominence given to heroes and martyrs, and the insistent stress which is laid on the role of the Khalsa. Among the heroes of the faith a position of particular affection is reserved for Maharaja Ranjit Singh, who during the first four decades of the nineteenth century ruled the Punjab in the name of the Khalsa. In view of this strong historical sense it is scarcely surprising that historical works should figure so prominently in the literature of the Panth. For the same reason the more important of these works must necessarily be accepted as primary sources for an understanding of its beliefs and doctrines. *[8*

1.8. NIRANKARIS AND NAMDHARIS

Although Ranjit Singh is remembered as one of the great heroes of the faith there were contemporaries who believed that many within the Panth had lost sight of the original teachings of the Gurus. Military struggle and political success, they believed, had obscured the message of the divine Name and the paramount need for the discipline of *nam simaran*. Two who evidently felt this concern were Baba Dayal of Rawalpindi and Balak Singh who lived in the neighbouring town of Hazro. Each attracted followers and the groups which were thus formed survive to the present day. The followers of Baba Dayal and his successors are known as Nirankaris (6.1). Those who trace their allegiance to Balak Singh (or more particularly to his successor Ram Singh) are called Namdharis or Kukas (6.2). *[1*

The Nirankari sect acquired its name from the stress which Baba Dayal laid upon the worship of God as the 'Formless One' (*Nirankar*). Because he was *Nirankar* he could not be incarnated nor could he be represented as an idol. The required response was for men to return to the teachings of Guru Nanak and to practise daily meditation on the divine Name.[11] For Baba Dayal and his followers the one book which mattered was the Adi Granth. Other literature was not required in order to practise devotion as the Nirankaris understand it, with the result that very little seems to have been recorded by members of the sect until comparatively recently. Only one document of any importance survives from the nineteenth century. This is the so-called *Hukam-nama* (6.1.2) which contains instructions issued by Baba Darbara Singh, first successor of Baba Dayal. The *Hukam-nama*, which is actually a rahit-nama, was probably issued before 1873 and certainly before 1884.[12] Nirankari literature remains very scanty until after the 1947 partition of the sub-continent had forced the sect to abandon its Rawalpindi headquarters and move to India. After settling in its new home the community initiated a publishing programme designed to communicate a wider understanding of Nirankari history and doctrine. Notable among the results of this programme is a history of the sect edited by Surinder Singh Nirankari and entitled *Nirankari Gurmat Prarambhita*. *[2*

Although the Namdhari or Kuka sect emerged in the same north-western area at much the same time as Baba Dayal's Nirankari following its membership has been drawn from a different section of the Punjabi community and its history has followed a very different course from that of the Nirankaris. Balak Singh's successor was Ram Singh, a carpenter from the village of Bhaini

Raian in Ludhiana District. Ram Singh met Balak Singh while serving in the army of Ranjit Singh and when he returned to Bhaini Raian after becoming the Namdhari Guru in 1862 the sect's influence travelled with him. His followers were increasingly drawn from the villages of Ludhiana District and adjacent areas, and were distinguished by the fact that most of them belonged to poorer and lower-status groups. In 1871–72 there was serious trouble with the British authorities which resulted in the deportation of Ram Singh to Rangoon. The Namdharis survived this serious blow and members of the community, with their white garments and distinctive turban, are still to be seen in the Punjab and elsewhere.[13]   [3

Although the Namdhari experience has been so very different from that of the Nirankaris their literary output has followed a similar pattern. Among the few documents which survive from the nineteenth century the most important is a rahit-nama issued in the name of Ram Singh (6.2.2). The same paucity of documents continues until very recent times, when the Namdharis, appreciating the importance of apologetics, began a publishing programme. A major contribution has been a liturgical manual published under the title *Namdhari Nitnem*. This work clearly indicates the extensive area of common doctrinal understanding which the Namdharis share with orthodox Sikhs and also the points at which they diverge. The most significant of the divergences concerns the doctrine of the Guru. Whereas orthodox Sikhs believe that the line of personal Gurus ended in 1708 Namdhari doctrine maintains that the succession still continues (6.2.1 [11]).   [4

1.9 THE SINGH SABHA MOVEMENT

While Ranjit Singh ruled the Punjab the Khalsa was patronised and in spite of the misgivings of such men as Baba Dayal and Balak Singh it retained all the marks of outward strength. After the Maharaja's death in 1839, however, the grounds for misgiving rapidly increased, particularly after the British annexed the Punjab in 1849. British observers were soon predicting the imminent demise of the Panth and many of its adherents seemed inclined to accept this gloomy view. They proved to be wrong. Although the reasons for their pessimism may have seemed obvious the actual outcome was very different. Far from slipping further into decay the Panth was in fact approaching a period of notable revival, a revival stimulated and sustained by a group of local associations known collectively as the Singh Sabha movement.   [1

Two major concerns evidently prompted the founding of the first Singh Sabha (Singh Society). One was the growing anxiety felt by many devout Sikhs concerning the manifold signs of erosion within the Panth. The second and more immediate reason was the announcement, issued in 1873, that four Sikh pupils of the Amritsar Mission School had decided to become Christians. Thoroughly alarmed by this news, a group of prominent Sikhs gathered in

Amritsar later in the same year and decided to form an association known as the Singh Sabha. This was followed by the formation of a similar society in Lahore. [2

Although the two groups were responding to the same impulse, rivalry soon developed and the early years of the movement were troubled by chronic disagreement between its leading constituents. As new societies were formed in other parts of the Punjab each affiliated to one or other of the parent organisations, thus producing two satellite systems. By the turn of the century, however, the earlier leadership was giving way to men with less interest in maintaining the division and in 1902 a co-ordinating committee was formed. This was the Chief Khalsa Diwan, an organisation which is still in existence.[14] [3

Notable amongst the early Singh Sabha leaders were Gurmukh Singh and Dit Singh, both of them members of the Lahore section. Gurmukh Singh was a professor at Oriental College in Lahore and Dit Singh, who proved to be a particularly prolific writer, was a Sikh of outcaste origins. Their backgrounds and interests help to explain the objectives of the Singh Sabha movement and also the methods which it employed. The dominant objective was the reconstitution of the Panth as the dedicated casteless society intended by the Gurus. The means to this end were to be preaching, education, social reform, and literature. [4

The result was a genuine renaissance, one which established doctrinal standards and attitudes still strongly influential in the Panth today. Literature attracted particular attention. Newspapers were established, books and tracts published, manuscripts collected, and libraries opened. Several of the books produced by Singh Sabha scholars are still treated as standard works, the most conspicuous example being Kahn Singh's invaluable encyclopaedia of Sikh literature and religion entitled *Gurusabad Ratanakar Mahan Kos* (commonly known simply as *Mahan Kos* or the 'Great Dictionary'). This monumental work remains an indispensable tool for all who study the faith of the Sikhs. Educational activities also produced impressive results, notably the celebrated Khalsa College in Amritsar. [5

Singh Sabha scholarship is distinctive both in terms of its general approach and also the forms which it favoured. Prior to its appearance there had been two scholarly traditions within the Panth, the Giani and Nirmala. Whereas the former emphasised strict adherence to sacred text and received tradition the latter tended strongly towards Vedantic interpretations. Although both were drawn into the Singh Sabha movement there emerged a preference for the Giani approach. It was, however, a transformed use of the old Giani style. Virtually all the prominent members of the Singh Sabha had been intellectually influenced by the British presence and the impress of Western scholarship can be easily recognised in their work. [6

The three disciplines which found particular favour among the Singh Sabha writers were history, scriptural commentary, and apologetics. The first of these was entirely predictable, both because of its traditional antecedents within the

Panth and as a result of the emphasis which it was receiving in contemporary Western education. The other two can also be regarded as natural developments in the circumstances of the time. In attempting to recapture the intention of the Gurus the reformers inevitably turned to the Adi Granth, and detailed commentaries resulted from the close attention which they bestowed on it. A vigorous apologetic was stimulated by the heady controversies of the late nineteenth century. The Singh Sabha reformers were confronted by Hindu counterparts in the newly established Arya Samaj as well as by Christian missionaries and traditional Muslim rivals. The one surprising feature was to be the lack of attention to systematic theology. Only one major work has been produced within this discipline and it, in a sense, can be regarded as an adapted form of scriptural commentary. This is Jodh Singh's *Gurmati Niranay*, issued in 1932 and still widely used (7.3). [7

The first of the scriptural commentaries to appear was *Adi Sri Guru Granth Sahibji Satik*, commonly known as the *Faridkot Tika* (the Faridkot Commentary) because it was commissioned by the Raja of Faridkot and published under his auspices. This work appeared in 1905. A lengthy gap separates it from the next complete commentary, *Sabadarath Sri Guru Granth Sahib Ji* (1936–41). Although its four volumes were issued anonymously *Sabadarath* is in fact the work of Principal Teja Singh, a distinguished commentator and apologist who wrote extensively in English as well as in Punjabi (7.4). Between 1958 and 1962 there appeared seven volumes of an incomplete commentary entitled *Santhya Sri Guru Granth Sahib*. This is a posthumous work by Vir Singh, the most famous of all the writers of the period[15] (7.5). The latest in the line, still set firmly within the Singh Sabha tradition, is Sahib Singh's distinguished *Sri Guru Granth Sahib Darapan*, published from Jalandhar between 1962 and 1964 (7.6). [8

Most of the apologetic material issued during the Singh Sabha period appeared in the form of ephemeral pamphlets or as a component part of ostensibly historical studies. One avowedly apologetic work stands out as particularly important. This was Kahn Singh's *Ham Hindu Nahin* ('We are not Hindus'), an attempt to demonstrate by means of extensive proof-text quotation that the Sikh Panth constitutes a religious and social system distinct from the Hindu tradition (7.2). First issued in 1898, the slender volume served as a significant milestone in the Sikh quest for identity. The Singh Sabha movement had raised the question of who is a Sikh and in *Ham Hindu Nahin* Kahn Singh provided the first part of the answer. Whatever Sikhs may be, he declared, they are certainly not Hindus. The remainder of the answer (the actual definition of a Sikh) was eventually supplied by the Sikh Gurdwaras Act of 1925 and *Sikh Rahit Maryada* (4.5 [7]). [9

The Singh Sabha movement produced an impressive list of contributors to religious revival. Others who deserve mention are the historians Karam Singh and Prem Singh Hoti; Bhai Takht Singh of Ferozepur, a proponent of female education; Bhai Mohan Singh Vaid of Tarn Taran; and the Englishman M. A.

Macauliffe. After four decades of activity, however, the movement found itself being increasingly overtaken by a radical style very different from its own stress on literature and education. This impulse emerged shortly before World War I and in the post-war period the initiative was firmly grasped by the Akali movement. Political agitation now became the dominant strategy of those seeking reform within the Panth.   *[10*

During this period the influence of the Singh Sabha movement receded, but it has yet to diminish to the point of insignificance. Although the Chief Khalsa Diwan is but a shadow of the associations which created it eighty years ago the impulse which they generated still exerts a considerable influence. Among those who seek to express the meaning of Gurmat for today this influence remains dominant. In intellectual terms the Singh Sabha period has yet to reach its conclusion.   *[11*

1.10 CHRONOLOGY

1469	Birth of Guru Nanak
....	Period of Nanak's compositions
1539	Death of Guru Nanak
	Development of oral tradition concerning Guru Nanak
	First collection of bani (Goindval *pothis*)
	Probable formation of early janam-sakhis
....	Period of Bhai Gurdas' compositions
1603–04	Compilation of Adi Granth
	Development of *Puratan* and *Miharban* janam-sakhi traditions
1658	Copying of earliest extant janam-sakhi (a *Bala* janam-sakhi)
1675	Execution of Guru Tegh Bahadur
	Period of Dasam Granth and Nand Lal compositions
1699	Inauguration of the Khalsa
....	
1701	Copying of earliest extant *Adi Sakhis* manuscripts
1708	Death of Guru Gobind Singh
	? *Gur Sobha*
1733	*The B40 Janam-sakhi*
	? *Gur Sobha*
	? *Chaupa Singh Rahit-nama*
	Mahima Prakas Kavita
1776	*Mahima Prakas Varatak*
1797	Sukha Singh, *Gur-bilas Dasvin Patsahi*
1799	Capture of Lahore by Ranjit Singh
....	
1823	Santokh Singh, *Nanak Prakas*
1839	Death of Ranjit Singh
1841	Ratan Singh Bhangu, *Prachin Panth Prakas*
1844	Santokh Singh, *Suraj Prakas*
1849	British annexation of the Punjab
1866	Namdhari Rahit-nama

Nirankari Hukam-nama
1873　Founding of Singh Sabha
1880　Gian Singh, *Panth Prakas*
1891　Gian Singh, *Tavarikh Guru Khalsa* (first portion)
1898　Kahn Singh Nabha, *Ham Hindu Nahin*

....

1905　Faridkot commentary on the Adi Granth
1909　M. A. Macauliffe, *The Sikh Religion*
1931　Kahn Singh Nabha, *Gurusabad Ratanakar Mahan Kos*
1932　Jodh Singh, *Gurmati Niranay*
1936–41　*Sabadarath Sri Guru Granth Sahib*
1950　*Sikh Rahit Maryada*
1958–62　Vir Singh, *Santhya Sri Guru Granth Sahib*
1962–64　Sahib Singh, *Sri Guru Granth Sahib Darapan*

2 THE GURUS

2.1 GURU NANAK (1469–1539)

Although one may encounter lengthy biographical studies of Guru Nanak the Guru himself tells us very little of his own life. Few details may be gleaned from his numerous compositions and in all cases these are presented to the reader as fleeting hints rather than as explicit information. The biographical studies of Guru Nanak rely for their material not on the Adi Granth but on the fund of popular anecdotes supplied by the janam-sakhis (1.5). Although several different groups of janam-sakhis can be identified there are extensive areas of overlap. None of the various groups or traditions is wholly independent of all the others and all may be shown to belong to a single network. A prominent example of common material appearing within distinctive traditions is provided by the Puratan, Adi Sakhis *and* B40 Janam-sakhi *versions of Guru Nanak's early life. The following account of his birth, childhood, and early adulthood is to be found in all three collections.*　*[1*

2.1.1 The birth and childhood of Nanak

A narrative of the events concerning the first Master which took place in the village of Talvandi, the village founded by Rai Bhoa the Bhatti.[1]

Baba Nanak was born in Talvandi, the son of Kalu, who was a Bedi Khatri by caste. In this Age of Darkness he proclaimed the divine Name (3.1.1 [7–13]) and founded his community of followers, the Panth. Baba Nanak was born in the year S.1526 on the third day of the month of Vaisakh [15 April 1469 A.C.]. He was born during the moonlit hours of early morning, that time of fragrant peace which is the last watch of the night. Celestial music resounded in heaven. A mighty host of gods hailed his birth, and with them all manner of spirit and divinity. 'God has come to save the world!' they cried.   [1

At the time of the birth Kalu Bedi was residing in Talvandi and Nanak was actually born in the village. As he grew older he began to play with other children, but his attitude differed from theirs in that he paid heed to the spiritual things of God. When he turned five he began to give utterance to deep and mysterious thoughts. Whatever he uttered was spoken with profound understanding, with the result that everyone's doubts and questions were resolved. The Hindus vowed that a god had taken birth in human form. The Muslims declared that a follower of divine truth had been born.   [2

When Baba Nanak turned seven his father told him that he must begin his schooling. Kalu took him to a teacher and directed him to teach the child. This the teacher agreed to do. He wrote on a wooden slate and Nanak studied with him for a single day. The following day, however, he remained silent. 'Why are you not studying?' the teacher asked him. 'What is it that you have studied and wish to teach me?' responded Nanak. 'I have studied everything. From accountancy to the sacred scriptures, I have studied them all,' answered the teacher. 'These subjects which you have studied are all useless,' declared Nanak. He then sang a hymn in the measure *Siri Rag* (3.1.1 [28–32]) . . . [Having heard the hymn and Nanak's explanation of its meaning] the teacher was astounded and did obeisance. Acknowledging that the child had already attained perfection he said, 'Do what you believe to be right.'   [3

Baba Nanak then returned home and remained sitting there. He did absolutely nothing. If sitting he merely sat and apart from sitting did nothing but sleep. He remained withdrawn and began associating with faqirs. Kalu was perplexed. 'What manner of child is this,' he asked himself, 'that he should act in this way?'   [4

When Baba Nanak turned nine he was invested with the sacred thread. He was set to learning Persian but soon reverted to sitting silently in the house, revealing his thoughts to no one. The people of the village said to Kalu, 'You should arrange a marriage for your son. Perhaps that will divert him from this fancy for renunciation.'   [5

Accepting their advice, Kalu set about planning a marriage for Nanak. A betrothal was negotiated with Mula, a Chona Khatri by caste, and when Nanak turned twelve he was duly married to Mula's daughter. But he showed no interest in these domestic arrangements. He would not speak to his parents or his wife, nor would he concern himself with household affairs. 'He spends his time with faqirs!' declared his disgusted family. One day Kalu said to him, 'Nanak my son, take the buffaloes out to graze.' Acknowledging his father's command, Baba Nanak drove the buffaloes out to graze and at dusk brought them home. Next day, when he took them out again, he left them unattended and fell asleep at the edge of a wheatfield. While he slept the buffaloes trampled the crop and ate the wheat.   [6

After the crop of wheat had been consumed its owner appeared and demanded an explanation. 'Why have you ruined my field? Explain this outrage,' he cried. 'Nothing of yours has been ruined, brother,' replied Baba Nanak. 'What harm is there in a buffalo grazing? God will make it a blessing.' This failed to mollify the owner, who began to berate Nanak, and, shouting all the way, he escorted him to the village headman, Rai Bular. When he had heard the owner's complaint the headman gave orders for Kalu to be summoned. The people who were standing near by agreed. 'Nanak is simple-minded,' they said. 'What can one say to him? Let Kalu be called.'   [7

They summoned Kalu and Rai Bular said to him, 'Kalu, rebuke your son. He has ruined another man's crop. You have let him become a simpleton. Recompense the owner for the damage which he has suffered or you will find yourself before the authorities.'   [8

'What can I do?' replied Kalu. 'He wanders around like a crazed fool.'   [9

'I pardon *your* offence, Kalu,' said Rai Bular, 'but you must make restitution for the damage which has been done.'   [10

Then Baba Nanak spoke. 'Nothing has been ruined,' he said. 'He is not telling the truth.'   [11

'Everything in my field has been ruined!' exclaimed the owner of the field. 'I have been robbed! Give me justice or I shall have him summoned before the authorities.'   [12

'Not a single blade of grass has been eaten,' said Nanak, 'nor even broken. Send your man to see.'   [13

Rai Bular sent his messenger and what should the messenger find when he went to inspect the field? He discovered that nothing had been touched. He returned and reported that there had been no harm done to the field. Hearing this, Rai Bular declared the owner of the field to be a liar and Nanak returned home with Kalu.   [14

In accordance with the will of God two sons, Lakhmi Das and Siri Chand, were born to Baba Nanak, but their arrival did nothing to cure his withdrawal from worldly concerns. Heedless of such things, he would go to the forest and sit there alone.   [15

One day Baba Nanak went to a grove of trees and fell asleep under a tree. Throughout the day he slept without stirring. Rai Bular had come out hunting and while passing that way he happened to observe someone sleeping under a tree. The shadows of the other trees had moved with the sun, but the shadow of that particular tree had remained stationary. 'Wake him,' said Rai Bular. 'Let us see who it is.' When they roused him they discovered that it was Kalu's son. 'I saw what happened previously,' said Rai Bular, 'and now this also I have witnessed. It is not without meaning. There is something of God's grace in it.' Rai Bular returned home and summoned Kalu. 'Do not maltreat this son of yours, Kalu, no matter what he may say. He has been divinely chosen and it is for his sake that my village exists. You too have been blessed, Kalu, for it is as your son that Nanak has been born.' Kalu remained bewildered. 'God alone knows what is happening,' he said and returned home.[2]   [16

2.1.2 The call to preach

In spite of Rai Bular's remonstrance Nanak's parents continued their attempt to involve him in worldly activity, and Nanak continued to resist. Thinking that perhaps his son might be ill, Kalu summoned a physician, only to have him silenced by a series of appropriate quotations from the patient. A solution was finally produced by Nanak's brother-in-law Jai Ram, husband of his sister Nanaki. Jai Ram, who was in the service of Nawab Daulat Khan, managed to persuade Nanak to join him in the town of Sultanpur. The Nawab agreed to employ him and Nanak became his steward. According to the janam-sakhis it was during this period of employment that Nanak received his call from God to undertake a life of preaching the message of the divine Name. Early one morning while he was bathing in the stream which flows past Sultanpur, the summons suddenly came. The prose version of the Mahima Prakas *describes the event as follows.*   [1

When Nanak reached Sultanpur he was warmly welcomed by Jai Ram. Taking him to the Nawab his brother-in-law declared him to be a most industrious worker and asked that he might be given employment. The Nawab put him in charge of his stores. Baba Nanak duly took his seat in the commissariat and gave complete satisfaction to all who needed supplies. Someone reported that Nanak was indulging in misappropriation, but when Nawab Daulat Khan came to investigate the allegation he discovered that everything had actually doubled in quantity. 'My steward is remarkably conscientious,' he said, heaping praise on Nanak.   [2

After returning home in the evening Baba Nanak would devote his nights to singing hymns, and when it came to the last watch of the night[3] he would go to the river and bathe. One morning, having gone to bathe, he entered the waters of the Vein stream but failed to emerge. His servant looked for him until mid-morning and then taking his clothes returned home to tell Jai Ram what had happened. 'During the last watch of the night Nanak went into the stream to bathe,' he said, 'but he has not emerged.' When he heard this news Jai Ram was greatly disturbed and went to the Nawab to report what had happened. The Nawab sent for nets and a thorough search was made, but to no avail.   [3

Eventually, however, Baba Nanak did return. After three days and three nights had passed he emerged from the stream, and having done so he declared: 'There is neither Hindu nor Muslim.' When the Nawab heard that Nanak had reappeared and that he was speaking in this manner he sent a servant to request an interview on his behalf. Baba Nanak went to the delighted Nawab who treated him with great deference.[4]   [4

This narrative from the Mahima Prakas Varatak *is much briefer than the* Puratan *version, which offers an account of what transpired during Nanak's three-day absence. Nanak's disappearance in the river was, it claims, the result of a summons to the presence of God. Appearing in God's court, he is*

*given a cup of nectar (*amrit*) to drink and is then charged by God himself*
with the duty of preaching the divine Name. In response he sings a hymn, one
which protests his unworthiness to discharge God's commission. God,
however, reassures him and after Nanak has recited Japji *and another hymn*
heavenly messengers return him to the river bank.[5]   [5*

The Puratan *version continues, in greater detail, to relate the events*
following Nanak's reappearance, stressing in particular the cryptic
declaration 'There is neither Hindu nor Muslim'. The pronouncement is
*greeted with much suspicion by the Nawab's religious administrator (*qazi*)*
and Nanak is summoned to give an explanation. This he does to the Nawab's
satisfaction and then accepts an invitation to join the midday Muslim prayer.
During the course of the prayer Nanak gives further proof of his divine
calling with an act which at first sight seems grossly offensive. The Mahima
Prakas Varatak version resumes its narrative at this point.   [6*

It came to the time for prayer and the Nawab stood up to pray. The Qazi also
stood up for the prayer, with Baba Nanak standing near him. When the Qazi
began to recite the prayer, however, Nanak laughed. As soon as the prayer had
been completed the outraged Qazi protested to the Nawab: 'You see! The Hindu
mocks our prayer!' The Nawab asked Baba Nanak why he had laughed while
the prayer was in progress. 'Because the Qazi's prayer was unacceptable to
God,' answered Nanak. 'A mare has foaled at the Qazi's house and he was
wondering if there would be anyone in the courtyard watching the filly. While
praying he let his attention wander there, hoping that the filly would not fall
into his well. That is why the Qazi's faith found no acceptance. And your mind
was on going to Qandahar to buy horses. That is why I laughed.'   [7

'It was a sin to summon Nanak,' said the Nawab to the Qazi. 'He is one close
to God.' Jai Ram took Nanak home and admonished him at length. 'Put on
your clothes,' he said. All was in vain, for Baba Nanak no longer took any
interest in worldly affairs. Mardana the Bard had come from Talvandi to visit
him. Taking him as a companion, Nanak assumed the renunciant way of life
and left Sultanpur.[6]   [8

2.1.3 The founding of Kartarpur

After leaving Sultanpur Baba Nanak and Mardana began a period of
wandering which was to last for twelve years. Many of the janam-sakhi
anecdotes are set in this period, but there is little agreement concerning the
itinerary followed by the travellers or the adventures which befall them.
Eventually they returned to the Punjab, where the Guru was briefly reunited
with his parents. After further travels Nanak found what was to be his
permanent home, a new village on the banks of the Ravi river upstream from
Lahore. Once again the B40, Puratan, *and* Adi Sakhis *texts tell the story in*
very similar words.   [1

It so happened that a high-ranking government official (a *karori*) resided
near the village where Baba Nanak was staying. One day he asked: 'Who is this

fellow whom everyone mentions? He has not merely corrupted Hindus. Even Muslims have been persuaded to betray their faith. What kind of faith can these Muslims have that they put their trust in a Hindu! Come, let us seize him and bring him here.' Having thus made up his mind, the karori prepared to depart. 'I shall go and bring that Hindu back a prisoner,' he declared. When he mounted his horse, however, it shivered under him and refused to move that day. Next day he mounted the horse again but as he proceeded on his way he was struck blind. He stopped, unable to see a thing.   [2

The people who observed his plight said, 'Sir, we are afraid and can say nothing save that Nanak is a great pir. You should show reverence towards him.' The karori began to praise Nanak, and all who were with him bowed in the direction of the place where Nanak was living. 'Nanak is a great man!' declared the karori.   [3

He mounted his horse again but immediately tumbled off, unable to see anything. 'Sir, you are forgetting,' protested the people. 'You are proceeding on horseback. Nanak is a great pir. Only if you go on foot will you receive blessing.' The karori proceeded on foot, and at the place where Baba Nanak's house came into view he stood and did homage. When he reached Nanak he fell at his feet. Baba Nanak was filled with joy. For three days he detained the karori and bestowed great favour on him. Before leaving the karori made a request. 'If you grant permission,' he said respectfully, 'I shall found a village in your name and call it Kartarpur. Whatever produce is grown will be contributed to the dharamsala.' The karori then took leave.   [4

When Kalu heard that Nanak had built a village and settled down he joined him with his family. Great was the rejoicing! A pattern of living was instituted, one which combined labour, charity and worship. Baba Nanak's seat was set apart under a peepul tree. He lived there for a lengthy period, during which time a large group of disciples gathered around him. Wherever he resided, there Mardana also stayed.[7]   [5

2.1.4 Panja Sahib

The founding and development of Kartarpur did not mean the end of Baba Nanak's travels. Although the janam-sakhis continue to provide widely divergent narratives they agree that Nanak spent much of his time away from the village. The later versions of the Bala janam-sakhi tradition include the story of how a jealous faqir tried to crush him with a huge boulder.   [1

While travelling to Kashmir the Guru came to the high hill which rises above the town of Hasan Abdal, approximately twenty *kos* from the Indus river. While he was resting near the town his companion Mardana became thirsty. Mardana asked the Guru for water but there was none to be found in the vicinity. When the thirsty Mardana became increasingly agitated the Guru said to him: 'At the top of that high hill there lives a Muslim faqir called Vali Qandhari. He has water close at hand, but nowhere else in this area will you find it. Go and ask him for some of his water. When he sees that you look like a

Muslim, he will probably let you have some.' [2

Mardana accepted the Guru's advice and set off to quench his thirst. With much difficulty he struggled up the hill and found Vali Qandhari sitting at the top. Beside him was a natural basin in which he stored water for his own use. Mardana told him that he was thirsty and politely asked for water. Observing his appearance and foreign dress, Vali Qandhari asked him, 'Where have you come from, thirsty fellow? What is your name and what brings you here? Are you alone or is there someone with you?' [3

'I have come with Guru Nanak, the celebrated holy man of the Punjab,' answered Mardana. 'He it is whom the Hindus regard as their guru and Muslims as their pir. Having travelled the entire world reclaiming lost souls he is now on his way to Kashmir. He is resting at the bottom of the hill. I am his minstrel companion and my name is Mardana the Bard. I accompany the Guru wherever he goes and sing his hymns.' [4

Vali Qandhari was furious when he heard the Guru praised in this manner. Burning with anger, he said to Mardana, 'If your holy man is so marvellous why doesn't he use his powers to produce water down there where he is sitting? One ought to give water to a thirsty person, but I'm certainly not giving any to you. Go back to your holy man and tell him to produce water for you. Let *him* be the one who quenches your thirst.' [5

The dejected Mardana tramped down the hill and told the Guru what had happened. 'When he was told how important you are Vali Qandhari became very upset and refused to give me any water,' he said. Having heard what had happened, the Guru smiled. 'Muslims like their fellow Muslims,' he said. 'Approach him humbly and bring some water back.' [6

Mardana returned to the Guru thoroughly upset. 'He won't give me any to him with humble courtesy. 'I am your fellow Muslim,' he said, 'and you possess great powers. Please give me some water so that I may satisfy my thirst.' Vali Qandhari angrily responded, 'Here you are writhing in anguish and that holy man Nanak, for all his supernatural skills, is unable to help you! Leave him and you will have water.' [7

Mandana returned to the Guru thoroughly upset. 'He won't give me any water,' he wailed, 'and here I am dying of thirst.' The Guru could read the inner thoughts of others and he knew what was in Vali Qandhari's heart. To quench Mardana's thirst he picked up a piece of wood and struck the ground at the foot of the hill. Instantly there appeared a spring of cool, clear water. At the same time Vali Qandhari's little reservoir of water sank into the hill and disappeared. Not a drop remained. [8

Overwhelmed with fear and anger, Vali Qandhari used his prodigious strength to send a huge boulder tumbling down the hill to where the Guru was sitting. Down it hurtled, crushing everything in its path. When he saw it descending on him the Guru raised his hand and stopped it in its tracks. As he did so his hand sank into the boulder leaving an imprint in the rock. Vali Qandhari, having witnessed the Guru open a spring of limpid water and then stop a boulder with his hand, was totally abashed. Humbly he acknowledged the Guru's mighty powers and, falling at his feet, begged for his blessing. The Guru responded affectionately. He urged the penitent Vali Qandhari to put aside his pride and having brought him peace he proceeded on his way.[8]   [9

2.1.5 The death of Baba Nanak

Kartarpur remained Nanak's base and it was there that he died in 1539. The Puratan text supplies the following account.   [1

Guru Baba Nanak then went and sat under a withered acacia which immediately produced leaves and flowers, becoming verdant again. Guru Angad prostrated himself. Baba Nanak's wife began to weep and the various members of his family joined her in her grief . . . The assembled congregation sang hymns of praise and Baba Nanak passed into an ecstatic trance. While thus transported, and in obedience to the divine will, he sang the hymn entitled *The Twelve Months*. It was early morning and the time had come for his final departure . . . His sons asked him, 'What will happen to us?' The Guru reassured them. 'Even the Guru's dogs lack nothing, my sons,' he said. 'You shall be abundantly supplied with food and clothing, and if you repeat the Guru's name you will be liberated from the bondage of human life.'   [2

Hindus and Muslims who had put their faith in the divine Name began to debate what should be done with the Guru's corpse. 'We shall bury him,' said the Muslims. 'No, let us cremate his body,' said the Hindus. 'Place flowers on both sides of my body,' said Baba Nanak, 'flowers from the Hindus on the right side and flowers from the Muslims on the left. If tomorrow the Hindus' flowers are still fresh let my body be burned, and if the Muslims' flowers are still fresh let it be buried.'   [3

Baba Nanak then commanded the congregation to sing. They sang *Kirtan Sohila* and *Arati* . . . Baba Nanak then covered himself with a sheet and passed away. Those who had gathered around him prostrated themselves, and when the sheet was removed they found that there was nothing under it. The flowers on both sides remained fresh, and both Hindus and Muslims took their respective shares. All who were gathered there prostrated themselves again.[9]   [4

2.2 THE SUCCESSORS OF GURU NANAK

2.2.1 Guru Angad (1539–52)

Indian tradition assumes that any religious teacher of renown who is not already within an established succession will initiate a succession of his own. This custom was widely observed in both Hindu and Muslim society. Hindu succession descended through lines of gurus, acharyas and sants, Muslim succession through the spiritual lineages (silsila) of Sufi pirs. Successors might be chosen by the teacher himself, or they might secure recognition following his death.   [1

The lineal succession of the ten Gurus is of crucial significance in the history of the Sikh Panth and in the development of its distinctive doctrinal system. Sikh traditions vary in their descriptions of how Guru Nanak's first successor was chosen, but all agree that he was designated by Guru Nanak himself and that the disciple whom he appointed was a man called Lahina. This disciple, chosen in preference to Nanak's two sons, received a new name and it was as Guru Angad that he succeeded to the gaddi. *The janam-sakhis of the* Puratan *tradition give the following account of the first meeting between Guru Nanak and his successor.* [2

It so happened, in accordance with the will of God, that there lived in the village of Khadur a Sikh who regularly chanted the Guru's name when performing his devotions.[10] This Sikh was a Khatri of the Bhalla sub-caste. Apart from this man all the inhabitants of Khadur believed in the goddess Durga and in the teachings of *hatha-yoga.* Near him there resided Lahina, the local priest. One day Lahina happened to overhear him reciting *Japji.* 'Whose composition is this?' he asked. 'It is the work of Guru Nanak,' answered the Sikh. [3

So impressed was Lahina that he went with the Sikh and prostrated himself before Guru Nanak. Having thus seen the Guru, he tore the ritual bells from his hands and feet, and having renounced his former practices he began to chant the Guru's name. He remained with Guru Nanak and devoted himself to the service of his new Master, humbly scouring pots and waving the fan.[11] [4

The Puratan *janam-sakhis also relate a gruesome test conducted by Guru Nanak in order to determine his disciples' worthiness.* [5

In accordance with God's purpose Gorakhnath[12] once visited Baba Nanak and asked him how his preaching had fared. 'You will see whether or not I have had any success,' answered the Guru. He then proceeded out of the village, attended by a group of devout followers. At his command copper coins appeared on the track. Many of those who were with him seized a share of the coins and departed. Farther along the track they found silver coins, whereupon many more of his followers grasped what they could and left him. Proceeding even further, they came to a scattering of gold coins, and almost all those who were still with him made off with these. Only two Sikhs remained. [6

They continued to follow the track until they reached a smouldering funeral pyre. Four lamps were burning on it and beneath a shroud there lay a corpse emitting a foul smell. 'Is anyone prepared to eat this corpse?' asked Baba Nanak. One of the two remaining Sikhs retched and fled. Only Lahina remained. In obedience to the Guru's command he went and stood beside the corpse. 'At which end should I begin?' he asked. 'Begin with the feet,' came the reply. [7

When Lahina raised the shroud whom should he find lying there but Guru Nanak himself! 'Nanak,' declared Gorakhnath, 'your successor as Guru will be this person, so loyal that he is as much a part of you as your own limb (*ang*).' Lahina was thereafter known as Angad, and Gorakhnath, having made his pronouncement, took his leave.[13]

2.2.2 Guru Amar Das (1552–74)

Following the death of Nanak the devoted disciple Angad duly succeeded him as Guru. As Nanak's heir he faithfully continued to preach the message of deliverance through the divine Name and the Panth continued to grow. One of the disciples attracted by Guru Angad proved to be the man who would succeed him as third in the line of succession. The Mahima Prakas Varatak *describes the manner in which the elderly Amar Das was chosen to succeed Guru Angad.* [1

Amar Das wondered what service he might perform for his new Master. It seemed that there were sufficient servants for all his needs, except for one. The Guru required someone who would bring water. And so Amar Das assumed the role of water-carrier, a task which he performed daily. Whenever anyone was thirsty he would immediately provide water, throwing out any surplus which remained. [2

In this manner six and a half years passed. Early one morning Amar Das was bringing water for the Guru's bath, carrying it through heavy rain. The path skirted a weaver's hut and while he was passing it Amar Das's foot slipped in one of the holes which weavers dig in order to work their looms. He managed to save the water-pot from falling, but the noise he made attracted the weaver's attention. 'Who is making that noise in our courtyard?' he asked his wife. 'It's only that poor homeless Amar Das,' she answered. When he heard her say this Amar Das called out, 'You are mad, woman! How can one who serves such a Master ever be homeless?' The weaver's wife immediately turned insane, while Amar Das went on his way with the pot of water and delivered it to his Master. [3

After he had bathed Guru Angad meditated until daybreak. He then called Amar Das and asked him what he had said to the weaver's wife during the night. Amar Das humbly replied that the Guru knows all things. The weaver and his wife were then summoned and when they appeared before the Guru he told them to relate truthfully what had happened. The weaver told him, 'I heard a noise in my courtyard and asked my wife what was happening. She replied that it was the homeless Amar Das, and he then called, "You are mad, woman! How can one who serves such a Master ever be homeless?" My wife immediately became insane.' [4

'You have been blessed,' the Guru said to him, and immediately his wife recovered. To Amar Das he said, 'You will be the pride of the humble and shelter of all who are homeless, protector of the defenceless with power to free men from their chains. To you I deliver the key to all that sustains mankind. Blessings upon you!' ... [5

Water was then brought and Amar Das was bathed. Guru Angad personally dressed him in fresh garments, placing a saffron turban on his head and the symbol of spiritual authority on his forehead. Before him he laid five copper coins and a coconut, [thus appointing him his successor as Guru].[14]   [6

2.2.3 Guru Ram Das (1574–81)

Having served as Guru for more than twenty-two years Amar Das died in 1574 at the age of ninety-five. He was succeeded by his son-in-law Jetha, known as Guru Ram Das. A particularly important event associated with Guru Ram Das was the founding of a new village which was eventually to become the city of Amritsar. Its founding is described in the Mahima Prakas Kavita.   [1

Mounting his horse, the Guru set forth to perform a wondrous deed. When he reached Sultanvind he paused there in its wasteland and gazed at the countryside around him. As he sat there on his horse viewing his surroundings the members of his retinue asked him to tell them about the area. 'This is a most sacred place,' replied the Guru. 'Behold its beauty. This, truly, is the gateway to deliverance. I shall now explain to you why this place will be for all people the source of true happiness in this present world and of deliverance in the world to come.' The Sikhs who were with him were filled with joy when they heard these words, knowing that whatever the Guru says must indeed be true.   [2

The Guru remained there and summoned the people who lived in the neighbouring village. All came and humbly prostrated themselves before him, willing to obey whatever command he might give. The Guru instructed them to excavate a pool at this most sacred of places. 'He who participates in the digging of the pool will find that devotion grows within him,' he promised them. 'Whoever resolves to join in the task will receive the merit which the deed must surely earn. How can I describe the glory of this supremely sacred place? In it God has revealed his glory to the world. The sun of righteousness has risen!'   [3

A host of people began to dig. All mysteries were revealed to them; all were rapt in the bliss of devotion. They continued to dig until the pool had been formed. All around there reigned a peace perfect and unbroken. All who had responded to the Guru's command found their reward in both the present and in the promise held out to them for the life to come. How can one find words to express the glory of that place, supremely blessed and sanctified as the dwelling place of the Guru?   [4

How grand the empty pool looked, a pure and beautiful bowl awaiting its sacred contents. As he surveyed it the Guru eagerly considered how it might be filled. With amrit he filled it, speedily completing the task, and having filled it with amrit he bestowed on it the name 'Amritsar'.[15]   [5

The Guru then pronounced his blessing on the sacred pool. 'He who bathes here with a heart filled with devotion to God shall thereby receive the deliverance which I confer. This will assuredly happen. Even a bird which flies over this pool shall attain to the same sure deliverance without any effort on its part. They who obtain this salvation will find blissful peace in mystical union with God. By the grace of our merciful Lord and Master this sacred pool has been filled with amrit, brought to this place for the deliverance of all. Our blessed Master, Giver and Sustainer of the Truth, has provided the source of joy in this world and the means of deliverance in the next.   [6

'Sing praises to this most sacred of all places dedicated to the Name of God, to the sacred water which banishes all pain and distress. Let all who come here sing its praises. Let them here discover the bliss of mystical union with God. Only those who know true devotion will come, for this is no place for hypocrites and deceivers. Here divine music will be sung, sublimely beautiful music which will bring joy to all who hear it. Here one will witness wonders; here one will meet the truly devout; here one will find peace.' . . .   [7

The Guru remained there for a lengthy period, receiving those who came for his blessing and conferring deliverance upon all who did so. All who came bathed in the sacred waters and appeared before the Guru. All praised the glory of his wondrous deeds. Eventually the Master returned to Goindval. Marvellous are the wonders which he has performed, deeds which no words can ever describe. The gods themselves, the mightiest of all, join in singing his praises.   [8

This, then, is the story of how the Guru so gloriously created the Lake of Amritsar. Let all who love the Guru hear and obey his words, for thus they shall know the joy of true devotion.[16]   [9

2.2.4 Guru Arjan (1581–1606)

Fifth in the succession of Gurus came Arjan, the youngest son of Guru Ram Das. Under his leadership the Panth grew larger, new villages were established, and new pools dug. In 1602–03 the pool of Ramsar was excavated near Ramdaspur (Amritsar) and in 1603 the task of compiling an authorised scripture was begun beside it (1.1[3]). Santokh Singh explains the decision to record the scripture and describes the manner in which it was done.   [1

One day the Guru sat before a large congregation [in Ramdaspur] and delivered a homily expounding the divine Name. A Sikh called out, 'Hear me, Guruji. Prithia[17] and others are circulating their compositions together with the authentic works of the Gurus (*gurbani*). Such compositions reflect their misconceived notions. Some can be recognised, but others cannot be distinguished from authentic works. How can we understand the Guru's truth if it is to be diluted by this material? How are we to recognise authentic compositions. If nothing is done about this situation the authentic Gurbani will be lost to us.'   [2

Hearing this, another Sikh said, 'Works which are not by the Gurus are spurious, yet here we have this serious doubt concerning their immortal words. How can ordinary Sikhs be expected to understand the difference between the spurious and the authentic? Cannot learned Sikhs such as Gurdas guide us? He is himself a writer, one who has revealed the glory of the Gurus' teachings. He has told us about God and about the mighty battles waged by those whom God has sent into the world.'   [3

Then spoke the Guru, the Lord of all mercies and solace of those who suffer. 'Each day we should all recite Gurbani,' he said. 'We must meditate on its meaning, fixing it in our minds and driving away all ignorance. During the early morning hour one should arise and recite Gurbani, gathering the wondrous benefits which it supplies and daily increasing the devotion which each must nurture in his heart. Any material which has been interpolated from the works of other poets must be distinguished from the divine truth which God communicates through his chosen messengers [the Gurus]. It is by studying Gurbani that one learns the Guru's will. Great is the comfort and great the joy which we derive from our reading or hearing of Gurbani, and from our regular repeating of it. There are innumerable compositions, but without the Guru's guidance there can be no distinguishing the difference between sin and virtue. He who neither hears nor recites Gurbani, or who fails in his love for it, must assuredly suffer. The test is whether or not it banishes distress and induces tranquillity. The works of Gurdas are filled with the Guru's praises. Read them attentively and you will acquire an understanding of what a Sikh should believe.' [4

A brief discussion followed, one which stressed the difficulties which would be encountered in future efforts to preserve the uncorrupted purity of the Guru's message. [5

The Guru replied, 'Guru [Amar Das] built the town of Goindval on the banks of the Beas river. His elder son Mohan still lives there, a man intoxicated with divine love and caring for nothing else. He has in his possession the works of the first four Gurus. He holds the entire collection and he must somehow be persuaded to part with it. It must all be recorded in a single volume so that it may be safely preserved for the benefit of mankind.' [6

Having persuaded Mohan to surrender the two volumes in his possession, Guru Arjan instructed Bhai Gurdas to act as scribe and amanuensis. [7

Guru Arjan summoned Gurdas and after inviting him to sit he told him what he planned to do. 'Listen while I tell you of my cherished ambition,' he said. 'I want you to prepare a large volume, a particularly fine one. Write in the Gurmukhi script, using the thirty-five characters which are enumerated in Guru Nanak's *Patti*.[18] Adorn your work with them. Record all the works of the Gurus in this script so that they may be easily read. All who desire enlightenment will then be able to obtain it. You have read and studied these works for many years and you understand their meaning. Present them in Gurmukhi and thereby satisfy this desire of mine.[19] [8

The sacred volume was thus prepared by Guru Arjan with the assistance of Bhai Gurdas, the task occupying their attention from 1603 until the late summer of 1604. The completed work was then installed in the Harimandir temple. [9

2.2.5 Guru Hargobind (1606–44)

A fundamental change in policy and practice took place during the period of Guru Hargobind. The first five Gurus had been spiritual guides who preached the message of the divine Name and stressed the devotional practice of nam simaran *as the primary response required from their disciples (3.1.1 [7–13]). The sixth Guru, however, was confronted by the active hostility of the Mughal authorities and adapted his policy accordingly. If their hostility were to be resisted the Guru and his followers would have to amend their life style drastically. Guru Hargobind accepted the Mughal challenge, with the inevitable result that the quietist approach gave way to a policy of militant action. The earlier stress on the divine Name was not abandoned, but the outward form of the Panth's life underwent a radical change.* [1

Guru Hargobind exemplified this change in his own personal life, and it is evident that the change which he introduced attracted considerable criticism from those who believed that religious leaders should adhere to the peaceful ways sanctified by tradition. Bhai Gurdas (1.4) was one who experienced the change and in a famous stanza from Var *26 he offers a loyal disciple's defence. The first six lines state the criticisms levelled at Guru Hargobind, and the two concluding lines give Bhai Gurdas's response.* [2

The earlier Gurus sat peacefully in dharamsalas; this one roams the land. || Emperors visited their homes with reverence; this one they cast into gaol. || No rest for his followers, ever active; their restless Master has fear of none. || The earlier Gurus sat graciously blessing; this one goes hunting with dogs. || They had servants who harboured no malice; this one encourages scoundrels. || Yet none of these changes conceals the truth; the Sikhs are still drawn as bees to the lotus. || The truth stands firm, eternal, changeless; and pride still lies subdued. 26.24 [3

2.2.6 Guru Har Rai (1644–61) and Guru Har Krishan (1661–64)

After Guru Hargobind's experience of Mughal hostility there followed a period of peace for the Sikhs. From 1644 until 1661 the Panth was led by Hargobind's grandson Har Rai, second son of the deceased Baba Gurditta. Guru Har Rai retired to the Punjab hills with a small retinue, emerging from time to time to visit his followers on the plains and to preach the Sikh message there. At his death he was succeeded by his infant son Hari Krishan. The child Guru died of smallpox in Delhi less than three years later, having indicated to his followers that the succession should revert to Tegh Bahadur, a surviving son of Guru Hargobind. [1

2.2.7 Guru Tegh Bahadur (1664–75)

Tegh Bahadur, the ninth Guru, was the second of the Gurus to be martyred. Sikh tradition attributes his death to the bigotry of the sixth Mughal emperor, Aurangzeb (1659–1707). It is not seen, however, as the result of a direct attack on the Panth or its leader. The tradition affirms that it resulted from Aurangzeb's hostility towards all non-Muslims, and specifically from an attempt to convert the Hindus of Kashmir to Islam. Gian Singh provides a detailed version of the tradition in his Tavarikh Guru Khalsa *(1.7 [8]). He records how the Brahmans of Kashmir, confronted by the fearsome threats of the Mughal governor, had gathered at the temple of Amarnath and were preparing to face death rather than conversion. Suddenly there appeared before them a sadhu who urged them to seek the protection of Guru Tegh Bahadur. The advice was accepted and a delegation left for the Punjab.* [1

When they appeared before the Guru in Anandpur the Hindu delegation explained their predicament with much weeping and wailing. Humbly they put their request to him. 'The river of Aurangzeb's brutality is engulfing the garden of Hindu dharma,' they declared. 'It threatens to destroy it root and branch. Cows are everywhere being slaughtered. If any cow or buffalo belonging to a Hindu is mortally ill the qazi comes and kills it on the spot. Muslims then flay it, cut it in pieces and carry it away. This causes us much distress. If we fail to inform the qazi when a beast is dying he punishes us, saying, "Why did you not tell me? Now its spirit has gone to hell, whereas had it been killed in the approved Muslim manner it would have gone to paradise." These, together with the *jizya* tax, are the kind of difficulties which we have had to endure and now it is their intention to convert us to Islam by force. We shall do whatever you say.' [2

This news of Aurangzeb's tyranny and of the suffering inflicted on the Hindu people greatly perturbed the Guru. After considering the matter at some length he declared: 'It will be very difficult to save the Hindu tradition unless some worthy person is prepared to sacrifice his life for its protection.' Before anyone else could respond to this pronouncement the Guru's son [Gobind Singh] prophetically answered his father. 'My Lord, who can be worthier than you yourself to make this sacrifice? Who else possesses the same piety or the same concern for the faith of others?' [3

The child was at that time only nine years old, but he possessed the mind and understanding of an adult. When they heard what he had said the others who were present were awestruck. The wise and learned, however, perceived the boy's true quality. What other child, little more than an infant, could advise his own father to sacrifice his head; and what father could be so gracious as to accept such advice with pleasure! Both the ninth and tenth Gurus possessed that strength of character and that belief in their own destiny which appear only in those whom God has sent for the defence and restoration of dharma. [4

The Guru realised that his son now possessed all the qualities required of a worthy successor, recognising in him a total willingness to submit himself to the will of God. Joyfully he told the Brahmans to present the following challenge to Aurangzeb: 'Our master and guide is Tegh Bahadur of noble Kshatriya descent. If the emperor can persuade him to become a Muslim then we too shall convert to Islam. If, however, he refuses, then we should be freed from the obligation to do so.' [5

The delegation hastened with all possible speed to present this message to Zalam Khan, Governor of the Punjab. [6

The Guru's challenge was duly communicated to Aurangzeb, who greeted it with expectant pleasure and gave orders for the Guru to be conducted to Delhi with all honour. This, however, was not in accordance with the Guru's own plans. He announced that he would make his own way to Delhi, and Aurangzeb, having been assured that the Guru's word could be trusted, permitted him to do so. [7

According to Gian Singh's account Guru Tegh Bahadur followed a circuitous route, visiting his sangats along the way. Eventually he reached Delhi and in the hope that he might be intimidated he was there imprisoned in a mansion believed to be haunted. Needless to say, the Guru was in no way disconcerted, nor was he persuaded by any effort which the emperor might make to convert him. Drawing on his own vivid imagination, Gian Singh considerably expands the received tradition with purported conversations between Guru and emperor. Blandishment and threats were both tried, and both failed. The execution of the Guru's personal attendants likewise failed to intimidate him. The Delhi drama moved to its tragic, triumphant climax. [8

That evening a proclamation was read in the city announcing that Guru Tegh Bahadur, the Hindu pir, would be executed the following morning at 7.30 a.m. The execution was to take place near the well in Chandni Chowk and all who wished to witness it were welcome to do so. Dread gripped the Sikhs of Delhi when they heard this announcement. Among those affected by the news was Bhai Jawahar Mal Arora, who had arrived in Delhi on business that very day, having vowed to give the Guru five hundred rupees. He managed to persuade Abdul the jailer to let him visit the divine Guru, and the Guru, after accepting his offering, distributed the entire sum to the needy. After darkness had fallen the same Sikh brought a feast of many different kinds of food. Appreciating this expression of love, the Guru shared the food with his followers and gave comfort to the generous donor. The Sikhs who were with him remained awake all night singing hymns. [9

The actual execution took place on Thursday, 11 November 1675. Having bathed at the usual hour, the Guru spent some time singing devotional songs. The heavens wept as grief-stricken Sikhs assembled for the final act in the tragedy. The Guru himself, however, remained serene. The royal qazi came and for the last time offered him the choice of conversion or death. His reply left the issue in no doubt. [10

When the qazi reported his clear and defiant answer to Aurangzeb the enraged emperor immediately ordered the chief executioner, Saiyyid Jalaluddin, to make preparations for the beheading of the Guru. The sight struck terror in the hearts of the people who observed what was happening. When the Guru, having completed five recitations of *Japji Sahib*, bowed his head to meditate on God the brutal Saiyyid from Samana struck him with a sword so sharp that his head was completely severed from his body. The assembled crowd shuddered and uttered a horrified groan. Then darkness fell and an earthquake rocked the city. Fresh green trees wilted in despair. Shouts of triumph were heard from heaven and cries of lamentation from the earth . . . Good men, both Hindu and Muslim, gave vent to their grief. Some wailed in anguish, some wrung their hands, some angrily called down vengeance on Aurangzeb.[20]   [11

2.2.8 Guru Gobind Singh (1675–1708)

Although Aurangzeb had executed the Guru he had certainly not extinguished the spirit of the Guru's followers. Under the leadership of the tenth Guru the Panth entered its heroic period, a period which initially exposed it to the might of the Mughal empire but which ended a century later in triumph for the Sikhs. It was Mughal authority that collapsed during the early decades of the eighteenth century, and within the Punjab it was Sikh power that took its place.   [1

From Guru Gobind Singh to Maharaja Ranjit Singh there extends a period of crucial importance in Sikh history. It is critically important because attitudes and conventions still powerfully present within the Panth of today owe their form and influence to the Panth's experience during this period. For more than a century it was occupied in intermittent warfare and increasingly in the acquisition of power. The experience was to fire it with confident ardour, with a sense of militant destiny which it has never since lost.   [2

The principal event within this period occurred at its beginning. For several generations the Gurus had delegated authority to agents known as masands. In 1699 Guru Gobind Singh summoned all Sikhs to acknowledge his direct personal authority, to accept initiation into a new order, and to observe thereafter a distinctive discipline. The order thus created was the Khalsa. Gian Singh provided a dramatic account of the crucial event which took place at Anandpur on the Baisakhi festival day of 1699 (30 March 1699).   [3

On the day before Baisakhi the Guru arranged for a large tent made of fine woollen fabric to be pitched on the area known as Kesgarh. Earlier he had given instructions for a large dais to be erected at the edge of the area. At that place he held a magnificent reception attended by five thousand Sikhs, all with eyes for none save the Guru. While they were gazing with rapture the Guru rose from his throne and in order to test them addressed the mighty assembly as follows. 'I want the heads of five Sikhs to offer as a sacrifice to God,' he proclaimed. 'Those Sikhs, beloved of the Guru, who cheerfully give their heads will enjoy in the eternal hereafter all the happiness that their hearts desire.'   [4

Terror gripped the hearts of all who heard him. All fell silent, the blood draining from their faces. The Guru drew his sword and called to them again. 'Why are you silent?' he cried. 'Who amongst you sincerely believes his body to be of no account? Let him stand up.' 			[5

Hearing this Daya Singh, a pious Khatri from Lahore, stood with hands respectfully joined. The Guru conducted him into the tent where five goats were secretly tethered. He felled one of them, letting its blood gush out. When he returned to the assembly the people were stunned by the sight of his bloodstained sword. When he proceeded to demand the head of another Sikh they stood petrified. 'He must have been bewitched by the goddess,' they said. 'Why elese should he demand the heads of Sikhs?' Some said one thing, some another. 			[6

Then Dharam Singh, a landowner, stood up. 'My Lord, here is your servant's head,' he said humbly. 'Are you not afraid to die?' asked the Guru. 'My Lord,' he answered, 'I gave you my head on the day I became your Sikh. It has already been entrusted to you. Do with it as you wish. This transitory body is but a morsel for Death to consume. Death is like a man carrying food in his pouch. Some he has already eaten, some he is actually munching, and the remainder he regards with anticipation. When all are thus condemned why should we hesitate to deliver our heads to the Guru?' 			[7

This response pleased the Guru greatly. Taking him into the tent, he seated him there, despatched another goat, and returned to the assembly. Blood could be seen trickling from the tent and when they again beheld the Guru with gleaming sword and fierce red eyes the crowd was panic-stricken. Timid Sikhs turned deathly pale. Agitated masands rushed to the Guru's mother protesting that her son was laying waste the noble work of his predecessors. . . . Meanwhile three more Sikhs had responded in turn to the Guru's summons. These were Himmat Singh, a Jhinvar by caste; Sahib Singh, a Nai; and Muhakam Singh, a Chhimbar. All were faithful disciples, pious men wholly given to worship and meditation who valued true wisdom and principle more than their own lives. When the Guru called for heads to be sacrificed these five Sikhs offered theirs. Faint-hearted Sikhs and masands, tricked by the goat ruse into believing that men were really being killed, whispered anxiously to each other, desperately wanting to flee. This they were unable to do. Overpowered by the radiant presence of the Guru, each was firmly rooted to the spot. 			[8

Although many more Sikhs, faithful and brave, were by this time clamouring to give their heads the Guru demanded only five. He did not call for a sixth. To those who had responded, the Cherished Five, he gave new garments and fine weapons so that their appearance should resemble his own. Then he led them from the tent, back to his assembled Sikhs. All were thunderstruck, believing that the Guru had restored to life those whom he had previously slain. 'Surely our Guru's power exceeds that of all other gurus!' they cried. 			[9

The Guru conducted the five to thrones set upon the dais and when they were seated he turned to the assembly . . . Hearing him and seeing the five resplendently alive, they who had been transfixed by fear now dissolved in rapturous relief. Many ruefully asked themselves why they had not stood up and offered their heads. The Guru comforted them, saying, 'You are all supremely precious to the Guru, all of you true and faithful. Remember how Guru Nanak tested the loyalty of his followers by feigning madness. The only one to pass the test was Guru Angad. By the grace of Guru Nanak there exists a mighty host of Sikhs. Five have now stood forth, with the result that countless others have been confirmed in their loyalty. Now it is clear for all to see that the Panth will win renown, that it will strike down the enemies of this land while it spreads abroad the message of the Sikh faith. All this will happen because God has made himself manifest in these five. As it has been said, "The chosen five are the five supreme; and the five find honour in the Court of God." By the grace of Guru Nanak all things will be fulfilled. We give thanks to God that he has destroyed the religion of Muhammad and his successors, replacing it with the supremacy of the Guru's chosen five.' . . .   [10

On the morning following this momentous event the Guru rose early. Having bathed and completed his period of meditation, he gave instructions for karah prasad worth one hundred rupees to be prepared and for another assembly to be held on the Kesgarh ground. When they heard the announcement from the Guru's stewards the sangat reassembled with eager anticipation. 'Let us see what the Guru will do today,' they said to each other.   [11

Meanwhile the Guru had donned white garments. Approaching the place of assembly, he took his seat on an impressive throne. To one side a contingent of five hundred mighty warriors sat armed and at the ready. After pouring water from the Satluj river into a large iron vessel the Guru gave instructions for the Cherished Five to be clad in white garments (including breeches) together with a sword and other symbolic items. He then had them stand before him and commanded them to repeat the divine name 'Vahiguru', fixing their minds on God as they did so. This they were to continue doing while he stirred the sanctified water (*amrit*) in the iron vessel with a double-edged sword held vertically. Before the recitation of *Japji Sahib* had been completed Mata Jito, the first of the Guru's wives, cast soluble sweets into the iron vessel and then sat at the Guru's left hand. After he had finished reciting *Anand Sahib* and *Ardas* The Guru commended her inspired contribution to the inaugurating of the [Khalsa] Panth. . . .   [12

The Guru then used the tip of his sword to take a small quantity of amrit from the iron vessel. This he did five times, letting each portion run from his sword on to his face. He then applied amrit to each of the Cherished Five in the following manner. Five times he poured amrit into the recipient's cupped hand. Five times he applied it to his hair, and five times he sprinkled it on his eyes. As he dispensed each handful he commanded the recipient to say, 'Vahiguru ji ka Khalsa, Vahiguru ji ki fateh' (4.5 [20]). This they repeated after the Guru. He then instructed each of them to recite the *Gur-mantra* five times (the first five stanzas of *Japji Sahib*). Next he gave them all karah prasad, every portion being taken from the same iron pan. Finally he promulgated the code of conduct which they were to observe. . . .   [13

Thus did the Guru lay the foundations of the Khalsa, determine its form, and define the obligations of its members.[21]   [14

*The inauguration of the Khalsa order was followed by a period of warfare,
terminating with the evacuation of Anandpur in 1705. During the course of
the fighting the four sons of Guru Gobind Singh were all killed, two in battle
and two by brutal execution. The Guru himself withdrew to Damdama in
southern Punjab. In 1707, having learnt of Aurangzeb's death, he visited
Agra and was honourably received by the new emperor, Bahadur Shah. He
agreed to join the emperor on an expedition to South India and during its
course died in 1708 at Nander in the Deccan.*   [15

*It is believed that prior to his death Guru Gobind Singh declared the
succession of personal Gurus to be nearing its end. After he had gone the
authority of the eternal Guru was to pass to the corporate community (the
Guru Panth or Khalsa) and sacred scripture (the Guru Granth). This
tradition is appended to the account of his death given in Sainapati's* Gur
Sobha.   [16

It is said that a certain Pathan came to the Guru with the intention of
assassinating him. He lingered for an hour or two, making pleasant
conversation, but was unable to carry out his plan because there were so many
people with the Guru. The Pathan returned to where he was staying and came
back again on two or three subsequent days. Each time he sat watching for an
hour or two, and he came to the conclusion that he would have to perform the
deed when there were few people present, returning on several occasions to
ensure that he understood the situation thoroughly.   [17

Having decided that the best time for the deed would be at night, the villain
came late one evening. The Guru heard him and called him into his room. He
invited the rascal to sit beside him and offered him food. The Pathan took some
and ate it. No Sikh was in the vicinity, except for one who was dozing. The
Guru himself soon lay down to sleep, whereupon the scoundrel drew his sword
and lunged for the Guru's heart. He struck a second time, but before he could
strike again the Guru retaliated. A single blow was sufficient.   [18

The Guru then called his followers, who appeared from all directions. Two
accomplices [who had come with the assassin] tried to escape, but both were
caught and killed. The encampment was in an uproar, and amidst the confusion
the Guru's followers, unaware that the Pathan was already dead, slashed at his
corpse. 'There is no need to do that,' said the Guru. 'He is already dead. Take
him away.'   [19

They carried away the wretch whom the Guru had slain. No one had yet
noticed that the Guru had actually been wounded. But then they saw him
swaying and when they examined his chest they discovered that he was indeed
wounded. Great was their alarm and dismay. The Guru assured them,
however, that God had protected him. This allayed their fears to some extent
and they summoned one of his attendants to sew up the wound. This was done,
but when the Guru sat up the stitches parted. The wound was stitched again,
and next morning ointment was applied. Three or four days passed, during

which time many Sikhs came to pay their respects. . . .   [20

Thus he received his followers and spoke with them; and they, having seen him, took leave and departed. Several days passed in this manner, but then the end drew near. The Guru ordered food to be brought. He ate some, drank some water, and reassured all who were with him. An hour and three quarters after midnight he began to recite the divine Word. Then he called to his Sikhs and having wakened them he bade them a final 'Vahiguru ji ki fateh.' They were bewildered when they heard him, and fear overtook them as they thought of all the things they should have asked him.   [21

The Sikhs gathered together and discussed what they should do. They decided that they would cremate the Guru's body and that they should do so before sunrise. The light that inhabited it had already returned to the infinite light from which it came. All this took place during the early morning hours of darkness on the fifth day of the waxing moon in the month of Kattak, S. 1765 [7 October 1708 A.C.] . . .   [22

On an earlier occasion the Guru had been approached by his Sikhs and had been asked what form the [eternal] Guru would assume [after he had departed this earthly life]. He had repled that it would be the Khalsa. 'The Khalsa is now the focus of all my hopes and desires,' he had declared. 'Upon the Khalsa which I have created I shall bestow the succession. The Khalsa is my physical form and I am one with the Khalsa. To all eternity I shall be manifest in the Khalsa. They whose hearts are purged of falsehood will be known as the true Khalsa; and the Khalsa, freed from error and illusion, will be my true Guru.   [23

'And my true Guru, boundless and infinite, is the eternal Word, the Word of wisdom which the devout contemplate in their hearts, the Word which brings ineffable peace to all who utter it, the Word which is wisdom immeasurably unfolded, the Word which none may ever describe. This is the light which is given to you, the refuge of all who inhabit the world, and the abode of all who renounce it.'[22]   [24

3 THE SCRIPTURES

3.1 THE ADI GRANTH

3.1.1 Guru Nanak

Having opened with a liturgical prologue, the Adi Granth turns to the sequence of ragas which provides the vast bulk of its material. The first of the ragas is Siri Raga *and as the works of the Gurus are recorded in chronological order it begins with a hymn by Guru Nanak. In this opening hymn Guru Nanak enunciates his fundamental doctrine. God is all-powerful and without him all hope is vain.*   [1

If I should own a priceless palace, walled with pearl and tiled with jewels; || Rooms perfumed with musk and saffron, sweet with fragrant sandalwood; || Yet may your Name remain, O Master, in my thoughts and in my heart.   [2

Refrain. Apart from God my soul must burn, || Apart from God no place to turn, || The Guru thus declares.   [3

If, in a world aglow with diamonds, rubies deck my bed; || If with alluring voice and gesture jewelled maidens proffer charms; || Yet may your Name remain, O Master, in my thoughts and in my heart.   [4

If with the yogi's mystic art I work impressive deeds, || Present now, then presto vanished, winning vast renown; || Yet may your Name remain, O Master, in my thoughts and in my heart.   [5

If as the lord of powerful armies, if as a king enthroned, || Though my commands bring prompt obedience, yet would my strength be vain. || Grant that your Name remain, O Master, in my thoughts and in my heart.[1]   [6

In this first hymn Guru Nanak refers to God's 'Name' in a manner which clearly suggests a concept of crucial importance. The divine Name of God is indeed a key concept, one which expresses the most basic of doctrines in the teachings of Guru Nanak (7.4). It is, moreover, a term which retains its primacy throughout the Adi Granth and beyond. All the Gurus make repeated reference to the Name, indicating in the clearest possible terms that man's hope of liberation depends on an understanding of what it means and on an actual grasping of the benefits which it confers. Because the Guru's make such frequent use of the term it inevitably recurs with corresponding frequency in the translations which follow. It is therefore most important that any reading of the works of the Gurus should be accompanied by an understanding of what they mean by the name.   [7

The actual word which appears in Gurbani is nam, *commonly used alone but sometimes in such expanded forms as* hari-nam *or* ram-nam, *'the Name of God'. Although the English word 'Name' is an exact translation it is obviously inadequate except as a convenient shorthand. It is, however, much closer to the actual meaning than our loose English usage might suggest. A name should be more than a mere tag. It should express something of the nature of whatever it designates, or at least point towards that nature. This is precisely the purpose which* nam *is intended to serve in the works of the Gurus.   [8*

The word nam *is a summary expression for the whole nature of God. Anything which may be affirmed concerning God is an aspect of the* nam. *Because he is all-powerful it follows that omnipotence is a part of the* nam. *Because he knows all things, omniscience is similarly a feature of the* nam. *The many and varied qualities which may be attached to God are all thereby to be regarded as aspects of the* nam, *the divine Name. And because God himself is infinite so too is the Name.[2]   [9*

This stress upon the Name as an expression of God's inherent nature should not imply that it is essentially passive. As far as the Gurus are concerned it is crucial that individuals should understand its active role. God in his mercy desires that all men should be freed from the anguish of transmigration and he sets before them the means to achieving this end. The means to liberation are enunciated by the Guru, and the message thus communicated by the Guru enjoins all men to bring their lives into harmony with the divine Name. By means of regular devotion coupled with strict virtue each person can develop a pattern of living which accords with the nature of God as expressed in his Name. This involves the earnest seeker in an ascent through progressively exalted levels of enlightenment and joy. In the end he attains to the supreme rapture, to the ineffable bliss of mystical union with God. It is this experience of blissful union which constitutes liberation from the cycle of transmigration; and it is this liberation which constitutes plenary salvation in the teachings of the Gurus.   [10

The fact that God in his grace proffers the Name to all who would accept it does not mean that it can be obtained without effort. He who wishes to appropriate the benefits conferred by a knowledge of the Name must undertake the regular discipline of nam simaran, 'remembrance of the divine Name'. At one level this involves the practice of nam japan, or 'repeating the Name', a long-established convention whereby merit is acquired by devoutly repeating a sacred word or mantra. This helps the devotee to internalise the meaning of whatever he may be uttering and in this sense the practice is explicitly enjoined by the Gurus. The Gurus also insist that the discipline must be practised in a corporate sense, with devotees gathering as a congregation (satsang) to sing hymns of praise (kirtan). A third level which is also required of the loyal disciple is meditation. God as expressed in the name is to be 'remembered' not merely in the repeating of auspicious words or the singing of inspired hymns but also in deep contemplation of the divine mystery of the Name. All three practices constitute legitimate and necessary forms of nam simaran.[3]   [11

It will be observed that this analysis of liberation through the divine Name has involved two separate usages of the word 'Guru', one singular and the other plural. This brings us to another key doctrine, one which is intimately associated with the divine Name. According to the Adi Granth God is a God of grace who actively communicates the truth which sets men free. The means whereby he effects this communication, the 'Word' of God, is mystically 'spoken' to man's inner understanding by the Guru. The Guru is thus, in a primary sense, the 'voice' of God and it is in this sense that it is used above in the refrain from Siri Raga 1. Because Nanak submitted himself to God in total obedience and achieved thereby a perfect enlightenment he became the human vehicle of the 'voice' of God. As such he is properly designated Guru Nanak. The same divine spirit similarly inhabited his nine successors, all of them bearing the same exalted title of Guru or Satguru (True Guru). With the death of Guru Gobind Singh the divine Guru ceased to occupy a human habitation and passed instead to the sacred scripture (the

Guru Granth) and the company of believers (the Guru Panth).[4] [12

This extension of the fundamental doctrine has introduced yet another basic term, the word shabad or 'Word'.[5] The introduction of the divine Word adds the final component to Guru Nanak's doctrine of revelation. God the Creator is revealed through his Name, expressed as the Word and spoken inwardly by the Guru. He who hears the Word and in obedience to the Guru lives a life which conforms to the nature of the Name will eventually achieve the blissful serenity of divine union. The actual obligations of a life of obedience find expression in the regular, disciplined practice of the various forms of nam simaran. Faithful performance of nam simaran lifts the disciple to that sublime condition known to experience but far transcending the power of telling. It is this experience which frees him for ever from the round of transmigration and thus brings him to eternal salvation.[6] [13

As one would expect, the three key words (nam, guru and shabad) recur again and again in the works of the Gurus. The second hymn in Siri Raga is another of the many Adi Granth compositions which exalt the absolute claims of the divine Name. [14

If in this life I should live to eternity, nourished by nothing save air; || If I should dwell in the darkest of dungeons, sense never resting in sleep; || Yet must your glory transcend all my striving; no words can encompass the Name. [15

Refrain. He who is truly the Spirit Eternal,[7] immanent, blissful serene; || Only by grace can we learn of our Master, only by grace can we tell. [16

If I were slain and my body dismembered, pressed in a hand-mill and ground; || If I were burnt in a fire all-consuming, mingled with ashes and dust; || Yet must your glory transcend all my striving; no words can encompass the Name. [17

If as a bird I could soar to the heavens, a hundred such realms in my reach; || If I could change so that none might perceive me and live without food, without drink; || Yet must your glory transcend all my striving; no words can encompass the Name. [18

If I could read with the eye of intelligence paper of infinite weight; || If I could write with the winds everlasting, pens dipped in oceans of ink; || Yet must your glory transcend all my striving; no words can encompass the name.[8] [19

Although the Guru is normally represented as the 'voice' of God or as his messenger, Nanak makes it clear that this usage should not imply any fundamental distinction from God. The Guru is in fact God, the Creator himself acting as Preceptor in order to communicate the message of salvation to needy mankind. This identity is clearly indicated in the following hymn from Sorath raga, a hymn which also stresses God's immanence. [20

All that has life must be subject to destiny, each one inscribed since creation began. || Only the Lord is immune from Fate's mastery, sovereign Creator and author of all. [21

Refrain. Let me repeat the blest Name of the Master; thus I find comfort and joy. || Constant the service I give to the Guru, God who is present in all.[9] [22

Dwelling within us, in all that surrounds us, God stands alone, for no other exists. || See him, the One, with the aid of the Guru, present within us as mystical light. *[23*

Stilling your spirit so restless and fitful, mark what the Guru reveals to us all. || Awed by his wonder behold the invisible, joy breaking forth as our woes melt away. *[24*

Drink the Lord's nectar, find peace beyond telling, peace that is blissful, unchanging, serene. || Sing to his praises, the Lord of creation; freed from the cycle of death and rebirth. *[25*

Essence of all things and light all-pervading, God lives in all and in him all things dwell. || He who is infinite, boundless in majesty, he is the Guru whom Nanak proclaims.[10] *[26*

The emphasis which Guru Nanak lays on the divine Name is present throughout the entire range of his works, and indeed through most of the Adi Granth. This does not mean, however, that his hymns contain little else. The divine Name theme is normally treated in conjunction with other issues or doctrines. In the next hymn Nanak contrasts the wisdom of the Name with the empty futility of worldly learning. The janam-sakhis set this particular composition in the context of a discourse between the child Nanak and a pundit engaged to teach him[11] (2.1.1 [3]). *[27*

Burn sensual craving, make ink with its ashes; as paper prepare heart and mind. || Take love as your pen and with reason the scribe enquire of the Guru and list his commands. || Write on that paper God's Name and God's praises; write of his infinite power! *[28*

Refrain. This is the record to learn how to write; || This is the record by which we are judged. *[29*

Where fame is conferred in the presence of God, where glory and rapture abound, || They who have treasured God's Name in their hearts bear the marks of his grace on their brows. || For grace is the means to obtaining the Name; all other is bluster and wind. *[30*

One may appear and another depart, each with his dignified title and name; || One may be born to beg food and his clothing, another to rule with renown. || Each as he passes shall surely discover that lacking the Name he is doomed. *[31*

In dread of your majesty, awesomely grand, my body must waste and decay. || They who were known as the lords of creation have withered and crumbled to dust. || Our ties with this transient world must dissolve when we rise and proceed on our way.[12] *[32*

Although the janam-sakhi story of Nanak and his teacher need not be treated as historical there can be no doubt concerning the Guru's attitude towards pundits who took a pride in their scholarly reputation. Brahmanical pretensions of whatever sort were roundly censured, for they exalted the external and the transient at the cost of the inward and the eternal. All conventional religion, whether Hindu or Muslim, was to be condemned for the sanction it gave to such external practices as mosque or temple worship, pilgrimage, and caste observance. Such practices were acceptable only if they

*involved an inner reality as well as an external observance; and if the inner
reality were present the outward observance ceased to be necessary. In
another typical sequence of metaphors Guru Nanak urges a Muslim to
reinterpret his traditional Islam in the light of inward reality.* [33

Make mercy your mosque and devotion your prayer mat, righteousness your
Qur'an; || Meekness your circumcising, goodness your fasting, for thus the true
Muslim expresses his faith. || Make good works your Ka'bah, take truth as your
pir, compassion your creed and your prayer. || Let service to God be the beads
which you tell and God will exalt you to glory.[13] [34

*Hindus and Muslims were not the only targets of the criticisms aimed at
conventional religion. During the time of Guru Nanak yogis of the Nath
tradition exercised considerable influence, respected for their ascetic
discipline and feared for the magical powers they were believed to possess.
Nath yogis claimed to be the disciples of the master ascetic Gorakhnath
and renouncing all worldly ties they devoted themselves to the practice of
hatha-yoga.[14] Their outward appearance was strikingly distinguished by a
number of prominent features, notably the large ear-rings which they wore.
(They were for this reason commonly known as Kanphat or 'split ear' yogis.)
Other items included a patchwork quilt, a horn, a begging bowl, and a short
crutch on which they might lean while sitting on the ground. Nath yogis lit a
fire wherever they stopped and regularly smeared their bodies with ashes.* [35

*The importance of the Naths during the time of Guru Nanak is plainly
indicated by the frequency of his references to them. In one fundamental
respect he shared with them a common conviction. The climax of the* hatha-
yoga *technique was held to be a condition of ineffable beatitude which in
Nath usage was known as* sahaj. *Guru Nanak agreed that the ecstasy of* sahaj
*was the ultimate objective, but disagreed with regard to the means whereby it
could be achieved. For Guru Nanak the only effective method could be* nam
simaran. *The Naths were mistaken in seeking it through* hatha-yoga *or
asceticism, and their distinctive usages were for him merely another example
of external futility. In hymns addressed to Naths he urges them to reinterpret
their beliefs in accordance with the Word of the Guru.* [36

I wear as my ear-ring the Word of the Guru, my robe with its patches the
patience I bear. || With gladness I welcome the will of my Master for thus we are
brought to the rapture sublime.[15] [37

Refrain. Blessed the yogi who mounts to this ecstasy, merged in the mystical
wonder of God. || Finding God's Name he knows bliss inexpressible, feeding his
soul on the wisdom divine. [38

Turning my eyes to the inner reality, casting aside all that blinds or distracts;
|| Bearing the horn of the Word of the Guru, hearing its music by day and by
night. [39

Thought is my begging bowl, wisdom my staff, with my ashes supplied by
God's presence in all.[16] || Singing to God is my regular discipline, faith in the
Guru my rigorous path.[17] [40

God's light is one though his forms be unnumbered; on it I lean as the crutch which I bear. || Hear me, O Bharathri,[18] Nanak has spoken: merge in the mystical being of God.[19]   [41

Guru Nanak's fondness for metaphor appears in a wide variety of contexts. Another selection is used to indicate the way of life which the disciple should follow.   [42

Let deeds be the soil, the seeding God's Word; let Truth be the water you daily apply || Let faith be the crop which you grow in your field, for thus you will learn of both heaven and hell.   [43

Refrain. Do not imagine that words are sufficient to raise us to heaven or save us from hell. || Seduced by possessions and sensuous pride we fritter our lives away.   [44

Sin is the slime which adheres to our bodies, minds like the frogs which no bloom can attract. || Follow the bee as it flies to the lotus, chiding our ignorant pride.[20]   [45

All that we say and whatever we hear is profitless wind if our minds are corrupt. || The grace of the Lord and the love which he bears is for those who remember the Name.   [46

You honour your fasts and you say all your prayers, believing that thereby sly Satan is foiled. || Why gather wealth and the goods of this world when the pathway to death lies ahead?[21]   [47

The perils of worldly temptation and the folly of external devotion are allied themes which appear repeatedly in the works of Guru Nanak. Assaults are also mounted against hypocrisy, particularly the variety which is associated with an outward display of piety. A famous example from Suhi *raga has produced three different janam-sakhi stories, each one describing the conversion of a pious villain.*[22]   [48

Bronze shines brightly and yet we find that it sheds an inky black. || Rub it a hundred thousand times and the blackness will still remain.   [49

Refrain. Constant the friends who stand firmly beside me, here and hereafter true; || They who can answer when Death shall demand that account which we all must produce.   [50

Beautiful houses, fine temples and palaces, each a delight to the eye; || Let them but fall and we see their true value, their frames gaping empty within.   [51

The heron so pious, in spotless white feathers, paddles in sanctified water.[23] || Pecking for food, it brings death to its victims, so how can we treat it as pure?[24]   [52

My body resembles the silk-cotton tree, falsely believed to be useful.[25] || Worthless the virtue I claim as its produce, outwardly spotless yet sterile.   [53

Doomed like the blind man encumbered with error, climbing a perilous slope; || Scanning the pathway I falter and stumble, crushed by my load of despair.   [54

What is the use of such service or virture, or wisdom devoid of the Name? || Nurture the Name in your heart with devotion; thus you shall cast off your chains.[26]   [55

The works of Guru Nanak embody a universal message, one which seldom refers to any particular time or circumstance. There is, however, a notable exception to this rule. It was while Guru Nanak was residing in Kartarpur that Babur, the Mughal ruler of Kabul, began the series of sorties into the Punjab which finally culminated in the battle of Panipat in 1526. At Panipat the Lodi forces under Sultan Ibrahim of Delhi were overthrown and the period of Mughal rule began. [56

The Mughal period commonly invokes an impression of glory and splendour, much of it associated with Akbar's reputation for tolerance and the magnificent architecture of Shahjahan. Guru Nanak presents a different view. In four famous hymns, collectively known as the Babar-vani *or 'utterances concerning Babur', he graphically depicts the suffering inflicted by the invaders.*[27] *The actual incidents are not specified, but the principal participant is named and the devastation is described in words which must surely have been those of an eye-witness.* [57

In spite of his destructive role Babur is seen by Guru Nanak to have been an unwitting instrument of the divine will. Because the Lodis had violated God's laws they were compelled to pay the penalty. Babur descended from Kabul as God's chosen agent, demonstrating the absolute authority of God and the retribution which must follow defiance of his laws. Guru Nanak's commentary on the events which he actually witnessed thus becomes a part of the same universal message. God is absolute and no man may disobey his commands with impunity. Obey him and receive freedom. Disobey him and the result must inevitably be retribution, a dire reckoning which brings suffering in this present life and continued transmigration in the hereafter. [58

Once they had heads of luxuriant hair, partings adorned with red.|| Now they must suffer the shears of brutality, throats filled with thick choking dust. || Driven away from the palace that sheltered them, now they must wander forlorn. [59

Refrain. Hail to the Lord, to the Lord of eternity, || Infinite Master, inhabiting all. [60

On the day they were wed, with their radiant grooms, proudly they sat in their marital splendour,|| Ivory bangles fresh on their arms, they were carried in palanquins, grandly arrayed. || Vessels of water waved over their heads,[28] in their hands they clasped glittering fans. [61

Sitting they gathered great masses of coins;[29] more they received when they stood.|| Feasting on nuts and on dates they were led to the joys of their marital beds. || Now they are lashed with the conqueror's rope, all their necklaces broken and scattered. [62

Riches and beauty, which once they admired, are enemies now to be feared.|| Angels of death, under orders to persecute, strip them and carry them off. || Glory or punishment, either we gather, as God in his purpose declares. [63

Freedom was theirs had they paused to consider it; grief was the fate which their sins must attract. || Heedless, the rulers,[30] distracted by merriment, followed the way which must lead to despair. || Now they must starve, for their foes have demolished them; now it is Babur who rules in their place.   [64

Muslims prevented from saying their prayer and the Hindus from offering worship;[31] || How can a woman observe Hindu custom, with bathing and frontal mark pure for her kitchen? || They who neglected remembrance of Ram are rebuffed if they call on Khuda.[32]   [65

Some may return from the field of disaster, greeted by those who will seek to console. || Others less fortunate, harried by destiny, sit in their anguish to grieve and lament. || All that God wills, Nanak, this we experience; all that God destines must surely prevail.[33]   [66

3.1.2 Guru Angad

The three principal forms in the Adi Granth are the shabad *(hymn), the* pauri *(stanza), and the* shalok *(usually a couplet but sometimes running to several lines).[34] Each shabad is a complete work, regardless of its length; and each pauri forms part of a sequence. The shaloks, however, are less regular. Many of them have been recorded under the names of their various authors in the epilogue which concludes the Adi Granth (1.2 [9]). Others are thickly scattered through the composite works known as* vars *(5.5. [1–4]).*   [1

Guru Angad's contribution to the Adi Granth consists exclusively of shaloks. Sixty-three of these compositions are identified as his work, most of them very brief. The following example, an exception to this rule, is one of the longest shaloks to be found in the Adi Granth.   [2

Through all the eight watches[35] we feed our desires, neglecting the spirit within. || Within us is treasure, God's wonderful Name, a storehouse of riches divine. || Blessed is he who sings praises to God, who led by the Guru is drawn to the truth. || In the watch which brings night to its tranquil conclusion[36] he senses a longing within. || We find ourselves drawn to some cool flowing stream, the Name on our lips, in our hearts. || Wondrous the blessings which there we receive, the grace which our Master bestows.   [3

Our bodies transfigured are turned into gold, assayed by the hand of the Lord. || If he is pleased by the test he applies he spares us thereafter the fire. || In the hours which remain follow goodness and truth, consorting with those who are wise. || Reflect with their aid upon virtue and sin, casting all falsehood aside. || There in their presence the bad are rejected, the noble held up to acclaim. || Pleasure and pain we receive as God orders; our words are all futile and vain.[37]   [4

3.1.3 Guru Amar Das

The pathway to God is revealed by the Guru, || A meeting which God decrees. || God knows the pathways which lead us to him, || The Order[38] his Word has revealed.   [1

Refrain. Fear of the Lord quells earthly fears, || That awesome fear which brings us to God. [2

God comes to us when we turn to the Guru, || Dear Master, beyond compare. || Praise him and worship his infinite Word, || The Giver of mercy and grace. [3

Truth we obtain when we come to the Guru; || The True One resides in our hearts. || When God dwells within all our deeds must be pure, ||All our actions prescribed by the Word. [4

We learn to serve God by the grace of the Guru, || Though few have discovered his Name. || May God live for ever, the Giver divine! || Our love for his Name shall endure.[39] [5

According to tradition Guru Amar Das was once visited by a learned Brahman, famed for his knowledge of the Hindu scriptures and for the substantial library which accompanied him on his travels. The hymn which follows is said to have been composed as a commentary on the visitor's arrogance.[40] It can also be read as a message addressed by the Guru to all Brahmans who took pride in their orthodox learning or who claimed special privileges on account of their traditional status. [6

Are we by nature worldly in spirit[41] or are we by nature detached? || Are our minds free from all social constraints, the spirit within us immortal? || Are our hearts restless or tranquil and free? || Why are they smitten by false worldly pride? [7

Refrain. Examine your nature, O wise learned Brahman. || All that you read is a wearisome weight! [8

Worldly attachments are given by God, pride and the lure of temptation. || This is the Order bestowed on the world, the Order which governs creation. || But wisdom is gained by the grace of the Guru. || Grasp it and with it the refuge it brings. [9

He who is truly a dutiful Brahman will cast off his burden of human desire, || Each day performing his God-given duty, each day repeating God's Name. || To such as submit God imparts divine learning, and those who obey him live virtuous lives. || He who is truly a dutiful Brahman wins honour when summoned to God. [10

Discerning the immanent nature of God he proclaims the Lord's presence in all; || Only the man who has eyes to perceive can attain to the knowledge required. || His spirit awakes if the Master is gracious; he comes to the Master's embrace. || Peace he finds waiting and wonderful happiness, now and for ever more. [11

What, asks Nanak, can man achieve, what methods avail with God? || Grace alone has the power to save, by grace alone are we freed. || Each day sing praises to God the Lord; each day sing hymns of joy. || The scriptures of old can do nothing to save us,[42] for only God's grace can avail.[43] [12

Guru Nanak's insistence on deliverance through the grace of the Guru and the power of the divine Name receives the same insistent emphasis in the works of his successors. [13

The Name of God is our merchandise, Truth is the trade we pursue || The Guru directs us in plying our trade, our goods of consummate worth || Blessed are they who can join in this trade, this trade with its prices so high || All are imbued with devotion to God, steeped in the glorious Name || All who would share in this trade in the Truth must inherit God's grace and must deal in God's Word. || Imbued with the Name they find deep satisfaction, these merchants who trade in the Truth. *[14*

Pride and desire [44] cause a grievous pollution, fouling the mind with their filth || The Guru directs us in cleansing our minds with a potion which God supplies. || As we drink from this potion there surges within us the Word of God's truth in our hearts. || Within us we harbour a well-spring of joy and the Word draws its pure nectar out. || All who would drink from this fountain of Truth must inherit God's grace, for by grace it is found. || Imbued with the Name they are cleansed from their filth, with the scum of their pride washed away. *[15*

Pundits and prophets who follow the stars try to impress with their shouts. || Worldly their trade, in false pride and attachment; filth the reward which it brings. || Worldly their trade, and seduced by desire they are caught in the round of rebirth || Poisonous worms, they take pleasure in vileness, ever absorbed in filth || None can erase what our fate has recorded; no one can wipe it away. || Rapt in God's Name we find joy overflowing, while fools waste their effort in noise. *[16*

If our hearts and our minds are seduced by desire wisdom is driven away; || But desire[45] is uprooted, it withers and dies, when the Guru arrives to stay. || Desire is uprooted while Truth is retained, our storehouse abundantly filled. || Blessed is he who gives ear to the Guru, heeding his message of Truth. || Only by grace can we come to the Lord, a mystery others ignore. || Deprived of God's Name we must wander astray; only the Name brings us joy.[46] *[17*

3.1.4 Guru Ram Das

Refrain. Wondrous Creator, Master eternal, you are my Lord and King. || Whatever may please you infallibly happens; our lot is whatever you bring. *[1*

All are your people, all in your hand; all turn to you in prayer. || He who receives your benevolent grace is blessed with the precious Name. || They who are led by the Guru will find you, leaving the wilful[47] forlorn. || Some you will draw to the joy of your presence, others you cast away. *[2*

You are the River of Life, O Lord; in you all beings dwell. || You are the One, no other exists, your presence encompassing all. || This world where we live is your realm of delight, here where you revel and play. || Here the bereft can be summoned again, restored to your loving embrace. *[3*

They alone know you who, blest with your grace, are brought to this knowledge divine. ||Enlightened by you they sing praises for ever, praise to the source of their joy. || They who serve God in their words and their deeds find the peace which alone he can bring. || Blissfully singing, their spirits enchanted;

mystically rapt in the Name.   *[4*

You are the Master, the Maker of all; all things are wrought by your hand.|| You are the One, for no other exists; your presence encompassing all.|| Having created, you gaze on your labours; all things you comprehend. || All that we need is revealed by your grace, for the Guru has shown us the way.⁴⁸   *[5*

Let him who is known as a Sikh of the Guru rise early and ponder God's Name. || Arising from sleep as the new day is breaking he washes his body and cleanses his soul.⁴⁹ || Repeat the Lord's Name as the Guru commands us, for thus are our sins washed away; || So greet every dawn with the words of the Guru and utter God's Name through the length of the day.   *[6*

Pleasing to God is the Sikh who is faithful, who utters the Name with each breath. || Our Lord shows us mercy, his grace all-bestowing, imparting his message to Sikhs who are true.|| Blessed are they who remember their Master; the dust of their feet I adore. || Blessed are they who lead others to freedom, joining their voices in praise to God's Name.⁵⁰   *[7*

God the Creator inhabits creation, free from all spot and stain; || Creation unfolds its continuing drama, governed by God alone. || The transient world with its many temptations is part of the purpose of God; || The Guru saves all who respond to his bidding, freed by his goodness and grace. || God's presence suffuses the whole of creation, all nature at one with his Truth.   *[8*

The Name of the Lord is our glorious treasure, source of our peace and our joy; || He who repeats the immaculate Name is led to his Father's home. || The Name is enshrined in the hymns of the Guru, these we must lodge in our hearts|| Our spirits subdued as a frightened bird quieted, stilled by the Guru's command. || When the Master shows mercy our spirits are tranquil, mystically rapt in the Name.   *[9*

The Name of our Lord is beyond comprehending; how can we understand?|| The Name of the Lord is our constant companion, how can we make it our own? || The Name of the Master pervades all creation, dwelling in every place; || Our Guru and Master discloses its mystery, present within our hearts.|| When God in his mercy extends us his grace the Guru will come to our aid.   *[10*

His body besmeared with renunciant ashes, yet darkness prevails within; || Though he wear the patched coat of the scrupulous yogi his mind is seduced by pride. || His spirit absorbed in his worldly affections, ignoring the claims of God's Word, || His inward desires having prompted delusion he foolishly wanders astray. || They who neglect to remember the Name must forfeit the chance life affords.   *[11*

They who bathe daily with scrupulous care yet nurture deceit in their hearts|| Shall earn for themselves the rewards of deception, their falsehood uncovered to all. || Whatever a man may conceal in his heart must assuredly come to the light, || And he who has fed upon falsehood and greed shall be doomed to the round of rebirth.|| The seed which we sow is the crop we must harvest, as God's sacred law has decreed.   *[12*

The Guru's disciple finds peace in his heart as the truth of God's Name is revealed; || And all his devotion, the service he renders, brings pleasure and joy to his Lord. || His heart is made pure by the service he offers, with radiant joy he sings praises to God. || Pleasing to God is such fervent devotion and all who perform it are saved. || The grace of the Guru has shown them the pathway; in glory they stand at his door.⁵¹   *[13*

3.1.5 Guru Arjan

A song of spring

Ponder devoutly the Name of God and bloom like the flowers in spring; || This is the season of blessed endeavour for those who receive his grace. || Nature is verdant through all of creation, ambrosia freely bestowed. || The Guru is ours with the peace that he brings, banishing every dark cloud. || Ponder the Name in your heart with devotion and sunder the round of rebirth.   *[1*

They who submit to the guidance of God find strength to control their desires.⁵² || In their hearts and their minds he bestows by his mercy the will to remember his Name. || They who obey him are freed from all sorrow, their sufferings ever erased; || His Name they remember in daylight, in darkness; the Name which will free them from death. || Man who has sprung from the spirit of God thus returns to the source of his birth.   *[2*

What is man's origin, where does he live, how can his spirit find peace? || God is the source of all life that has being; who can take stock of his worth? || Blessed are they who give praise to their Master, who daily remember his Name. || Awesome is God and his wonder unbounded, a glory no other commands. || Such is the truth which the Guru discloses; such is the truth we proclaim.⁵³   *[3*

In this spring shabad Guru Arjan sings of the joy of living. Elsewhere he acknowledges its woes, though always with the same insistent stress on the divine Name as their infallible remedy. The quest for the divine Name is not an enterprise to be conducted in isolation. He who hopes to achieve deliverance from suffering and transmigration must seek it in the congregation of the faithful (the sadh-sangat *or* satsang*). (3.3.1[21]).*   *[4*

Refrain. Tell me, my mother, tell me the way, the way to discover my Lord.[5

Coarse in appearance, witless and feeble, a foreigner come from afar, || I have no wealth nor the freshness of youthfulness; helpless I cry to my Lord. || Pleasure forsaken I spend my days seeking, in craving the sight of my Lord. || My Master is gracious, all yearning is over; his faithful have banished my woes.⁵⁴   *[6*

The same dominant themes are repeated throughout the entire range of Guru Arjan's works, the largest of all the individual contributions to the Adi Granth. He who is faithful in his devotion to the divine Name is assured of deliverance, for the Guru is merciful and his promises sure.   *[7*

Blissful, my friend, is the life to come, || A joy in the future as in the past. || All is the gift of a Master who cares. || Why should my heart be afraid?   *[8*

Refrain. Eternal Lord, my joy, my delight!|| I see you in all your creation. *[9*
All living things are yours, O God; || Your gracious hand supplies our needs. ||
Wondrous your majesty, wondrous might!|| I praise and adore your Name.[55]*[10*

God is my constant companion; || Death's messengers dare not approach. ||
God holds me close in his keeping|| For I trust in the Guru's Word. *[11*
Refrain. The perfect Guru fulfils all my needs.|| My enemies smitten, God's
truth revealed. *[12*
God's presence diffused through the whole of creation,|| Has brought me his
peace and his joy.|| Nanak dwells safe in the hands of the Lord,|| Of the Master
who conquers all pain.[56] *[13*

Refrain. Without the Lord's blessing our actions are futile; all are rejected by
God.|| Mystical mantras, restraint and austerities, works of devotion, all fail at
life's end. *[14*
He who puts faith in his fasting and discipline trusts a misguided belief. ||
In the hereafter such deeds count as worthless, for none can go with us at
death. *[15*
Bathing on pilgrimage, piously wandering, wasting our efforts in vain −|| In
the hereafter such deeds earn no recompense, none can assist at the end. *[16*
Learning the Vedas must likewise be useless, earning no credit or gain.|| All is
dishonour, a wretched pollution; all but God's glorious Name. *[17*
Nanak declares that the man who is worthy, who crosses life's turbulent sea,||
Is he who gives heed to the Guru's commandments and humbly remembers
God's Name.[57] *[18*

The Guru has shattered the shell which is falsehood, his light has illumined
my soul!|| Gone from my feet are the shackles which bound me; the Guru has set
me free. *[19*
Refrain. My wanderings have ended, my restless soul stilled;|| The cauldron,
once seething, now cooled by the Name. *[20*
From the moment I turned to God's faithful disciples the minions of Death
fled away.|| If he who imprisoned me sets me at liberty how can mere warders
protest? *[21*
The burden of earlier deeds is removed and the chains of my past are
destroyed, || Thanks to the grace of the Guru who carried me over life's
turbulent sea. *[22*
The truth which God gives is the land I inhabit, his Truth is the goal which I
seek;|| Truth is my capital, Truth is my trade, and the produce I store in my
heart.[58] *[23*

If life is a gamble then gamble away all your lust and your anger, your envy
and pride. || Take as your winnings those God-given virtues of truth and
contentment, of mercy and faith. *[24*

Refrain. Gone is the burden we bring from our past, the burden we carry through death and rebirth. || In the midst of God's faithful our spirits are cleansed, set free by the Guru's grace. [25

All men are brothers, let blessings abound, the blessings which goodness bestows.[59] || All men are part of God immanent presence, all are sustained by his grace. [26

God is the One and our Master alone; from him creation proceeds. || All who adore him, repeating his Name, are set free from the pains of rebirth. [27

Boundless your majesty, infinite Master, none can encompass your span. || Nanak gives praise to your grace and your mercy as humbly he ponders your Name.[60] [28

The vast majority of the hymns recorded in the Adi Granth make no reference to recognisable individuals, nor do they bear any evident relationship to contemporary events. The Gurus' intention was to preach the merits of God's divine Name, a timeless message expressed in a poetry which makes few concessions to actual events. Even the recurrent references to human depravity and social discord must be set in this timeless context. In most instances they are clearly to be construed as descriptions of the Kaliyuga, the cosmic era of darkness and strife currently running its demonic course. They are not normally to be interpreted as comments on conditions current during the actual lifetimes of the Gurus, at least not in any specific or exclusive sense. [29

There are, however, occasional exceptions to this general rule. The earliest consists of a cluster of four hymns by Guru Nanak which specifically refer to Babur and his invading Mughals (3.1.1 [56–66]). Another exception is provided by references in the works of the fourth and fifth Gurus to malicious rivals who challenged their authority. One of these rivals was Prithi Chand, the eldest son of Guru Ram Das. Prithi Chand openly challenged the right of his younger brother Arjan to succeed their father and the methods which he used to further his claims were by no means scrupulous. Tradition affirms that the following couplet by Guru Arjan refers to an occasion when a Brahman servant, charged with the care of the Guru's son Hargobind, unsuccessfully attempted to poison the child at Prithi Chand's bidding. [30

Failed the attempt, he tried in vain. || The wicked Brahman died in pain.[61] [31

Although the couplet does not actually refer to Hargobind, Guru Arjan elsewhere mentions him by name. These references to the sixth Guru constitute another of the rare exceptions to the Adi Granth rule. One of them records Guru Arjan's profound gratitude for his child's deliverance from a serious illness. [32

Refrain. God is my Helper, my certain Protector, my refuge and trustworthy aid. || By his grace Hargobind is saved from this illness, saved by his merciful hand. [33

His fever subsiding, its heat has abated, cooled by the grace of the Lord || My honour is saved by the prayers of the faithful; humbly I bow before God. [34

Here and hereafter the Lord is my Keeper, heedless of virtues and sins. ||
Firm is your promise my Guru and Master; blest be your merciful hand.[62]   *[35*

3.1.6 The works of the bhagats (*bhagat bani*) (1.2[8])
3.1.6.1 Kabir

Twelve years of ignorance spent as a child, twenty neglecting my penance; ||
Thirty more years without homage or worship, now age brings its flood of
regrets   *[1*
Refrain. Selfish concern for my personal profit has wasted the whole of my
life. || The pool of my life has now dwindled to nothing, all vigour and strength
at an end.   *[2*
Why dam a pond which has lost all its water; why fence a harvested field? ||
Foolish is he who keeps watch on the stable when Death has made off with his
horse.   *[3*
Faltering feet and a head always nodding, tears ever seep from my eyes. ||
How can I hope to perform what is needed with quavering voice now so faint? *[4*
He who by grace can repeat the blest Name will enraptured receive his
reward. || Led by the Guru he gathers God's riches, true wealth which for ever
endures.   *[5*
Hear what Kabir says to God's faithful followers: all other wealth must
decay. || All must relinquish this worldly existence when God sends the call to
depart.[63]   *[6*

Words of wisdom, inner foulness! || Why churn water when all is deceit?   *[7*
Refrain. Why scrub your body with earnest zeal || When filth remains
within?   *[8*
Wash a gourd at all the tiraths, || Bitter taste will yet remain.   *[9*
Thus Kabir implores his Master: || Help me cross life's troubled sea.[64]   *[10*

3.1.6.2 Namdev

What do I gain if you give me a kingdom? Worthless the glory it brings. || Why
should the beggar be humbled or taunted; why should he suffer contempt?   *[1*
Refrain. Let me with gladness give praise to my Master; this is the pathway
to bliss. || Thus we are ransomed from death and returning, our wanderings
brought to an end.   *[2*
All that exists, all its doubt and delusion, is caused by your sacred design. || He
who is granted the blessing of grace is the one who can know what it means.   *[3*
He who is brought to the feet of the Guru will find that his doubts have been
stilled. || God is the One whom alone I have witnessed; whom else can I worship
and praise?   *[4*
One piece of stone will attract pious faith, while another is trampled and
kicked. || If one is a god then the other is also; my Master alone will I serve.[65]   *[5*

3.1.6.3 Ravidas

Refrain. A lowly cobbler lacking skill, || Yet others bring their broken shoes.   *[1*

I have no awl to pierce the holes;|| No knife have I to cut a patch.   *[2*

Though others patch they yet know pain; || I lack their skill and yet know God.   *[3*

Thus Ravidas repeats God's Name;|| And thus eludes Death's evil grasp.[66] *[4*

3.1.6.4 Sheikh Farid

Why leave your home, why roam the wild, why spike your feet on thorns?|| Why seek him in the jungle waste, the Lord who dwells within?   *[1*

I thought that I alone had pain, yet what should meet my gaze,|| When from my rooftop looking out I saw the world ablaze.[67]   *[2*

3.1.7 Guru Tegh Bahadur

The version of the Adi Granth recorded by Bhai Gurdas in 1603–04 is not the text in current use today. At some stage later in the seventeenth century or very early in the eighteenth a collection of works by the ninth Guru, Tegh Bahadur, was added to the original compilation (1.2[2]). This supplement comprises fifty-nine hymns and fifty-seven shaloks. The traditional explanation for the appearance in the standard text of these compositions by Guru Tegh Bahadur is that his son, the tenth Guru, added them when dictating a fresh copy of the sacred scripture in 1705 or 1706. It is, however, evident that the addition had been made prior to this date, probably during the closing years of the seventeenth century.[68] *[1*

The fifty-seven shaloks by Guru Tegh Bahadur enjoy a particular popularity. This is largely due to the beauty of cadence and expression which they possess, but it has been considerably reinforced by the position which they occupy at the end of the Adi Granth. Because they occupy this terminal position the shaloks figure prominently in the bhog *ceremony with which each reading of the Adi Granth concludes. Their dominant theme is well suited to their location in the sacred volume and in the* bhog *ceremony. The principal message which they contain stresses the promise of God's protection in the midst of tribulation, a theme which supports the belief that the shaloks were composed shortly before the Guru's execution in 1675.* *[2*

If we neglect to sing God's praise we live our lives in vain.|| Let your heart be steeped in praise to God, like a fish which swims in the sea.   *[3*

Why this fondness for evil and vice, a passion never abandoned?|| Let your heart be steeped in praise to God and escape death's fatal noose.   *[4*

Youth we wasted and now we submit to the drag of advancing years.|| Let your heart be steeped in praise to God for your life is ebbing fast.   *[5*

Your years have advanced but not your wisdom; death now waits at hand.|| Why so foolish, why so neglectful, why no praise to God?   *[6*

Your riches, your woman, and all your possessions – all that you name as your own –|| None can accompany you, all must remain; this is the truth you must learn.   [7

Raising the fallen, calming our fears, Lord of the helpless and weak; || See him beside us, always at hand, present for ever our Lord.   [8

God gave you life and the riches you own; why is affection withheld? || Foolish man, why shake and quiver? Why are you trembling with fear?   [9

Your body, your riches, and all your possessions, your pleasures, the home you adore – || Why no respect for the Giver of mercies? Why no remembrance of God?   [10

All our contentment we gather from God; no other Lord can we own. || Pondering God and repeating his Name we attain that ineffable bliss.   [11

Bliss he confers upon all who remember him; sing to his glory, my friend. || Let me be prompt to sing praises to God, for my life hastens on to its end.   [12

I fear only that which can strike without warning, that which can awe and confound. || Nothing survives from this path we are following; nothing we take from this world.   [13

He who is born must assuredly die, now or in days yet to come. || Sing to God's glory, sing praise to his Name, and strike off the chains of this world.   [14

My limbs are in fetters, my strength has decayed; futile my hopes of escape. || The elephant fled by the mercy of God;[69] I pray that I too my be freed.   [15

My strength is restored and my fetters are broken; all is within my power! || Everything flows from your mercy, O Lord, your strength my infallible aid.[70]   [16

All have deserted me, stealing away; none has remained at my side. || Only the hand of my merciful Lord will support me in times of need.   [17

The Name remains, God's people too; the Lord himself stands firm. || They who are loyal find strength in this world, repeating the Guru's Word.   [18

He who enshrines God's Name in his heart, the Name beyond compare, || Is freed from all that suffering brings, blessed by a vision of God.[71]   [19

3.2 THE DASAM GRANTH

3.2.1 Guru Gobind Singh's prayer
Strengthen me, O Lord, that I shrink not from righteous deeds, || That freed from the fear of my enemies I may fight with faith and win. || The wisdom which I crave is the grace to sing your praises. || When this life's allotted course has run may I meet my death in battle.[72]   [1

3.2.2 *Akal Ustat*. In Praise of the Eternal One
The nature of this poem is clearly indicated by its title. Guru Gobind Singh's Akal Ustat is a sustained hymn of praise, one which expounds a doctrine of God in terms which repeatedly stress the splendour of his many attributes. Following a brief invocation the poem immediately takes up its central

theme. [1

The Eternal One is my Protector, all-powerful Lord in steel incarnate. || Master of Death and Lord of Steel, my Shield, my eternal Protector.[73] [2

I bow before the Primal One, || Immanent in sea, in earth, in sky; || The Primal Being, formless and everlasting, || Whose light illumines all creation. [3

Dwelling within both elephant and ant, || Viewing alike both king and pauper; || The One unique, beyond our comprehending, || Yet knowing the secrets of every heart. [4

Ineffable, eternal, formless and thus devoid of raiment, || Devoid of passion, colour, shape or lineament, || Needing no sign to designate his caste, ||[The Primal One, alone, without spot or stain. [5

Immune from caste and the marks which proclaim it; || Neither father nor mother, friend nor foe; || Distant from all yet close beside them, || Immanent in sea, in earth, in sky. [6

Infinite his form and soundless his speech; || At his feet even Durga finds refuge. || Neither Brahma nor Vishu encompass his bounds. || 'Not this, not this,' Brahma declares. [7

Thousands of gods has he created, thousands of Indras and deities of lesser power. || Brahma and Shiv are his creation, both of them created and both to be destroyed. || The fourteen worlds are the products of his pleasure, || All to be drawn within him again. [8

Countless demons, gods, divine serpants – all are the works of his creation || Celestial musicians and Kuber's attendants,[74] wondrous examples of the beauty he confers. || All that can happen is known to him, the past, the present, the future yet to come. || All this he knows and all that lies within, reading the deepest secrets of every human heart. [9

He has no parents, neither caste nor lineage, || No single mood ordains the pattern of his deeds. || Present within the light which lightens every soul, || Behold him immanent in every place, visible to all. [10

Beyond the reach of death, immortal; || Beyond our comprehending, formless and detached; || Unmarked by symbols designating caste or family line, || The eternal Lord, for ever true. [11

Destroyer of all, Creator of all, || He who disperses illness, grief and guilt. || Reflect on him for a fleeting moment, || And thus escape death's snare.[75] [12

These opening stanzas comprise the first of the poem's eleven cantos. The cantos vary in length from ten to thirty stanzas and employ a variety of poetic forms, but all carry forward the same fervent message of praise to the Eternal One. Insistently they repeat that there is but one God, all-powerful yet supremely merciful, dwelling immanent in his own creation. The third canto stresses the futility of traditional doctrines and rituals as means of finding God or of satisfying him.[76] Other portions of the poem lay particular emphasis on the eirenic belief that the differences which divide men are in reality meaningless. They are meaningless because all people are

fundamentally the same and because all are under the same Lord. A famous
sequence from the seventh canto gives pointed expression to this view. These
verses also declare God to be both the source and ultimate resting place of all
mankind, and reinforce the claim that the practices of traditional piety are
useless as a means of access to him. [13

If self-inflicted suffering leads to the Lord of peace and tranquillity, what
then of the blows received by the wounded? || If repeating sacred words can
bring one to the ineffable Lord, why not the warbler's constant *tuhi* cry?[77] || If
God be found by roaming the skies, what then of the bird which remains for
ever on the wing? || If burning oneself is the means of liberation, freed is the
widow who mounts her husband's pyre; and if it be attained by living beneath
the ground then blessed indeed is the snake! [14

Some shave their heads and become sanyasis, others adopt the style of the
yogi; some abstain from connubial pleasure, or claim to be totally chaste. ||
Some are called Hindus, others are Muslims, members of sects such as Shia or
Sunni. Let it be known that mankind is one, that all men belong to a single
humanity. || So too with God, whom Hindu and Muslim distinguish with
differing names.[78] Let none be misled, for God is but one; he who denies this is
duped and deluded. || Worship the One who is Master of all; worship and serve
him alone. See him present in all creation, a single form, an all-pervading
light. [15

There is no difference between a temple and a mosque, nor between the
prayers of a Hindu or a Muslim. Though differences seem to mark and
distinguish, all men are in reality the same. || Gods and demons, celestial beings,
men called Muslims and others called Hindus – such differences are trivial,
inconsequential, the outward results of locality and dress. || With eyes the same,
the ears and body, all possessing a common form – all are in fact a single
creation, the elements of nature in a uniform blend. || Allah is the same as the
God of the Hindus, Puran and Qur'an are one and the same. All are the same,
none is separate; a single form, a single creation. [16

As sparks fly upwards in their thousands from a fire, each separate and
distinct then reuniting with its source; || Or earth when pulverised to fine-
ground dust ascends as a cloud of particles and then subsides again; || As waves
rise endlessly in the ocean's vastness, their water one with all around them; || So
from the natural world the living and inanimate emerge, and having thus
appeared return to it again. [17

Countless tortoises and fish, with the predators which consume them;
countless the birds which are born to fly. || Countless their enemies, seeking
food, which snatch them on the wing; and countless more, hunting the hunter,
which seize and eat those birds of prey. || Whether they live in water or on land,
whether they fly in the air, all are created by the Master of Death and by him all
are brought to destruction. || As light dawns from darkness and returns to it
again, so does all proceed from God, its source and final destination. [18

Many cry as they wander the land, others wail themselves to death; many submerge themselves in water while others choose the agony of fire. || Many dwell by the Ganga, in Mecca or Medina; others follow the ascetic way, roaming the world as renunciants. || Many are sawn apart, others are buried, interred in the ground alive. Others prefer to be skewered on stakes, enduring the pain of impalement. || Many fly in the skies above, others live in the water. Vain is their effort without knowledge of the truth; fire is the fate which awaits them.   [19

The gods have failed in their quest for perfection, the demons in their rebellion. Wise men have failed in their search for wisdom, the devout in their hope of contentment. || Preparing and dabbing on sandal paste, sprinkling the fragrance of attar, worshipping idols, offering sweets – all are futile and worthless. || Visiting graves, seeking comfort from tombs, piously smearing walls, plastering on them auspicious symbols – none can achieve its end. || The music-makers of the gods have failed, those who sing and those who dance. Pundits have failed, ascetics have failed; none knows the way to God.[79]   [20

The remaining cantos continue the themes already enunciated, maintaining the same stress on the manifold glories of the eternal, all-pervading bountiful Creator Lord. Such wonders are beyond the wit or understanding of even the mightiest of sages. Failure must inevitably await any who seek to circumscribe the boundless or give expression to the ineffable.   [21

He has no beginning, no middle, no end; no past, no present, no future. || He is the Master of all four ages, Lord of all that they span. || The deepest meditation of the noblest ascetics, the songs of the numberless heavenly host, || All have failed, all are defeated, for none can encompass the infinite.   [22

Countless sages of mighty stature, the rishis Narad and Vyas, || Practised meditation and fearsome austerities, yet in the end tired of their task. || With them have failed the celestial musicians, those who sing and those who dance. || Mighty gods have struggled in vain, ignorant still of the answer.[80]   [23

3.2.3 Bachitar Natak. The Wondrous Drama

Bachitar Natak (or Vichitar Natak) is a lengthy work comprising fourteen cantos. Although the principal interest of the poem derives from Guru Gobind Singh's description of his upbringing and early wars this autobiographical material is not introduced until the sixth canto. The first canto comprises another of the Guru's hymns of praise. It opens with an invocation to God represented as the Divine Sword.   [1

Reverently I salute the Sword with affection and devotion. || Grant, I pray, your divine assistance that this book may be brought to completion.   [2

Thee I invoke, All-conquering Sword, Destroyer of evil, Ornament of the brave. ||Powerful your arm and radiant your glory, your splendour as dazzling as the brightness of the sun. || Joy of the devout and Scourge of the wicked, Vanquisher of sin, I seek your protection. || Hail to the world's Creator and Sustainer, my invincible Protector the Sword![81]   [3

As in the Jap *and* Akal Ustat *Guru Gobind Singh incorporates in* Bachitar

Natak *a lengthy catalogue of the divine attributes. Particular attention is devoted to the martial splendour of God and to his awesome power as Master of the Sword. This militant emphasis dominates the first canto. It is, however, accompanied by recurrent reference to his role as merciful protector of those who fear him. The following stanzas illustrate these features, juxtaposing them to form a striking paradox. They also serve to illustrate the clipped brevity of the style which predominates in this canto.* [4

When he takes up bow and arrow || Fear assails the proud; || When he wields the sword || Mighty warriors quail. [5

With the battle fiercely joined || He fights with deadly skill, || Treasure of kindness and mercy, || Giver of eternal grace.[82] [6

A typical hyperbole concludes the first canto.

If all the continents could serve as paper, the seven oceans as ink; || If all the trees on earth were felled and turned into pens for writing; || If for countless ages Sarasvati dictated, with every word recorded by Ganesh; || Without our submission nothing would please you, Lord of the death-dealing sword.[83] [7

In the next three cantos Guru Gobind Singh relates the traditional history of the Sodhi and Bedi lineages. One of the most important sections of Punjabi society is the Khatri caste. This is a mercantile caste, but the word itself is a cognate form of Kshatriya, and Khatris trace their origins as well as their etymology to the warrior caste of the Kshatriyas. Like all major castes that of the Khatris is divided into numerous sub-castes. Two of the most important are the Sodhi and Bedi sub-castes, and it is their traditional history which Guru Gobind Singh narrates in cantos 2–4.[84] [8

According to this tradition Ram and Sita, hero and heroine of the Ramayana, had two sons. These were Lav and Kushu, founders of the Punjabi cities of Lahore and Kasur respectively. Rivalry between their descendants eventually led to war and to the defeat of Lav's lineage. Their chief, Kalrai, retreated to Sanaudh, south-east of Delhi. The son born to him there was named Sodhi Rai and it was from this leader that the Sodhi sub-caste took its name. [9

Sodhi Rai later brought his forces up to the Punjab and retook Lahore from the usurping Kushu lineage. The vanquished descendants of Kushu fled to Banaras, where they earned renown as expositors of the Vedas. They thus acquired the name of Vedi (Bedi). A Sodhi ruler of Lahore eventually invited the Bedis to return and was so impressed by their Vedic learning that he renounced his authority in their favour. In gratitude the newly installed Bedi ruler promised that when he was reincarnated as Nanak he would confer the highest of dignities on the Sodhi lineage. After he had been thrice incarnated as Guru (as Guru Nanak, Guru Angad, and Guru Amar Das) the fourth incarnation was to appear within the Sodhi lineage (Guru Ram Das). [10

Factional fighting and a confounding of traditional caste roles subsequently overtook the State, with the result that the Bedis lost the sovereignty of Lahore. All they were able to retain was a patrimony of twenty

*villages and it was in one of these that Nanak Bedi, the first Guru, was
eventually born. He makes his appearance in the fifth canto, seal of the
earlier prophecy and liberator of suffering mankind. A brief eulogy relating
his spiritual achievements is followed by a summary account of the eight
Gurus who succeeded him. The canto concludes with a stirring version of the
ninth Guru's martyrdom, one of the most famous passages in Sikh literature
(2.2.7).* [11

Frequent disputes took place amongst them, quarrels which no one could
settle. And so the Almighty took action against them, depriving them of their
land. [12

Shudras were acting as if they were Brahmans, and Vaishyas as if they were
Khatris. Khatris behaved like Vaishyas, and Brahmans in the manner of
Shudras. [13

Twenty villages remained to them, and there they tilled the soil. A lengthy
period passed in this way until finally Nanak was born. [14

Nanak Rai was born a Bedi, born in that house and line; born to bring
comfort to all his disciples, guidance both here and hereafter. [15

Here, to this Dark Age, he brought true belief, pointing the way for the pious
to follow. He who sets out to follow this path shall never be troubled by sin. [16

He who chooses to follow this path is released by God from all sin and pain.
Freed from all hunger and suffering, he is saved from the snare of death. [17

Nanak then entered the body of Angad, still spreading the truth far and wide.
Next his name became Amar Das, successive lamps but a single flame. [18

When the time came for the promised blessing the title of Guru was conferred
on Ram Das. Having fulfilled the ancient pledge Amar Das took the path to
heaven. [19

Thus was Nanak known as Angad, and Angad was seen in Amar Das. Amar
Das was transformed into Ram Das, as the pious know but never fools. [20

The foolish see them as separate persons; how few the wise who know them to
be one! They who know it grasp the ultimate truth, the mystery which they
alone can comprehend. [21

When Guru Ram Das went to God the succession passed to Arjan. When
Arjan, in turn, proceeded to heaven Hargobind assumed his place. [22

Hargobind passed on to the realm of God, and Har Rai took his place;
followed in turn by his son Hari Krishan, and he by Tegh Bahadur. [23

For their frontal mark and their sacred thread he wrought a great deed in
this Age of Darkness.[85] This he did for the sake of the pious, silently giving his
head. [24

For the cause of truth he performed this deed, giving his head in obedience to
his resolve. Bogus tricks are for counterfeit conjurors, deceits which God's
people must spurn.[86] [25

Dashing himself on the ruler of Delhi, he departed for God's abode. Such was
the achievement of Tegh Bahadur, the feat which he alone could perform. [26

At the death of Tegh Bahadur lamentation swept the earth. From below came anguished wailing, from heaven triumphant cries![87]   [27

The death of his father, the ninth Guru, brings Guru Gobind Singh to his
own life story. This he begins in the sixth canto, commencing with the period
which preceded his actual birth. Prior to his birth he dwelt high on a remote
mountain, immersed in devout austerities. It was here that he received from
God the command to enter the world of mortals.   [28

And now my own story I tell, how from rigorous austerities I was summoned
by God; called from the heights of Hem Kunt where the seven peaks so grandly
pierce the sky.   [29

Sapat Sring is the name they bear, the place where the Pandava king
practised yogic rites. There I performed harsh austerities in service to the
Almighty Lord.   [30

Through constant practice of strict austerities my being had merged in the
spirit divine. My parents too had followed this path, devoutly serving the
ineffable Lord.   [31

Such was the piety of the worship they performed that God was pleased [and
heeded their cry]. Receiving thus the divine command I was born in this Age of
Darkness.   [32

God commanded, yet I was unwilling, for my mind was immersed in the bliss
of contemplation. But God insisted that I must go, and speaking thus
despatched me to this world.[88]   [33

There now follows a discourse in which God unfolds before his chosen
servant the history of times past and of the failures which it has produced.
Lesser gods who had been sent to serve mankind grew proud and demanded
worship. Men of exalted spiritual understanding declined into self-centred
pride and lost their way. Dattatreya, Gorakhnath, Ramanand and
Muhammad were all sent to lead men to enlightenment but all had been
deflected from their task. The need thus remains and it is to answer the need
that Guru Gobind Singh is being despatched into the world.   [34

You I now exalt as my chosen son; summon men to the path which all must
follow. Preach to them the way of truth, and purge them of every evil way.   [35

Guru Gobind Singh responds:
Reverently I stood with palms together, head respectfully bowed. 'With your
gracious aid to sustain my endeavours I go into the world to preach the way of
truth.'   [36

This was the charge entrusted to me, despatched by God to take birth in this
world. The words which he spoke are the words which I deliver, inspired by
enmity to none.   [37

If anyone should claim that I am God he shall burn in the fires of the fiercest
hell. See me only as the slave of God. Let this be known without shadow of
doubt.   [38

I am the servant of the Master Supreme, here in this world to witness its
drama. I speak to the world as God commands, cowed into silence by none.[89][39

The remainder of the sixth canto is largely devoted to a description of the religious practices which the Guru rejects. The way which he preaches is neither the ascetic path of the yogi nor the ignorant worship of avatars. Muslims may read the Qur'an and Hindus the Puranas, but both are doomed to a futile quest. Death must be their fate. Liberation awaits only those who focus their minds and affections on God's divine Name. In canto 7 the Guru takes up the story of his human life. This short canto, comprising only three stanzas, briefly sketches his birth and childhood.　　　　　　[40

When my father turned his steps to the east he visited places of pilgrimage, bathing in their waters. Travelling on he reached the sacred confluence[90] and there spent many days performing pious rites.　　　　　　[41

There it was that my conception took place, and my actual birth in the city of Patna. From there I was taken back to the Punjab, nursed with affection by many attendants.　　　　　　[42

As I grew in stature my body was trained, and my mind was stored with understanding. It was when I had reached the age of responsibility that my father was summoned to heaven.[91]　　　　　　[43

The eighth canto continues to narrate the Guru's growth to maturity. This it does very briefly, saving its detailed treatment for the wars which the Guru fought with chieftains of the Punjab hills.　　　　　　[44

Summoned thus to the exercise of power I tried, as best I could, to spread the message of truth. Many the hunts which we followed in the wastelands, pursuing the bear, the antelope and the boar.　　　　　　[45

Eventually I left that area and transferred to the town of Paunta. Happily reposing on the banks of the Kalindri, I enjoyed all manner of amusement.[92][46

There I hunted and killed many tigers, and also antelopes and bears. Fateh Shah, the local ruler, angered by my presence, attacked me without cause.[93] [47

The poem now describes in considerable and vivid detail the battle of Bhangani which the Guru successfully fought with Fateh Shah in 1688. The account concludes:　　　　　　[48

When the arrow struck me it roused me to anger. Seizing the bow I returned the fire, loosing a hail of arrows.　　　　　　[49

The enemy turned and ran as the arrows showered upon them. Taking aim I shot again, despatching another of their number.　　　　　　[50

Hari Chand was slain as his soldiers struggled to escape. So too the ruler of Kotlehar, his life cut short in battle.　　　　　　[51

And so they fled from the field of battle, running in fear of their lives. Victory was mine, the battle won, the enemy crushed by the grace of the Lord.　　　　　　[52

Having carried the day in battle we sang the songs of triumph. Rewards were showered on the victors as joy embraced us all.　　　　　　[53

The victory won we could scarce contain our exaltation. Returning now to Kahlur I there restored Anandpur town.　　　　　　[54

All who had shrunk from supporting my cause were refused admission to the town, whereas honour was bestowed on all those warriors who valiantly fought on my behalf.　　　　　　[55

Thus did a lengthy period pass, the pious sustained and the evil destroyed. The wicked were slain, rended limb from limb, dying like dogs the death they deserved.[94]   [56

Cantos 9–12 continue the narrative of Guru Gobind Singh's struggles with the chieftains of the Punjab hills. Canto 13 briefly mentions an expedition despatched to the Punjab by the Mughal emperor Aurangzeb and roundly denounces all who cravenly deserted the Guru on that occasion. The poem concludes with a final salutation to God in canto 14.   [57

3.3 OTHER WORKS APPROVED FOR RECITATION IN GURDWARAS

3.3.1 Bhai Gurdas

The theme of Bhai Gurdas's first var is appropriately the mission of Guru Nanak. Bhai Gurdas first sets the scene for the coming of the founding Guru by stressing the wretched condition of the world prior to his birth. Having briefly sketched its past history and present infirmity, he turns to the life of the Guru and devotes the greater part of the var to a retelling in verse of some of the more popular anecdotes from current tradition. The substance of the var is thus a brief janam-sakhi.[95]   [1

The var opens with a salutation to the eternal Guru.

Hail to the blessed Guru divine, to him who reveals the message of the Name,[96] || To him who has brought us deliverance and peace, plucking us from the perils of life's dread ocean;[97] || Saving us from the fear of death and rebirth, from all sickness of body and separation from God. || Vain and deceitful is the world in which we live, source of our woes and the wearisome round of rebirth.|| Death's punishment awaits the false and the perverse, fools who have squandered their lives. || But all who seek the Guru's mercy are saved, and seeking they receive the Word of Truth. || Blessed are they who show love and devotion, who honour the Guru and follow the threefold path,[98] || For we reap the harvest of the seed which we sow. (1:1)   [2

This opening stanza serves as both an invocation and as a summary of the message which Bhai Gurdas wishes to communicate. Immediately thereafter he turns to the creation of the world and of man (1:2–4), the instituting of the cycle of four yugas (1:5–7), and the development of the six systems of Hindu philosophy (1:8–14). This is followed by brief descriptions of the other major systems which have appeared in India. The degeneration of both Hindu and Muslim observances brings him to the dawning of the new age, the rising of the glorious sun which will scatter afar the darkness of ignorance and strife.   [3

Thus there exist the four Hindu castes, and with them the four sects of Muslims; || All of them involved in vanity and avarice, in pride, in discord, in violence. || Hindus turn to the Ganga and Banaras, Muslims to Mecca and the

Ka'bah; || Muslims cling to the rite of circumcision, Hindus to the *tilak* and *janeu*.⁹⁹ || Though Ram and Rahim are one and the same, Hindu and Muslim follow paths that are separate. || Forgetting the words of their own sacred scriptures, both have succumbed to the world's satanic greed. || Brahman and maulvi, spurning the truth, destroy themselves in malicious feuding. || Death and rebirth is the fate which awaits them. (1:21)   *[4*

God himself prescribes our actions, a way of life for every era. || He is the slate, he is the pen, and he is the scribe who records it. || Yet without the Guru all is darkness, a woeful tale of strife and death. || Sin rules supreme, covering the earth, as the Bull of Righteousness lows in anguish.¹⁰⁰ || Starved of grace, it grows ever weaker, powerless to rise from the pit of hell. || Grievously crippled, it struggles to stand, crushed by its burden of sin. || Where are the pious to give it support, the faithful who follow the truth? || Agony-stricken it bellows in vain, for none can be found to assist it. (1:22)   *[5*

Hearing the cries of a world in anguish the Lord of Grace sent Guru Nanak. || Acknowledged as Master by his loyal disciples, he sealed their obedience with the time-honoured rite.¹⁰¹ || Here in this era of darkness and strife he revealed that God is one. || Firmly establishing true belief he fused together the four great castes. || King and beggar he treated as equal, publishing abroad the virtue of humility. || See how the ways of the world are transformed, the proud brought low in humble submission! || Preaching the message of the one True Name, he brought redemption to the Age of Darkness. || This was the purpose for which he came, to liberate all under sentence of death. (1:23)   *[6*

Divinely commissioned in the Court of God, Baba Nanak went forth to serve. || His food was sand and the pod of an *ak*, and his bed he spread on stones.¹⁰² || Harsh the austerities which he performed, earning thereby the approval of God. || In the Court of God he was robed with honour, adorned with the Name and the mantle of humility. || In deep meditation Nanak looked forth and beheld the world in flames. || Without the Guru all was confusion, rent with the cries of people in anguish. || Assuming the form of an ordinary man he lived a life of pious simplicity. || Thus did he come, here to this world, to restore it again to the pathway of virtue. (1:24)   *[7*

In the next two stanzas Bhai Gurdas describes how Guru Nanak searched the world for true piety but met with utter failure in his quest. Men and gods, all were sunk in pride and superstition.   *[8*

Visiting the places of sacred pilgrimage he searched in vain for a true believer. || Hindus and Muslims he saw them all, pirs and prophets, and men of the sword. || The blind were thrusting the ignorant blind into the darkness of a well! (1:26)   *[9*

With the coming of Nanak, however, the grievous condition of the world is instantly transformed.   *[10*

When Satguru Nanak appeared on earth the darkness fled, dispelled by the light, || As at the rising of a new day's sun the stars are hidden and darkness flees away, || As at the roar of a prowling lion a herd of deer takes instant flight. ||

Sacred shrines mark every place sanctified by the presence of Baba Nanak. || Siddhs in their centres throughout the world heard and submitted to the teachings he brought. || Numberless homes became places of worship where kirtan was sung as in an endless festival. || To all the world he brought peace and deliverance, spreading the truth to every corner. || Thus did the Guru enter our world, here in this Age of Darkness. (1:27)   [11

In the stanzas which follow Bhai Gurdas relates six anecdotes from the janam-sakhi traditions concerning Guru Nanak. These are the discourse with Siddhs on Mount Sumeru, the Guru's visits to Mecca and Baghdad, the discourse with Siddhs at Achal Batala, the encounter with the pirs of Multan, and the choosing of Lahina to succeed Nanak as Guru Angad.[103] *This sequence is interspersed with brief panegyrics and a stanza supplying details concerning the Guru's life in the village of Kartarpur.*   [12

In Kartarpur he made his home, putting aside the garments of renunciation. || Assuming the garb of the people around him, he lived amongst them as teacher and guide.[104] || Reversing the accepted order of succession, he appointed Angad to follow him as Guru, || For his sons had refused to own his authority, proving themselves to be rebels and deserters. || The words which he spoke brought light to his people, driving afar the darkness of untruth. || Wisdom abounded in all that he uttered, joy beyond telling reigned endlessly supreme! || *Sodar* and *Arati* were sung every evening, and *Japji* recited in the early morning hour. || Thus was the burden of ancient tradition shed and forsaken by all his disciples. (1:38)   [13

The var concludes with three stanzas which briefly exalt Nanak's five successors, thus carrying the eulogy forward to the author's own day.   [14

In the remaining vars Bhai Gurdas faithfully reflects the doctrines taught by the Gurus and enshrined in the sacred scripture. God is described in the following terms.   [15

When God took form in his own creation no concept existed of time or of sequence. || Without taking form he who is formless continues unmanifest, wholly unknown. || Thus it was he created himself, assuming the Name by which he is known. || Hail to the Master of time and eternity, he who is now and for ever shall be. || Boundless is he, without end or beginning, his infinite forms beyond hope of computing. || Causing creation to come into being, immanent he dwells within (18:7)   [16

In the above stanza God is called Oankar and Ekankar (the one God), Nirankar (the Formless One) and Adi Purakh (the Primal Being). The creation which he brings into being as a visible manifestation of himself is summarily described as his nam (3.1.1[7]). In the following stanzas from var 9 he appears as Puran Braham (the Supreme Being), mystically present in every heart and accessible to all who seek his presence through contemplation.   [17

God dwells within us as reflection in a mirror, || Present within as the moon on water produces a multitude of separate images. || As ghee is present in the milk of a cow, || As scent in a flower or juice in fruit, || As fire glows red in burning wood, as water is held in the bosom of the earth, || So God resides in every heart, revealed in the lives of his faithful. (9:6)   [18

Rare is he who in contemplation directs his mind to the Guru's wisdom. || He it is who acquires the skill to assay the value of spiritual jewels, || To know the worth of that precious pearl which is found in the company of the Guru's faithful. || The faithful disciple is a string of jewels, a thread for the Guru's pearls of wisdom. || Dying to self he attains immortality, dwelling for ever in blissful peace. || Mystically blending in the Guru's light he comes to a knowledge of the One who knows all. (9:7)   [19

In his vars Bhai Gurdas lays repeated stress on a cluster of fundamental doctrines, two of which appear in the latter stanza. These are the grace of the Guru, who alone can impart the truth which brings deliverance; and the importance of the satsang *as the place where that truth is received. The* satsang *or* sadh sangat *is the congregation of the pious, the gathering for corporate worship of those who seek the Guru's guidance (5.6[20]).*   [20

The central activity of the gathered satsang is the singing of hymns (kirtan). *These hymns record the actual words of the Gurus (gurbani) and Bhai Gurdas is entirely faithful to the Sikh tradition in maintaining that this particular form of devotional activity is uniquely effective as a means of invoking the Guru's grace. Literal meaning and spiritual experience, intellect and sentiment, join in penetrating both mind and heart. Where inner conviction and affection lead, outward behaviour must necessarily follow. The pious seeker is irresistibly drawn to the Guru and in the ecstasy of surrender he finds the path to liberation open before him.*   [21

He who receives the Guru's teachings must live a life which reflects their truth. || Let him take his place in the company of the faithful, absorbing their virtue in the presence of the Word, || As sesame mingled with sweet-smelling blossom produces a perfume of wonderful fragrance. || Led and guided by the Guru's halter he walks without fear, secure and unafraid. || Rising early and devoutly bathing he lives his life in a world of beauty. || Faithfully repeating the words of the Guru he opens his heart to the coming of the Lord, || For the Guru comes to those who love him, to those who fear and follow his truth. || Daily his follower rises renewed, freshly robed in the garments of grace. || Serving thus the Giver of all goodness he lives for ever in the presence of his Lord. (3:9)   [22

The gathering of the faithful is the Realm of Truth,[105] that state of bliss where the pious abide, || There where they contemplate God the All-powerful, their minds absorbed in the Name which is truth. || Dazzling the light which shines in their presence, the refulgent light of ardent devotion. || They who seek shall see him revealed, alone and immanent in all creation. || They who find him escape Death's rod, safe in the shelter which God provides, || Safe from the fearsome horrors of hell, their deadliest sins forgiven. || They alone can know this bliss, for the Realm of Truth has no place for the false. || As rice is stripped and its husks abandoned the false are cast away. (22:18)   [23

Although the Guru is not always mentioned in stanzas which enunciate the way of deliverance his role is always assumed if not actually stated. In the works of Bhai Gurdas an extract read in isolation may leave one wondering whether the author is referring to the mystical Guru who exists from eternity or to one of the living Masters physically present during Bhai Gurdas's own time. The answer is, of course, that he refers simultaneously to both. The living Guru embodies the spirit and authority of the eternal Guru, and as the following stanza indicates the eternal Guru is to be identified with God himself. [24

Finding peace in the company of the faithful the true disciple is freed from worldly affections, || As the lotus rooted in water and slime yet turns its face to the heavenly sun, || Or the sandal tree entwined by snakes extends its fragrance and cooling shade. || Though the company of the faithful must dwell upon the earth they turn their faces to the heavenly Word. || In the joy of union, mystically sublime, they accomplish in this life eternal deliverance.|| God is one, whether near or far; and the Guru is one with God.|| By his grace the wondrous tale is told, the message of salvation unfolded here today. (15:21) [25

Repeatedly the role of the Guru is stressed. He alone can reveal the truth; he alone can break the shackles which bind men to the wheel of transmigration. Freedom is obtained only by those who put their trust in the Guru. [26

Our true King is the Guru; all the kings of the earth are false.|| The Master Nath is the Guru; the nine Naths wander homeless and lost.[106] || Supreme is the Guru as Giver of gifts; all other givers lag feebly behind. || The Guru is he who has fashioned creation, revealing the Name whereby he is known. || To protect our possessions we turn to the Guru; all earthly bankers must fail. || The Guru alone can heal all our ailments; no other physician will serve. || Without the Guru we stray unguided, ignorant, helpless and lost. (15:1) [27

The same insistent message is repeated in a variety of ways.

Without the Guru none can be freed; a house without walls must surely collapse. (36:13) [28

In exalting the Guru's role Bhai Gurdas contrasts his sublime power with the futility of conventional religious practices. External observances, he declares, are useless. Only the Guru can bring deliverance. [29

If bathing at tiraths procures liberation, frogs, for sure, must be saved;|| And likewise the banyan, with dangling tresses, if growing hair long sets one free.|| If the need can be served by roaming unclad the deer of the forest must surely be pious; || So too the ass which rolls in the dust if limbs smeared with ashes can purchase salvation. || Saved are the cattle, mute in the fields, if silence produces deliverance. || Only the Guru can bring us salvation; only the Guru can set a man free. (36:14) [30

The gift which is proffered by the Guru requires a practical response from the disciple who wishes to accept it. The nature of this response is another of the issues to which Bhai Gurdas repeatedly returns. [31

Rise from sleep during night's last watch[107] and discharge the disciple's threefold task.|| Speak with courtesy, walk in humility, practise virtue by aiding others.|| Obey the Guru by acting with restraint, sleeping and eating with strict moderation and saying no more than occasion demands.|| Live by your labour, performing honest toil; never take pride in status or achievement.|| Daily join with the company of the faithful, singing God's praises by day and by night.|| Seek for joy in the Guru's Word, the means whereby he delights the soul. || Abandon the ties of worldly concern; let your only hope be the Guru's grace. (28:15)   [32

A similar stanza from the concluding var paraphrases a similar composition by Guru Ram Das.[108]   [33

A Sikh should rise as night draws near to dawn and begin each day with an early-morning bathe. || Devoutly reciting the Guru's words he goes to the dharamsala to hear eternal truth.|| Joining the sangat there assembled he hears with deepest reverence the Guru's sacred songs.|| Let doubt be driven far from his mind, his thoughts turned instead to the service of others.|| Let honest toil be his sacred duty, adding to this the sharing of its fruits.|| When giving food to the Guru's Sikhs he first serves others and for himself takes only what remains.|| In this Age of Darkness he reveals the truth that Guru and Sikh are one. || The Sikh who lives according to this rule treads safely the path of life. (40:11)   [34

Some stanzas provide summaries of the complete message which Bhai Gurdas seeks to communicate. In the following example he returns to the popular metaphor of the lotus.   [35

Though it live in a slough the lotus stays pure, unsullied by all that surrounds it. || At night it attracts the black bee near, drawn by its cool and fragrant presence.|| By day it turns its face to the sun, joyfully spreading its petals wide. ||The disciple lives like the lotus flower, joyously tranquil wherever he may be.|| Others may strive to perform good works, directed by custom and venerable texts.|| The disciple gives heed to the Guru's wisdom, following the path which leads to deliverance. || Safe in the company of the blessed faithful, he puts his trust in the Guru's Word. (16:2)   [36

A number of particular issues attract Bhai Gurdas's attention. One which he treats with vehemence concerns the harm inflicted by the sectarian allegiances of Hindu and Muslim. Their separate paths lead only to suffering and to continued transmigration. Hindu and Muslim, he insists, should recognise the perversity of their mutual antagonism and join in following the irenic way of the Guru. The theme is one which he has already enunciated in the first var. He returns to it in var 33.   [37

Born of the union of matter and spirit, two kinds of people with two separate paths.|| Ram is the name which Hindus repeat while Muslims call him Khuda.|| Hindus turn to the east when praying, Muslims bow to the west.|| Hindus revere the Ganga and Banaras, Muslims the city of Mecca.|| Each has four scriptures, four castes and four sects,|| Yet both are derived from the same basic source. || The world is but one, [its Creator is one]; only the names are different. (33:2)   [38

The weaver, from a single yarn, weaves both warp and woof. || If the tailor tears the cloth apart who will pay its price? || When the blades of his shears are opened wide they are harshly ground on stone. || Yet his thread can draw the fragments together, joining the pieces as one. || God is one, yet through his world run the separate paths of Hindu and Muslim, || One exalting his guru's teachings, the other the words of his pir. || Separate roads have no destination save only pain and confusion. (33:4)   [39

Bhai Gurdas also repeats the Guru's teachings with regard to caste. In a much quoted couplet Guru Nanak declares:

Worthless is caste and worthless an exalted name. || For all mankind there is only one refuge.[109]   [40

Bhai Gurdas faithfully reflects this teaching.

All four castes he mingles as one, blending the colours as betel turns to red.[110] || The eight base metals all become one, a mystery the scriptures can never explain.[111] || The scent of sandalwood spreads to all, even the flowerless absorbing its fragrance. || That which was iron is turned to gold and, wonder of wonders, the gold becomes fragrant. || He who was base has now become precious, transformed to gold by the touch of the Guru. || Within himself he sees treasure agleam, diamonds and pearls and the rare red coral. || These jewels are the gems of the Guru's Word, mystically seen with the eye of wisdom. || The true disciple receives his reward in peace and contentment, in joy and in love. (11:7)
                                                                              [41

3.3.2 Bhai Nand Lal Goya

The Divan-i-Goya *or 'Ode sequence by Goya' opens with a* ghazal *in praise of God.*

Only the longing to worship God has brought me into the world; || But for the joy of offering praise why should I ever come? || Happy the life of the man who spends his days in remembering God; || Without that remembrance why should we linger, under the dome of heaven? || Without that remembrance life is death, remembrance alone can sustain me. || Without that remembrance all that life offers is empty and futile for me.   [1

All that I am, my heart, my life, I offer in humble abasement, || Taking the dust from the blessed feet of the one who has led me to you. || No trace of you had I ever seen in heaven above or on earth below || Until the desire to behold you, Lord, laid me prostrate in awe and devotion. || Without the remembrance of God, O Goya, how can I ever live? Grant that deliverance soon may be mine, that released I may meet my Beloved.   [2

In his Zindagi-nama *Nand Lal again takes up the theme which dominates the entire range of his poetry.*

He is the Master of all below, Lord of the heavens above; || He who gives life to all that breathe, to man and to every beast.   [3

The dust from his feet is the balm we apply, humbly anointing our eyes; || The glory men win, whether kings or faqirs, is given by him alone.   [4

If a man should engage in remembrance of God, his name on every breath,|| He will owe it all to the One he adores, for the impulse to praise is from God. *[5*

If you, my soul, dwell eternally rapt in unceasing remembrance of God; || Then, O my soul, that perfection is yours, a life that is whole and complete. *[6*

Clouds descend and hide the sun, its brightness veiled and dimmed; || But then like the moon it returns again, its radiance unconfined. *[7*

Your body is like the clouds on high which spread and conceal the sun;|| Yet the light may be found if you turn your mind to the praise and remembrance of God. *[8*

He who discerns the mystery, who sees the gifts God brings;|| Will know no need save only one, to offer endless praise. *[9*

Remembrance of God is the meaning of truth, and thus is truth defined; || Even the lowllest clod of eai th can learn of the greatness of God. *[10*

If by fortune's grace you find a band of pious souls,|| You also find, beloved friend, eternal treasure, timeless wealth. *[11*

One finds this wealth in serving those who offer humble praise to God;|| To God each soul surrenders all, from beggar mean to mighty king. *[12*

Learn to be like them, O brother, learn to be like them; || Treat them with respect, O brother, ever with respect. *[13*

He who has learnt how to show this respect, how to serve the faithful who glorify God,|| Here and hereafter he shines like the sun and glows like the moon by night. *[14*

Praising God is the means he supplies to gather that treasure which never decays;|| Praise and adore him, praise and adore him, praise and adore him, the Lord! *[15*

Clothe yourself in the raiment of worship and kingly power is yours;|| From the moon on high to the fish below, all is within your sway. *[16*

Foolish is he who is slothful in praise, who neglects his remembrance of God; || Foolish the beggar remiss and uncaring, foolish the master and king. *[17*

Most precious is the love God gives, its worth transcending all;|| A canopy his outstretched hand, a royal sign of grace. *[18*

Repeat the sacred Name of God, for thus we show our love for him; || Our lives transformed by God's good grace, an alchemy divine. *[19*

God's love supports the life within us, safe within his care; || Repeat the sacred Name of God and fill faith's treasure-house. *[20*

Every Friday loyal Muslims, those who faith is firm, || Come together praising God and offer him their prayer. *[21*

Thus to the satsang we are drawn, this is our custom and rule;|| There in its midst to give glory to God, there to enjoy his love.[112] *[22*

4 KHALSA AND RAHIT

4.1 THE KHALSA

During the time of the early Gurus the Panth was comparatively small and all who joined it owed their allegiance directly to the Guru. As its numbers increased, however, the task of pastoral care and tithe-collecting was partially delegated to regional supervisors called masands. Sikhs who remained under the Guru's direct supervision were collectively known as his Khalsa. All others were entrusted to the masands. [1

For many years the system evidently worked satisfactorily, but by the time of the tenth Guru many of the masands were asserting claims to independent authority. Confronted by this growing problem, Guru Gobind Singh took a twofold decision. The authority of the masands was to be terminated and all Sikhs were to be brought under the Guru's direct supervision as members of his Khalsa. At the same time the Panth was to be transformed. The Khalsa was to become a new order, its members subject to a new and demanding discipline. Entry to the Khalsa was to involve a distinctive style of initiation, and all who accepted this initiation were to swear obedience to a specific code of conduct (2.2.8). Ratan Singh Bhangu explains to the English enquirer Murray why the Guru decided to transform the Panth in this manner. [2

Murray then asked me to explain in detail why the Guru had created a [new] Panth. 'The Muslims ruled an immense empire, ' he said, 'and their writ ran through its twenty-two provinces. It included islands in the ocean, and extended through the mountains of the south and the east. Everyone was under their control. How could this community of Singhs continue to grow? How could the subjects [of such an empire] raise a rebellion and where was its army? How could the rulers remain unaware of the activities of the Sikhs? Surely they would regard the Guru and his followers with the greatest of hostility? Had they become friendly towards them? Why did they not recognise the Sikhs as a third panth [distinct from both Hindus and Muslims]? Did they have no counsellors wise enough to recognise their significance? Had not the Panth claimed sovereignty? How could it possibly remain concealed from the authorities?' [3

Fellow Sikhs, I answered him as follows. 'From its very birth the [new] Panth was unconcealed. From the very beginning its members were as sharp as thorns. When was the Sikh Panth ever concealed? The Sikhs could never hide themselves! It was a Panth created to fight, its members bearing arms from birth. Its Sikhs are given the baptism of the sword, and the *gurhati*[1] which they receive is likewise administered with the sword. In their turbans they carry steel quoits and daggers. How can they who sport lions' claws ever remain concealed? The Supreme Guru created the Panth in order that it should fight! Sovereignty cannot be won without struggle. From the very outset the Guru provided the means of waging war.   *[4*

'Hostility between the Gurus and the Emperors had become increasingly serious, and after Guru Tegh Bahadur had sacrificed his life how could the Sikhs be restrained? The Guru went down to Delhi and was there executed by the Emperor. Guru Gobind Singh appreciated the significance of the event. "The root of Muslim rule has decayed," he declared, "but the tree will not fall unless it is cut down or unless it is shaken by a mighty storm. A storm of swords will now assail it and thus it shall be felled."   *[5*

'And so the Guru took up the sword, recognising that the time had come to destroy the rule of the Muslims. As he did so he reflected on what might follow. "What use have I for an empty kingship?" he asked himself. "The throne which I occupy is the spiritual throne of Guru Nanak. This earthly empire cannot compare to it and for such temporal sovereignty I have no use. I shall confer it on my servants."   *[6*

'As he thus planned the destruction of Muslim rule the Guru considered the possibility of transforming the hill chiefs into true warriors.[2] But then he realised that this could not succeed. "They will never become my Sikhs," he said. "Why give them a priceless gift for nothing? . . . They worship idols of stone and they themselves are like stone unaffected by water. The history of their dealings with the Gurus had been a sorry one. Because they call themselves Rajputs and regard themselves as soldiers they can scarcely bring themselves to accept sovereignty from the Guru. It would be much better to bestow it on the poor, for they will truly appreciate the Guru's gift. . . . If these poor Sikhs are given authority they will acknowledge that I am the Guru." *[7*

'And so the Guru summoned his Sikhs to take up arms and slay the Muslims. But they shrank from the task, for they feared the Muslims. "The Muslims have a huge army," they protested. "Why should they surrender their authority?" They refused to listen to him. "When were we ever able to defeat the Muslims? We are sparrows, they are hawks. We are goats and they are wolves. How can deer be made to kill lions? It would be like expecting rainwater to run up a roof! They are Mughals and Pathans, soldiers since time immemorial. We are peasants, barbers, and carpenters. You have gathered low-caste people who do not bear arms. Summon the Rajput chiefs. Let them assist you in your purpose."   *[8*

' "What can I do with these Sikhs?" The Guru asked himself. "They refuse to accept the sovereignty which I want to confer of them." The omniscient Guru who knows all things discerned the reason. "The form of baptism which they receive is to blame," he reflected. "*Charan-amrit*[3] encourages a docile nature. It does not inspire the spirited fervour which alone can meet the need. They deck their hats with woollen rosaries and take submissive names such as 'Das' [slave]. Such meekness does not produce warriors who will wield weapons. They must therefore be transformed. They must be infused with a spirit which will strike fear in the hearts of others. They must assume martial names and they must receive a baptism which will impart this spirit."   *[9*

'Thus the Guru reasoned and from thought he proceeded to action. His followers were to emerge as splendid warriors, their uncut hair bound in turbans; and as warriors all were to bear the name 'Singh' [lion]. This, the Guru knew, would be effective. He devised a form of baptism administered with the sword, one which would create a Khalsa staunch and unyielding. His followers would destroy the empire, each Sikh horseman believing himself to be a king. All weakness would be beaten out of them and each, having taken the baptism of the sword, would thereafter be firmly attached to the sword. [10

'Thus the Khalsa would itself be God, possessor of all divine attributes and subject only to the Guru. All superstition would be cast aside. Sikhs would no longer worship spirits, tombs or cremation grounds, nor would they pay homage to popular deities. [They would set themselves apart from Hindu society], renouncing the frontal mark and refusing to wear either sacred thread or dhoti. Together they would constitute a single caste, all eating from the same vessel and all united in the same resolve.'[4] [11

4.2 THE RAHIT

Ratan Singh Bhangu supplements the dominant tradition concerning the origin of the Khalsa as a distinctive order. The dominant tradition emphasises the importance of a visible identity, one which makes it impossible for any Sikh to remain anonymous or concealed. When Guru Tegh Bahadur was executed most of the Sikhs who were present in Delhi shrank from their duty of assisting and defending their Master (2.2.7[11]). This they could do because they were outwardly indistinguishable from the general populace. The nature of the discipline required by membership of the new order ensured that concealment would no longer be possible. A Sikh of the Khalsa was to be visibly and unmistakably a Sikh, his identity proclaimed for all the world to see. [1

The actual inauguration of the new order took place on the Baisakhi festival day of 1699 (2.2.8[3]). All who responded to the Guru's summons and all who have subsequently accepted initiation into the Khalsa are amrit-dhari *('Sikhs who have taken amrit').[5] As such they are required to observe a distinctive code of conduct, one which specifies normative behaviour, outward appearance, social obligation, and ritual observances. The code is known as the Rahit and the manuals which record it are called rahit-namas. The first of the extant rahit-namas was evidently recorded several decades after the actual inauguration of the Khalsa. Before this happened, however, Rahit injunctions had been incorporated in earlier works describing the life and mission of Guru Gobind Singh. An early example is Sainapati's Gur Sobha (1.7[5]). The portion of this work which is devoted to the founding of the Khalsa includes the following lines.* [2

Spurn the masands, repeat the Lord's Name: this was the guidance he gave.||

The faithful should dwell in the spirit of God as a fish in the depths of the sea. [3

Let all discharge their daily duty, repeating the Name of God. || He who utters the Name but once shall receive abundant joy.   [4

This I proclaim, let all take heed, that he who knowingly slanders the Khalsa shall find himself in hell.   [5

Shun all those who have cut their hair;[6] spurn and avoid the Five.[7] || Let no Sikh ever consort with such people, even in funeral rites.   [6

Scorn the hookah, sing God's praises; his Name will supply all the food we desire. || Shun those who tonsure the heads of their corpses; proclaim this to all who are Sikhs.   [7

Never observe this tonsuring, brothers; razors must never be used. || Whenever a mother or father should die follow the Guru's tradition.   [8

Keep in your house a casket for alms, deposit therein your tithe. || Keep it away from the hands of masands; have nothing to do with such men. || Whatever the offering made for the Guru, all that you wish to give, || Take it direct to the Guru himself, offer it only to him.   [9

This is the Rahit, the custom to follow, the way which the faithful hold dear. || He who can witness the sangat at worship finds comfort and marvellous peace.   [10

Thus he declared, the Guru supreme: 'All in the sangat belong to my Khalsa. || He who obeys me is truly a Sikh, and he who denies me a rogue. || Banish the Five, embrace the true sangat; cherish God's grace and resist all temptation. || Abstain from the hookah, let hair stay uncut, and thus be a Sikh of the Guru's own Khalsa.'[8]   [11

The primary purpose of this section of Gur Sobha *is to denounce the masands and to insist that all loyal Sikhs must transfer their allegiance from these corrupt intermediaries to the Guru himself. As followers directly subject to the Guru they will be members of his Khalsa and it is thus membership of the Khalsa which the writer is primarily concerned to stress. This membership is, however, dependent on more than a mere affirmation of direct allegiance to the Guru. All who acknowledge the allegiance must also observe the distinctive code of conduct incumbent on a Sikh of the Khalsa. To renounce the masands and pay homage directly to the Guru requires loyal observance of the Rahit. The author's stress on the Khalsa allegiance is therefore accompanied by specific examples of Rahit observance. A Sikh of the Khalsa must never associate with the Guru's enemies. He must rigorously avoid the polluting hookah and he must never cut his hair.* [12

4.3 THE RAHIT-NAMA OF CHAUPA SINGH

Because these injunctions are strictly incidental to the author's main purpose Gur Sobha *cannot be regarded as a rahit-nama. Its fifth section is, however, a clear pointer to the emergence of the formal rahit-nama. The earliest of the formal rahit-namas still extant is probably the collection of injunctions attributed to Chaupa Singh, a servant of the tenth Guru. This manual has survived as part of a composite work which was evidently compiled and recorded near the middle of the eighteenth century. The dominant view concerning this extant version is that it represents an authentic work subsequently corrupted by mischievous supplements. Its acceptable injunctions include the following items:* [13

A Gursikh should not observe the custom of wearing a sacred thread or frontal sect mark. [14

A Gursikh should render service to others Sikhs with all his heart and without hesitation. [15

A Gursikh should never be arrogant, deceitful or wanton. He should be neither lustful nor prone to anger, neither a slanderer nor one puffed up with pride. [16

From the proceeds of his labours the Gursikh should put aside a tenth part for the Guru and use it to feed other Sikhs for the sake of the Guru. [17

Whenever a Gursikh joins other Sikhs he should choose his seat with care. Sit in a line, never in front of another Sikh . . . At such gatherings a Gursikh should lay the shoes of his fellow Sikhs in a straight line, for thus he is kept humble. [18

A Gursikh should never commit theft or adultery, nor should he ever indulge in gambling. [19

A Gursikh should protect the dignity of his *kes* and thus preserve the honour of the Sikh faith. The *kes* is the outward symbol of the inward faith of a Sikh.[9] [20

4.4 NAND LAL AND PRAHLAD SINGH

The Chaupa Singh Rahit-nama *has been little used during the past century. Items are occasionally quarried from it, but it is usually treated with marked caution or total neglect. There have also been clear signs of caution in the use made of the brief rahit-namas attributed to Nand Lal, Prahlad Singh, Desa Singh, and Daya Singh. It is, however, a more relaxed caution and in one respect this cluster of rahit-namas has made a notable contribution to Sikh doctrine. The versions attributed to Nand Lal and Prahlad Singh contain clear emphatic statements concerning the nature of the eternal Guru. Nand Lal's* Prasan-uttar *is largely devoted to an explanation of this key doctrine* [1

4.4.1 Prasan-uttar: the Catechism of Bhai Nand Lal

The Guru speaks. 'Hear, my friend, the pattern of behaviour (*rahit*) which should be observed by a Gursikh. [1

'Arise with the dawn and lovingly direct your thoughts to God. Repeat God's sacred words. Having bathed repeat both *Japji* and *Jap* (5.1.1–2). See me and meditate with reverence and with love. In the mid-afternoon listen with loving attention to katha and at sunset join in *Rahiras* (5.2). Hear both kirtan and katha, and join in praising God. The Sikh who regularly observes this discipline shall be brought to eternal joy. He who practises this five-fold discipline shall ensure deliverance for all his descendants, even up to the twenty-first generation; and they who are thus delivered shall no more suffer the round of death and rebirth.'   [2

Nand Lal speaks. 'You say that we should see you, O Master. Tell me where we are to find you.'   [3

The Guru speaks. 'Listen attentively, Nand Lal, and I shall explain. I am manifested in three ways: the formless or invisible (*nirgun*), the material or visible (*sargun*), and the divine Word (*gur-sabad*). The first of these transcends all that is material. It is the *neti neti* of the Vedas, the spirit which dwells in every heart as light permeates the water held in a vessel. The second is the sacred scripture, the Granth.[10] This you must accept as an actual part of me, treating its letters as the hairs of my body. This truly is so.   [4

'Sikhs who wish to see the Guru will do so when they come to the Granth. He who is wise will bathe at dawn and humbly approach the sacred scripture. Come with reverence and sit in my presence. Humbly bow and hear the words of the Guru Granth. Hear them with affection and alert attention. Hear the Guru's Word of wisdom and read it that others may also hear. He who wishes to converse with me should read or hear the Granth and reflect on what it says. He who wishes to hear any words should attentively read or hear the Granth. Acknowledge the Granth as my visible presence, rejecting the notion that it is other than me.   [5

'The Sikh himself is the third form which I take, that Sikh who is forever heedful of the words of sacred scripture (*gurbani*). He who loves and trusts the Word of the Guru is himself an ever-present manifestation of the Guru. Such a Sikh is the one who hears the Guru's words of wisdom and reads them so that others may hear. It is he who attentively recites both *Japji* and *Jap*, who regularly visits the gurdwara, and who strictly avoids adulterous liaisons. The Gursikh who is faithful in serving his Master will find himself cleansed from all sense of self-dependence. He who is scrupulous in performing these obligations is the Sikh in whom I am made manifest.   [6

'Worthy is the Sikh who devoutly serves his Master, expressing his obedience to me in the generous offerings which he makes. Such is the service which I gladly receive from a loyal Sikh, Nand Lal, service which earns him deliverance and leads him to heaven.'   [7

Nand Lal speaks. 'You have told me of three forms, Master, the three being the invisible, the visible, and the Word of the Guru. The first of these we cannot see and the second we witness in the person of the obedient Sikh. Merciful Lord, how can we comprehend the infinity of your invisible form? You are the supreme Guru our Master, and your presence mystically pervades every soul, [but how can we perceive that presence]?'   [8

The Guru speaks. 'You are a devout Sikh, Nand Lal. Hear this divine message which I impart to you. First you must recognise the Guru as visibly present in his Sikhs and serve me by diligently serving them. Next you must serve me by singing the divine Word, accepting it as truly a manifestation [of the Guru]. He who regularly sings portions of the sacred scripture shall thereby come to an understanding of the infinite being [of the Guru].   [9

'He who reads or hears this homily and pays careful heed to it will find himself the object of much admiration. He will also find that he is worthy to be united with me, his spirit mystically blended in mine.'   [10

This message of comfort and joy was delivered on the ninth day of the waxing moon in the month of Maghar, S. 1752 [4 December 1695 A.C.]. Let the Guru's praises be everywhere sung, declares Nand Lal. Repeat the name of God and the Guru. Meditate on the greatness of God. The Gursikh who truly has faith in his heart shall assuredly win deliverance.[11]   [11

4.4.2 The Tanakhah-nama

The other verse rahit-nama attributed to Nand Lal offers guidance of a much more specific nature. It begins by briefly stating that Nand Lal once questioned the Guru concerning the correct behaviour of a Sikh and then launches into a vigorous defence of regular attendance at gurdwara worship.   [1

'Tell me,' Nand Lal asked the Guru, 'what should a Sikh do and what should he avoid?' The Guru answered him: 'These are the deeds required of a Sikh, Nand Lal. Let him perform only those which reflect the threefold rule of the divine Name, charity and purity (*nam dan isnan*). He who does not attend the satsang early each morning should be treated as a grievous offender; and he who attends but lets his mind wander will find no peace in this world or the next. He who continues to talk while listening to the singing of God's praises is, I declare, bound for hell. He who refuses to have a poor person sit beside him commits an offence. He who utters the divine Word without understanding it gains nothing; and he who neglects to bow after completing a reading from the sacred scripture will find himself cut off from God.'[12]   [2

Having dealt with gurdwara behaviour and the procedure to be followed when preparing karah prasad (4.5[12]) the Tanakhah-nama *devotes the remainder of its text to a list of miscellaneous items. Some are distinctively Sikh in nature; others amount to little more than elementary rules of hygiene.*   [3

The Sikh who ventures out unarmed shall be doomed to continued transmigration. . . .   [4

He who combs his hair twice a day, reties his turban afresh each time he removes it, and daily cleans his teeth will be saved from suffering.   [5

Gobind Singh declares that one should never trust the selfish person who witholds the Guru's tithe, nor should he trust the person who utters lies. *[6*

Cursed is he who violates his sacred duty by commiting any of the following offences: (1) Bathing in water that is not cold. (2) Eating without having recited *Japji.* (3) Permitting an evening to pass without participating in Rahiras. (4) Retiring to bed at night without singing *Kirtan Sohila.* (5) Inflicting harm on another by maligning him.[13] *[7*

The Tanakhah-nama concludes with a stirring summons by the Guru, one which dramatically evokes the martial spirit of the Khalsa. *[8*

Hear me, Nand Lal, for I speak the truth. I shall establish my rule. I shall merge the four castes into one. I shall turn men to repeating God's sacred Name. My Sikhs shall mount swift horses and I shall have them fly like hawks. When confronted by a Muslim they will never turn and flee. One Sikh will confront a host of 125,000 *(sava lakh)* and he who fights will win salvation. Banners will wave, resplendent elephants will march, music will resound at every gate. When a mighty artillery discharges its guns the Khalsa shall arise and all enemies of the truth will be overthrown.[14] *[9*

The final couplet epitomises the spirit of the eighteenth century and the triumphant climax of the early nineteenth century. It incorporates the celebrated slogan raj karega khalsa *('the Khalsa shall rule'), powerful words which still challenge and inspire the followers of Guru Gobind Singh.* *[10*

The Khalsa shall rule, no enemy shall remain. All who endure suffering and privation shall be brought to the safety of the Guru's protection.[15] *[11*

4.4.3 The rahit-nama of Prahlad Singh

Like the Tanakhah-nama the rahit-nama attributed to Prahlad Singh is largely devoted to catalogues of pithy injunctions. After briefly claiming that it represents guidance given by Guru Gobind Singh during his visit to Abchalnagar in Central India the rahit-nama commences the listing of items so typical of this kind of manual. *[1*

If a Sikh wears a cap [in the Muslim style] he shall seven times be born a leper. The Sikh who wears the sacred thread [of the Hindus], plays at dice, or visits a prostitute shall be reborn as a dog countless hundreds of times. The evil seed which he sows must inevitably produce its evil fruit. The Sikh who removes his turban before eating shall find himself destined for hell.[16] *[2*

Virtually the whole of the rahit-nama is written in this manner. Two separate couplets together provide an unusually clear statement of the developed doctrine of the Guru. *[3*

Accept the Khalsa as Guru, for it is the manifest body of the Guru. The Sikh who wishes to find me should seek me in its midst. . . . *[4*

The Panth was founded at the command of Akal Purakh. Every Sikh is bidden to accept the Granth as Guru.[17] *[5*

This represents the ultimate form of the doctrine. The divine Guru, present within each of the ten personal Gurus, now dwells eternally in the corporate

community (the Guru Panth) and in the sacred scripture (the Guru Granth).
[6

4.5 SIKH RAHIT MARYADA

Although these early rahit-namas have been influential as guides to conduct they proved to be insufficient for the needs and understanding of the Singh Sabha reformers (1.9). They were neither systematic nor comprehensive, and they included items which the rational modernising instincts of the reformers found unacceptable. Some appeared to be mere superstitions: [1
It is an offence to extinguish a light by blowing it out, or to douse a fire by pouring the remains of drinking-water on it.[18] [2
Others breathed a crusading spirit more appropriate to eighteenth-century warfare than to the enlightened views of the Singh Sabha: [3
The true Khalsa is one who carries arms and slays Muslims.[19] [4
An early solution to this problem was to expurgate the received versions. This was justified on the grounds that injunctions inconsistent with reason or sound morality must surely be interpolations. It was, however, an unsatisfactory answer and early in the twentieth century the compiling of a new rahit-nama was begun. No one questioned the tradition that Guru Gobind Singh had promulgated a rahit. The need was for a systematic statement of the authentic Rahit as it had actually been delivered by the Guru in 1699 and during the remaining nine years of his life. [5
Predictably the task proved to be a very difficult one. A book of order for Khalsa rituals was issued in 1915 under the title Gurmat Prakas Bhag Sanskar, *but this manual never attracted widespread acceptance. In 1931 another attempt was made, this time under the auspices of the Shiromani Gurdwara Parbandhak Committee.[20] The result eventually appeared in 1950 as* Sikh Rahit Maryada *('The Sikh Code of Conduct'). This manual succeeded where its 1915 predecessor had failed. It soon secured general acceptance as an authoritative statement of the Rahit and has ever since been regarded as the standard guide.[21] It includes the following items:* [6

Definition of a Sikh
A Sikh is any person who believes in God (*Akal Purakh*); in the ten Gurus (Guru Nanak to Guru Gobind Singh); in Sri Guru Granth Sahib, other writings of the ten Gurus, and their teachings; in the Khalsa initiation ceremony instituted by the tenth Guru; and who does not believe in any other system of religious doctrine. [7
A Sikh should rise early (3 a.m. to 6 a.m.) and having bathed he should observe *nam japan* by meditating on God. Each day a Sikh should read or recite the order known as the 'Daily Rule' (*nit-nem*). The Daily Rule comprises the following portions of scripture: Early morning (3 a.m.–6 a.m.): *Japji, Jap,* and

the *Ten Savayyas* (5.1) . . . In the evening at sunset: *Sodar Rahiras* (5.2) . . . At night before retiring: *Sohila* (5.3). At the conclusion of the selections set down for early morning and evening (*Sodar Rahiras*) the prayer known as *Ardas* must be recited (5.4).   [8

The influence of the Gurus' words is best experienced in a religious assembly (*sangat*). Each Sikh should therefore join in sangat worship, visiting gurdwaras and drawing inspiration from the sacred scripture in the sangat's presence. In each gurdwara the Guru Granth Sahib should be opened daily. . . . The Guru Granth Sahib must be treated with great reverence while it is being opened, read, or closed. When it is to be opened it should be laid under a canopy in a place which is clean and tidy. It should be set on a stool or lectern over which a clean cloth covering has been spread. Cushions should be used to support it while it is open and a mantle should be provided for covering it when it is not being read. A whisk should be provided for use when it is open. . . . Shoes must be removed before entering a gurdwara. Feet, if unclean, should be washed. . . . Whenever a Sikh enters a gurdwara his first duty must be to bow before the Guru Granth Sahib, touching the floor with his forehead. . . . No Sikh may sit bareheaded in the presence of the sangat or an opened Guru Granth Sahib. . . .   [9

The only works which may be sung as kirtan in a sangat are those which are recorded in the sacred scriptures (1.2–3) or the commentaries on sacred scripture composed by Bhai Gurdas and Bhai Nand Lal (1.4).   [10

A practice to be commended is for each Sikh regularly to read right through the entire contents of the Guru Granth Sahib, planning his daily instalments in such a way that he completes the task in four to eight weeks (or whatever period may be convenient for him). . . . An unbroken reading of the Guru Granth Sahib (*akhand path*) may be held in time of distress or to mark an occasion of particular joy. Such a reading takes approximately forty-eight hours, the actual reading continuing without interruption.   [11

Karah prasad [sanctified food] which has been prepared in the prescribed manner may be brought to a gurdwara for distribution. The prescribed method for preparing karah prasad is as follows. Equal portions [by weight] of wholemeal flour, sugar (the best available) and ghee should be mixed in a clean [iron] vessel while passages from the sacred scriptures are sung or recited.   [12

Each Sikh should live and work in accordance with the principles of Gurmat. Gurmat may be defined as follows: [13

(a) To worship only the one supreme God (*Akal Purakh*) spurning all other gods and goddesses.   [14

(b) To accept as the means of deliverance only the ten Gurus, the Guru

Granth Sahib, and the works of the ten Gurus.   [15

(c) To believe that the same spirit was successively incarnated in the ten individual Gurus.   [16

(d) To reject caste distinctions and untouchability; magical amulets, mantras, and spells; auspicious omens, days, times, planets and astrological signs; the ritual feeding of Brahmans to sanctify or propitiate the dead; oblation for the dead; the superstitious waving of lights; [traditional] obsequies; fire sacrifices; ritual feasting or libations; sacred tufts of hair or ritual shaving; fasting for particular phases of the moon; frontal marks, sacred threads and sanctified rosaries; worshipping at tombs, temples or cenotaphs; idol worship; and all other such superstitions . . .   [17

(g) A knowledge of Gurmukhi is essential for Sikhs (1.2[10]) . . .   [18

(i) Do not cut a child's hair . . .   [19

(r) When Sikhs meet they should greet each other by saying, 'Vahiguru ji ka Khalsa, Vahiguru ji ki fateh' [Hail to the Guru's Khalsa! Hail to the victory of the Guru!]. This is the correct form for both men and women . . .   [20

(t) A Sikh must wear a kachh (4.5[43]) and a turban. Apart from these garments he may wear whatever he chooses. The turban is optional for women.   [21

Sikh Rahit Maryada includes rubrics for a birth and naming ceremony, marriage, Khalsa initiation, and cremation. The birth and naming ceremony is conducted as follows: [22

Following the birth of a child in a Sikh home the family and relatives should visit their gurdwara as soon as the mother is able to rise and bathe. (There is no particular period fixed for this purpose.) They should take karah prasad with them or arrange to have it prepared on their behalf. While they are in the gurdwara they should celebrate the event and give thanks by singing such hymns as Guru Arjan's 'God has broken every barrier' (*Sorath* raga), and his 'God has sent this wondrous gift' (*Asa* raga) (5.7.3). If a complete reading of the Guru Granth Sahib has been undertaken [to mark the occasion] the concluding ceremony should be performed [at this time]. A passage should be chosen at random and the officiating granthi should propose a name beginning with the same letter as the first word of the randomly-chosen shabad. If the suggested name meets with the sangat's approval it shall be the name bestowed on the child. To a boy's name 'Singh' should be added, and to a girl's name 'Kaur'. [23

After the six prescribed stanzas of *Anand Sahib* have been read the child's birth is celebrated with an appropriate *Ardas* and the distribution of karah prasad.   [24

Sikh marriages are solemnised in accordance with an order known as the Anand rite (5.7.6).   [25

At the time for the actual marriage the congregation should assemble in the presence of the Guru Granth Sahib and kirtan should be sung, either by professional singers (*ragi*) or by the congregation. The bride and bridegroom should be seated in front of the Guru Granth Sahib, the bride on the groom's left. Having first secured the consent of the assembled sangat the Sikh (either man or woman) who is to conduct the marriage ceremony should instruct the couple to stand, together with their parents or guardians, and should then recite the *Ardas* with which the ceremony begins.   [26

The officiant should then instruct the couple in the teachings of Gurmat concerning the duties of marriage. . . . To signify their assent to these injunctions the couple should bow before the Guru Granth Sahib. The bride's father or senior relative should then place in her hand the hem of one of the garments worn by the bridegroom. The person serving as reader then sings the *Lavan* hymn, Guru Ram Das's *Suhi Chhant* 2.[22] After each of the four stanzas the couple walk around the Guru Granth Sahib, the bridegroom followed by the bride who continues to hold his hem. While they are thus proceeding around the Guru Granth Sahib either the ragis or the entire congregation repeat the appropriate stanza. After completing each of the first three rounds the couple bow before the Guru Granth Sahib and then stand erect to hear the next stanza. Following the fourth round they bow and resume their seats. The ragis or others appointed for this particular purpose then sing the first five stanzas and the last stanza of *Anand Sahib*. The ceremony finally concludes with *Ardas* and the serving of karah prasad.   [27

The order for the conduct of funeral ceremonies includes the following instructions.

When a death takes place there should be no excessive lamenting, no beating of breasts or grief-stricken wailing. The best method of reconciling oneself to the will of God is to read the sacred scriptures or repeat God's name . . .   [28

A corpse should be bathed and clad in clean garments, complete with all five Ks (4.5[43]). It should be laid on a bier and *Ardas* (5.4) should be recited. The bier should then be carried to the cremation ground to the accompaniment of appropriate hymns. At the cremation ground a funeral pyre should be erected and before consigning the body to the flames *Ardas* should be recited. The corpse should then be laid on the pyre, and the pyre lit by a son, some other relative, or a close friend. The assembled sangat should meanwhile sit some distance away and sing hymns appropriate to a funeral (5.7.7) . . . When the pyre is well ablaze *Kirtan Sohila* should be recited (5.3), followed by *Ardas*. [29

After the cremation a reading of the Guru Granth Sahib should be initiated on behalf of the departed soul, either in the house of the deceased or in a neighbouring gurdwara. When the funeral pyre has cooled the body's ashes, together with any remaining bones, should be gathered and should either be cast into running water or buried at the place of cremation. No memorial should be erected to mark the spot where the cremation took place.   [30

Prayers of intercession may also be offered on appropriate occasions.

In addition to the ceremonies detailed above there may be occasions of particular joy or sadness which warrant a special intercession. Examples are the first entry into a new building, the opening of a new shop, or a child's first day at school (5.7.1). On such occasions a Sikh should invoke God's blessing by reciting *Ardas* (5.4). Readings from the scriptures and *Ardas* are essential components of all Sikh rituals. [31

The manual concludes the section on 'personal discipline' with an exhortation to perform seva, or 'service'.

Seva is a fundamental feature of Sikhism. Gurdwara maintenance provides a means of inculcating this essential virtue. Common examples are the sweeping of a gurdwara, serving water to members of a sangat or fanning them, serving food in the gurdwara dining-hall (*langar*), and cleaning the shoes [of worshippers]. [32

The Guru's langar serves two purposes. It inculcates the spirit of *seva* in Sikhs; and it breaks down false notions of status and caste. Anyone may eat in a langar, regardless of his status or caste. When all take their places in the same line [to receive their food] there should be no discrimination on the basis of nationality, caste or religion. The only qualification is that food which is given to initiated members of the Khalsa (4.5[34]) must be served from a separate dish. [33

*Having dealt with 'personal discipline' (which includes 'personal' rituals) Sikh Rahit Maryada takes up 'panthic discipline'. This concluding portion of the manual consists almost exclusively of the order for initiation into the Khalsa. The rite of Khalsa initiation (*amrit sanskar*) is conducted in the following manner.* [34

An open copy of the Guru Granth Sahib is required at the place of initiation together with at least six baptised Sikhs, each of them bearing all five of the Khalsa symbols. One of the six will sit with the Guru Granth Sahib while the remaining five will administer the actual initiation. Either men or women may serve in both capacities. Prior to the ceremony they should bathe and wash their hair. . . . [35

Any man or woman who affirms belief in the Sikh faith and vows to live according to its principles may receive initiation, regardless of nationality, [previous] creed, or caste. Those who are to receive initiation should be old enough to understand the meaning of the ceremony. They should bathe and wash their hair, and should present themselves wearing all five Khalsa symbols. These are uncut hair (*kes*), a sword or dagger (*kirpan*) suspended from the shoulder, a pair of shorts (*kachh* or *kachhahira*), a comb (*kangha*), and a steel bangle (*kara*).[23] No symbols associated with other faiths may be worn. The head must be covered, but not with a hat or cap. Ear-rings and nose ornaments must not be worn. Prior to receiving initiation the candidates should stand reverently before the Guru Granth Sahib with palms together. [36

One of the five officiants should then address those who are seeking initiation, explaining to them the principles of the Sikh faith in the following terms: 'The Sikh faith requires you to abandon the worship of man-made objects. Instead you should direct your love and devotion to the one supreme

Creator. This obligation is discharged by attending to the words of sacred scripture; by serving the sangat and the Panth; by acting benevolently towards others; by maintaining love for the divine Name; and after receiving initiation by living in accordance with the Rahit. Do you gladly accept this faith?' [37

When an affirmative answer has been given one of the officiants should offer an appropriate prayer and take a *hukam*.[24] The five officiants should then take their places beside the large bowl [which is to be used for the baptism]. The bowl should be made of iron and should be set on something clean and appropriate, such as a gilded stool. Fresh water should be poured into the bowl and soluble sweets added. Having done this the five officiants should sit around the bowl in the 'heroic posture'.[25] The following passages from scripture should be recited: *Japji, Jap*, the *Ten Savayyas, Benati Chaupai* and the six prescribed stanzas of *Anand Sahib* (5.1, 5.2.4–7). [38

The officiant who performs this recitation should do so with his left hand placed on the rim of the bowl. With his right hand he should stir the water with a two-edged sword (*khanda*), keeping his attention intently focussed on the task he is performing. The other officiants should gaze intently into the water with both hands resting on the rim of the bowl. After the appointed passages have been completed one of the officiants should recite *Ardas*. . . . [39

The candidate should now be instructed to adopt the 'heroic posture', turning their thoughts to the Tenth Master as they do so. Each should cup his hands, placing the right hand over the left. Five times the sanctified water (*amrit*) is poured into the candidate's cupped hands. As he does this the officiant shall say to him, 'Say, "Vahiguru ji ka Khalsa, Vahiguru ji ki fateh" ' (4.5[20]). After drinking each portion the recipient shall repeat, 'Vahiguru ji ka Khalsa, Vahiguru ji ki fateh.' Amrit is then sprinkled onto his eyes five times, and five times it is sprinkled over his hair. After each sprinkling the officiant shall call, 'Vahiguru ji ka Khalsa, Vahiguru ji ki fateh,' and the recipient shall repeat the words after him. The amrit which still remains is then consumed by the initiates (both men and women), all drinking from the same vessel. [40

Next the five officiants should impart the Name of God to the initiates by reciting the Basic Credal Statement (*mul mantra*) in unison and by having the initiates repeat it after them (5.1.1[1]) . . . [41

One of the five officiants should then expound the Rahit as follows: 'As from today you are "born to the Guru and freed from rebirth". You are now a member of the Khalsa. Guru Gobind Singh is your spiritual father and Sahib Kaur[26] your spiritual mother. Your birthplace is Kesgarh Sahib[27] and your home is Anandpur Sahib. Because you are all children of the same father you are spiritual brothers, one with another and with all others who have received the amrit initiation. You must renounce your former lineage, occupation, and religious affiliation. This means that you should put aside all concern for caste status, birth, country and religion, for you are now exclusively a member of the sublime Khalsa. You must worship God alone, spurning all other gods, goddesses, incarnations and prophets. You must accept the ten Gurus and their teachings as your only means of deliverance.   [42

'You can already read the Gurmukhi script (if not you must learn how to do so) and at least once a day you must read or hear the following works which together constitute the Daily Rule: *Japji, Jap* the *Ten Savayyas, Sodar Rahiras*, and *Sohila*. You should also read or hear some additional passage from the Guru Granth Sahib at least once a day, and you must always wear the Five Ks. These are uncut hair (*kes*), a sword or dagger (*kirpan*), a pair of shorts (*kachh*), a comb (*kangha*), and a steel bangle (*kara*).   [43

'There are four sins which are particularly serious and which must be scrupulously avoided: (1) Cutting one's hair. (2) Eating meat which has been slaughtered according to the Muslim rite. (3) Sexual intercourse with any person other than one's spouse. (4) Using tobacco. Anyone who commits any of these cardinal sins must be re-initiated, unless the act has been unintentional in which case no punishment should be administered.   [44

'Have no dealings with initiated Sikhs who cut their hair, nor with Sikhs who smoke.   [45

'Always be prepared to support the Panth and to provide whatever assistance may be required in a gurdwara. Set aside a tenth part of whatever you earn and dedicate it to the Guru. Let all that you do be done in accordance with the principles of Gurmat.   [46

'Observe at all times the discipline required of those who belong to the Khalsa. If you violate the Rahit in any respect you should present yourself before a congregation of the Khalsa and request a penance. . . . The following offences warrant a penance: [47

1. Associating with Minas, Masands, Dhir-malias, Ram-raias,[28] and other enemies of the Panth; or with smokers, those who murder baby daughters, or initiated Sikhs who cut their hair.   [48

2. Eating from the same dish as a person who has not received the Khalsa initiation or an apostate Sikh (*patit*).   [49

3. Dyeing one's beard.   [50

4. Giving or receiving a cash dowry in return for a son's or a daughter's hand in marriage.   [51

5. Consuming any drug or intoxicant (cannabis, opium, alcohol, cocaine, etc.).   [52

6. Performing any rite or ceremony which conflicts with Sikh belief, or commissioning anyone else to do so.   [53

7. Neglecting to fulfil any part of the Rahit.'   [54

At the conclusion of this homily one of the five officiants should recite *Ardas* (5.4). The person sitting in attendance on the Guru Granth Sahib should then take a *hukam*. If any of the newly initiated bears a name which was not selected from the Guru Granth Sahib he should now receive a new name [chosen in the approved manner] (4.5[23]). Finally karah prasad should be distributed. All who have enlisted in the Guru's service, both men and women, should take karah prasad from the same dish. [55

5 LITURGICAL TEXTS

5.1 THE EARLY MORNING ORDER

Each morning a Sikh should rise early and bathe. He should then repeat Guru Nanak's Japji, Guru Gobind Singh's Jap, *and the* Ten Savayyas *(4.5[8]).* [1

5.1.1 Japji

The Basic Credal Statement (mul mantra). There is one Supreme Being, the Eternal Reality. He is the Creator, without fear and devoid of enmity. He is immortal, never incarnated, self-existent, known by grace through the Guru. [1

The Eternal One, from the beginning, through all time, present now, the Everlasting Reality. [2

1. Through ritual purity he can never be known though one cleanse oneself a hundred thousand times. Silent reflection will never reveal him though one dwell absorbed in the deepest meditation. Though one gather vast riches the hunger remains, no cunning will help in the hereafter. How is Truth to be attained, how the veil of falsehood torn aside? Nanak, thus it is written: Submit to God's Order (*hukam*), walk in its way. [3

2. God's order is far beyond our describing though all that exists is its visible expression. All forms, all life is its creation, and it alone determines greatness. Some are exalted, some abased; some must suffer while others find joy. Some receive blessing, others condemnation, doomed by God's Order to endless transmigration. All are within it, none beyond its power. They who comprehend it, Nanak, renounce their blind self-centred pride. [4

3. They who are strong sing of God's might; they who perceive his gifts sing of his grace. Some praise his majesty and the wonders he performs; others laud his wisdom in their scholarship and learning. Some praise his power made manifest in creation, how he brings to life, restores to dust, and reincarnates anew. Some sing of his distance, of how he dwells afar; others of his presence, immanent in all creation. Countless numbers tell of him, describing him in endless ways. None can ever hope to succeed, for none can encompass his infinite being. Continually he gives, bestowing gifts beyond our power to receive. He cares for us, supplying our needs down the endless ages. God commands and by his Order directs our path. For ever joyous is he, declares Nanak, for ever free from care. [5

4. The eternal Master whose Name is Truth speaks to us in infinite love. Insistently we beg for the gifts which he by grace bestows. What can we offer in

return, what gift will gain us entrance to his court? What words can we utter to attract his love? At the ambrosial hour of fragrant dawn meditate on the grandeur of the one true Name. Past actions determine the nature of our birth but grace alone reveals the door to liberation. See him therefore, Nanak, dwelling immanent in all. Know him as the One, the eternal, changeless Truth. *[6*

5. He cannot be made and installed as an idol, he the Supreme One devoid of spot or stain. Whoever serves him wins honour, Nanak, so sing of him and his boundless excellence. Sing his praises, hear them sung, and nourish love for him within your heart. Thus shall your suffering all be banished and peace take its place within. The Guru's word is the mystic sound, the voice of the scriptures immanent in all. Shiva, Vishnu, Brahma and Parvati, all are but manifestations of the one divine Guru. Were my mind to comprehend him my words would surely fail, for he is far above describing, far beyond all power of human telling. One thing only I ask of the Guru. May the gracious Lord, the Giver of all, constantly dwell in my thoughts and recollection. *[7*

6. I would bathe at a place of pilgrimage if that would please God, but without his blessing nothing is gained. Throughout all creation nothing can be gained except by means of his grace. He who accepts but a single word from the Guru shall find within himself a treasure trove of jewels. Grant me, Master, that single perception, the constant remembrance of the Giver of all. *[8*

7. If one were to live through all four yugas or even ten times their span; if one were to be famed throughout the world, acknowledged as leader by all; if one were to earn an exalted name and a glory which covered the earth, yet would it all be futile and wasted without the blessing of God. If God's gracious glance avoids such a person all turn their faces away from him. He will be treated as the lowest of worms, scorned and blamed by all. The worthless he converts to virtue, Nanak, to the virtuous he imparts yet more. He alone has the power so to do, for no one confers virtue on God. *[9*

8. By listening to the Word one gathers all the qualities of the spiritually adept. By listening to the Word one comprehends the deepest mysteries of the universe. When one listens to the Word the vastness of the world comes into view, its continents, its realms, and under it the nether regions. If one listens to the Word the power of Death is overcome. The devout, declares Nanak, dwell in everlasting bliss, for suffering and sin must flee from all who hear the Word. *[10*

9. By listening to the Word one matches the gods, the equal of Shiva, of Brahma, and of Indra. From listening to the Word even the wicked turn to praise. Through listening to the Word one attains deep understanding, learning the mysteries of the yogic art and the wisdom of the scriptures. The devout, declares Nanak, dwell in everlasting bliss, for suffering and sin must flee from all who hear the Word. *[11*

10. Listening to the Word one finds truth, contentment, spiritual perception. Listening to the Word secures all that pilgrimage can achieve, the merit earned by bathing at every sacred site. By listening to the Word one

D

acquires the fame of the learned scholar. Listening to the Word one knows the rapture of deep meditation. The devout, declares Nanak, dwell in everlasting bliss, for suffering and sin must flee from all who hear the Word. [12

11. Listening to the Word one plumbs the ultimate depths of virtue. Listening to the Word one comprehends the wisdom of the Sufi masters. Listening to the Word the blind find their eyes have been opened. Listening to the Word one fathoms the unfathomable mysteries of our existence. The devout, declares Nanak, dwell in everlasting bliss, for suffering and sin must flee from all who hear the Word. [13

12. None can describe the believer's bliss; he who tries will rue his folly. Though one sit engrossed in strenuous thought no paper nor pen can serve the need, no scribe discharge the task. For such is the wonder of the Name of God, free from all spot and stain. Only he who truly knows the Name can ever be accounted a believer. [14

13. By believing one gains inner sight and wisdom. By believing one wins access to the mansions of the mind. Death no longer smites the believer, freed by faith from the summons to depart. Such is the wonder of the Name of God, free from all spot and stain. Only he who truly knows the Name can ever be accounted a believer. [15

14. No obstacle stands in the believer's path; unchecked he advances with honour and acclaim. For him the broad highway, no narrow track he follows, obedient to the call of his sacred duty. Such is the wonder of the Name of God, free from all spot and stain. Only he who truly knows the Name can ever be accounted a believer. [16

15. By believing one finds the door to liberation, and he who finds it shows the way to all his family and kin. The master leads, his disciples follow. He who has faith and believes, Nanak, need never wander as a beggar. Such is the wonder of the Name of God, free from all spot and stain. Only he who truly knows the Name can ever be accounted a believer. [17

16. The truly devout win God's acceptance, supreme as the leaders of men. Honoured in the Court of God they stand in glory at his royal door, gazing upon their Master alone and thus directed by him. If we should seek to speak of God or turn to him in contemplation our attempts to encompass him must surely fail. Wondrous are the Creator's deeds, far beyond our computing! Faithfulness, the offspring of grace, is the Bull which supports the earth (3.3.1 [5]). Serenity is the rope by which it is tethered. Enlightened is he who truly knows the burden born by the Bull. Beyond this earth there are countless more. Who stands beneath them, what bears their weight? Beings of various kinds, colours, and names, he recorded all with a flowing pen. If one might know how to score their sum what a mighty account it would be! What power, what beauty, what bounteous giving! Who can comprehend them! With a single command he unfurled creation and by that command a host of streams sprang forth. How can I, abject and worthless, ever describe your mighty power? Worthy is that which pleases you, eternally constant Nirankar.[1] [18

17. Countless those who repeat your Name, countless those who adore you. Countless those who offer you worship, countless those who perform austerities. Countless those who intone the scriptures, countless the ascetic practitioners of yoga. Countless the devout contemplating goodness and wisdom. Countless the faithful and the givers of charity. Countless the warriors scarred by battle. Countless those who observe vows of silence. How can I, abject and worthless, ever describe your mighty power? Worthy is that which pleases you, eternally constant Nirankar. [19

18. Countless the fools, the thieves, the swindlers; countless those who have ruled by force. Countless the cut-throats, violent murderers; countless those who live lives of sin. Countless the liars, reborn to lie again; countless the polluted subsisting on filth. Countless the slanderers, weighed down by infamy. Nanak the lowly, having pondered now declares: Worthless am I to be offered as sacrifice. Worthy alone is that which pleases you, eternally constant Nirankar. [20

19. Countless your names and countless your dwellings, numberless worlds beyond man's comprehending. Even declaring them numberless falls sinfully short of the truth. Yet by words alone can we utter the Name, with words alone can we give you glory. With words alone can we tell of your wisdom, with words sing hymns of praise. With words we write and recite the scriptures, and words must be used to record our destiny. He who records it is free from its trammels; whatever he commands must surely come to pass. Whatever he has made gives form to his Name. Nothing exists except that which expresses it. How can I, abject and worthless, ever describe your mighty power? Worthy is that which pleases you, eternally constant Nirankar. [21

20. If hands, feet and body are smeared with grime water will wash them clean. Clothes may be stained with the traces of urine, but soap will restore them again. If the mind be soiled and defiled by sin it is cleansed with love of the Name. Virtue and sin are more than mere words, for each of us carries the fruit of his deeds. As we have sown so shall we reap. Each must transmigrate, Nanak, as God's divine Order decrees. [22

21. Pilgrimage, austerities, charity and alms earn no more merit than a paltry sesame. Hear, believe, nurture love in your heart, for thus one is cleansed by the waters within. All virtue is yours, O Lord, none do I possess. Helpless am I unless you confer it, unable even to love you. All praise to you Master of all, Creator Lord made manifest in the Word. You are Truth, you are Beauty, you are the One eternally blissful. What was the time, what the occasion, what the date and what the day; what the month and what the season when first creation took its birth? No pundit knows, for no Purana contains it; no qazi will find it recorded in the Qur'an. No yogi knows the date or day, no man can tell the season or the month. Only the Creator knows the answer; he alone knows when creation began. How can I tell of him, how utter his praise? How can I describe him, how comprehend his might? Everyone tries to describe him, Nanak, each claiming wisdom beyond his neighbour. He is the Master, Supreme in his

greatness, Maker and Lord of all! He who claims to encompass him, Nanak, can win no glory in the hereafter. *[23*

22. A hundred thousand worlds below, countless heavens above! He who would count them must certainly fail as the Vedas so curtly confess. Eighteen thousand, say the Muslim scriptures, their foundation the Creator's deed. Yet none can compute them, no words will suffice; no language can ever describe them. Let God be praised and magnified, Nanak, for he alone can comprehend. *[24*

23. Though men may praise you, endlessly praise you, none may perceive the true measure of your being. Rivers and streams merge with the ocean, each unaware of its boundless extent. Kings may own empires vaster than oceans, with wealth heaped high as mountains. Yet none can hope to match the ant which ever remembers God. *[25*

24. Infinite are his praises, uttered in ways unnumbered; infinite his works and infinite his gifts. Infinite is his sight, infinite his hearing, infinite the workings of his mind. His creation is boundless, infinite its span. Though many may try none can ever comprehend it. None there be who know its bounds; though much be said much more remains. Great is God and high his station, higher than high his Name. Only he who matches its height can ever aspire to understanding. God alone can scan it, Nanak. All we receive is by his grace. *[26*

25. Grace abounding, beyond recording! Great the Giver, seeking no return. At his door beg warriors unnumbered, with countless more beyond describing. Many there be who misuse his gifts, turning his bounty to their own destruction. Many receive while denying the source; others accept without gratitude or thanks. Many endure constant suffering or hunger, yet even these are your gifts, O Lord. Our bonds are broken, if such be your will, by the word which you alone can speak. If any fool should assume this right retribution must follow, a fate beyond telling. God alone knows, God alone bestows. Rare is he who acknowledges this. Endowed with the power to offer praise, Nanak, one stands supreme, an emperor amongst kings. *[27*

26. Priceless the stock, incomparable the merchants, conducting their trade from a store beyond valuing. Peerless are they who take up this commerce, boundless the profits they carry away. Priceless the devotion they give to their Master, priceless the unity all share with him. Priceless his laws, priceless his court, priceless the scales which balance our merits. Priceless his blessing and the tokens he bestows; priceless his grace and priceless his commands. God himself is beyond our appraisal, all our descriptions must falter and fail. Men may try, seeking words to express him. The end is the silence of mystical union. The scriptures have tried and so too have scholars, attempting descriptions in text and in commentary. Brahmas tell of him, so too do Indras; Krishna and gopis all join in the task. Shiva speaks of him and likewise the Siddhs, numberless others whom God has enlightened. Demons and gods, the inspired, the ascetic – all speak of him and all fail in the telling. How many men have sought to describe him, endlessly striving yet finally failing. Though countless

more be brought into being their efforts too would all be in vain. He is as mighty as he may choose; he alone knows his own greatness, Nanak. Should anyone boast that he too can know let him be branded the feeblest of fools.   [28

27. Where, O Lord, is the place where you dwell, with its gate where you sit keeping watch over all; there where the music resounds to your glory, the heavenly strains of a host without number? Boundless the range of your glorious harmony; infinite they who unite in your praise. The wind and the waters, the whole world of nature, unite in your praises and join in the song. With them your scribe and his tireless attendants, praising your greatness while listing men's deeds. Blest by your grace all the gods and their consorts, a mighty array singing hymns to your praise. So too the Siddhs in their deep contemplation, and others of wisdom, austerities, strength. They who are learned sing hymns to your glory, with rishis who study the scriptures of old. Ravishing beauties add joy to the harmony, music in heaven, on earth and below. Spirits most precious give voice to their gladness, their music resounding where piety dwells. Heroes and warriors, famed for their victories, sing with creation one vast song of praise. They who enraptured lend voice to this harmony all win your love for the praises they sing. Boundless, unnumbered, an infinite chorus, mighty assemblies which none may conceive. Master eternal, our Lord and Creator, with Truth as your Name and unfailingly true; all that exists in its forms and its colourings, all is your handiwork, all you sustain. None may command you, none challenge your purpose, whatever you choose comes to pass. You are the Master, our King all-prevailing, before whom all creatures must bow.   [29

28. Yogis wear ear-rings, let yours be patience, with honest labour for begging bowl and pouch. Cover yourself with contemplation as the yogi applies his ashes. Clothe yourself in the remembrance of death as the yogi dons his blanket. Let purity be your yogic discipline and lean for support on the staff of faith. Accept all as brothers, be strong in self-discipline. He conquers the world who conquers self. Let the yogi's cry be our joyous greeting, to you the Master of all. From time's beginning, through all eternity, you are the pure, the eternal Lord.   [30

29. With wisdom your food and compassion the giver let the mystic music resound in every heart. God is supreme, the Master of all. Put your trust in him, not in magical powers. Such powers are futile, for all power is God's. He summons or despatches as our destiny decrees. Let the yogi's cry be our joyous greeting, to you the Master of all. From time's beginning, through all eternity, you are the pure, the eternal Lord.   [31

30. In some strange way (so people believe) a Mother gave birth to three appointed sons – one the world's creator, one its sustainer, one to sit in judgement and pass the sentence of death. But all is under God's control, all functions according to his command. Wonder of wonders, God witnesses all, yet to all remains invisible, unseen. Let the yogi's cry be our joyous greeting, to you the Master of all. From time's beginning, through all eternity, you are the pure,

the eternal Lord. *[32*

31. God dwells in every realm of the universe, every realm a portion of the storehouse divine. All that exists he created once for ever, keeping vigil over all that he thus brought into being. Eternally steadfast is he, O Nanak, and his works endure for evermore. Let the yogi's cry be our joyous greeting, to you the Master of all. From time's beginning, through all eternity, you are the pure, the eternal Lord. *[33*

32. Let every tongue become a hundred thousand; let each be multiplied twice ten times more. Let this multitude of tongues then join together, each repeating a hundred thousand times the name of creation's Lord. This path is a stairway leading to the Master, an ascent to the bliss of mystical union. All may follow it, even the lowliest, if they but heed the word from above. They who receive grace will find the path, Nanak, leaving the braggart to wander astray. *[34*

33. We have no power to speak or be silent, neither to beg nor give to another. The power to live, the power to die, the strength to possess kingdoms, spurs to arrogance – none is ours to claim or command. We have no power to gain wisdom or enlightenment, neither spiritual skill nor the means of liberation. God alone possesses power, he alone can wield it. Before him all are equal, Nanak. None are exalted, none abased. *[35*

34. God created the night and the day, the days of the week and the seasons of the year. With them he created wind and water, fire and the regions established below. Amidst them all he set the earth, the place where men are confronted by duty. Wondrous the creatures there created, boundless variety, countless their names. Each must be judged for the deeds he performs, by a faultless judge in a perfect court. Those who are justified stand radiant in glory, bearing upon them the mark of his grace. All who enter are recognised, Nanak, the false distinguished from those who are true. *[36*

35. Such is the law in the Realm of Duty. Hear now the nature of the Realm of Knowledge – the infinite variety of wind, water, fire, numberless Krishnas, countless Shivas, endless Brahmas creating endless styles of form, of colour, of outward attire. All are present in infinite array – the earth and sacred mountains, each with its Dhruva uttering sermons without end; the Indras, the moons and suns, infinite spheres and lands without number; Siddhs and Buddhas, Naths and devis, gods and demons, men of silence, precious jewels and mighty oceans! How deep the mines, how varied the speech, how grand the dynasties of rulers and kings! Infinite forms of meditation, numberless those who perform them. Boundless, limitless, infinite, O Nanak. None can perceive its end. *[37*

36. Enlightenment shines in the Realm of Knowledge, music and spectacle, wonder and joy. Beauty prevails in the Realm of Endeavour, beauty of form unique in its splendour. Words will not serve, for none can describe it. Were one to try one would surely be humbled. Perception is sharpened, wisdom grows deeper, powers far transcending the knowledge of mortals. *[38*

37. Mastery rules in the Realm of Fulfilment, for there God's will prevails. There one encounters mighty heroes, filled with the spirit of God's pervading power; and virtuous women, praised as was Sita, women of beauty no words can describe. Death cannot touch them nor any deceit, for God himself resides in their hearts. God also dwells in the hearts of his faithful, host upon host enraptured by his presence. God's ultimate dwelling is the Realm of Truth, the ineffable home of eternal bliss. There the Creator keeps watch over all, imparting grace, bestowing joy. Within that realm are continents and universes, their vastness far beyond power of telling. Worlds upon worlds and endless forms, all of them acting as God has decreed. Joyously he watches, guiding their courses. To describe it, Nanak, is as hard as steel. *[39*

38. Let continence be the forge and tranquillity the goldsmith, intelligence the anvil and knowledge the tools. Let fear be the bellows, austerities the fire, and love the crucible wherein the amrit is poured. In such a mint the divine Word is cast, the daily task for all who receive his grace. They who receive his grace, Nanak, are blessed with transcendent joy. *[40*

Epilogue. Air is the Guru, water the Father, and earth the mighty Mother of all. Day and night are the caring guardians, fondly nurturing all creation. In the court of God all stands revealed, the record of deeds both good and evil. As we have acted so we are recompensed, the devout brought near to the presence divine, the reprobates banished afar. They who have faithfully followed the Name have run their course, their labours done. Freed are they and others with them. Radiantly, Nanak, they go to glory.[2] *[41*

5.1.2 Jap
By the grace of the Eternal One, the True Guru

He has no visible sign, neither caste nor lineage; || None may describe his form, neither features nor attire. || He is the Eternal One, self-enlightened and of infinite power. || God of Gods, the King of kings; Master of the three worlds, the Lord of creation; ruler of all beings, demon, human and divine; || His nature affirmed by the mantle of the forest, his infinity proclaimed by every blade of grass. || Who can recount your names, O Lord? By your deeds alone can you be known. *[1*

Hail to the Eternal One, hail to the Lord of Grace! Hail to the Formless One, incomparable, unique. *[2*

Hail to him the invisible Lord,[3] immune from judgement's writ. Hail to him the incorporeal, beyond the cycle of birth and death. || Hail to him the imperishable One, to the One beyond destruction or decay. Hail to him the nameless One, to the One no single place can hold. *[3*

The poem continues in this manner through a total of 199 brief stanzas, each naming a cluster of divine features or qualities. The result is a lengthy catalogue of descriptive terms, some designating negative concepts but most expressed as positive attributes. Epithet is heaped on epithet as the Guru develops his extended statement of God's nature and being. God is formless, uncreated, and deathless, fearless, pure, and beyond all desire. He is immanent, infinite, resplendent, unbound. Absolute in power he is yet benign and merciful, wholly just and supremely generous. The Light of Truth, he is also the ultimate mystery. The paean concludes: [4

Invincible, immortal, fearless, unchanging. [5

Without beginning, unborn, eternal, all-pervading. [6

Invulnerable, unyielding, ineffable, self-sustaining. [7

Timeless, merciful, inexpressible, unbound. [8

Nameless, without desire, beyond comprehending, unyielding. [9

Subject to none, destroyer of all; free from the cycle of birth and death, from the need to observe any vows of silence. [10

Wholly detached, without colour, form or sign. [11

Untrammelled by karma, unhindered by doubt, enduring for ever, beyond all power of telling. [12

Hail to the One who is worthy of reverence, hail to him the Destroyer of all.|| Hail to him the Invincible Lord, the Nameless One, dwelling within. || Hail to the One free from passion's control, our dearest treasure, immanent in all. || Scourge of the wicked, cherished guardian of the obedient, hail all hail to him. [13

Eternally true, eternally blissful, Destroyer of all who challenge his might.|| Bestower of blessing, Maker of all things, Creator Lord pervading all. || Awesome in wealth, the dread of his enemies. || Destroyer, Creator, compassionate Lord. [14

Around us lies God's dwelling-place, his joyous presence on every side.|| Self-existent and supremely beautiful, he dwells as a presence immanent in all creation. || Birth and death are abolished by his power, by the grace made manifest in his being|| Eternally present within all humanity he reigns in glory for ever.[4] [15

5.1.3 The Ten Savayyas

The 'Ten Savayyas' which are appointed for daily recitation after Japji *and* Jap *form a segment of Guru Gobind Singh's* Akal Ustat.[5] *In their* Dasam Granth *setting the 'Ten Savayyas' are preceded by the heading* tavprasad savayye, *literally 'By your grace savayyas'. They are sometimes known by this name, a title which may be translated as 'The Invocatory Quatrains'.* [1

Scrupulous Jains and hosts of Siddhs, ascetic yogis – I have seen them all.|| Warriors and demons, gods who drink amrit, devout believers in a multitude of doctrines.|| All these have I witnessed as I travelled the world, yet never a true follower of the Lord. || Without the love and grace of God their devotion is trivial, worthless, lost. [2

Mighty elephants in gorgeous array, magnificently decked with gold; || Thousands of horses nimbler than deer, their speed even swifter than the wind; || Though their masters be powerful emperors, potentates before whom countless bow.|| In the end such greatness crumbles to nothing as barefoot they go on their way.   *[3*

They march victorious across the world, beating their drums in triumph, ||
Their splendid elephants vibrantly trumpeting, their legion of thoroughbreds
proudly neighing. || Kings of the past, of the present, the future, their numbers
beyond comprehending, || Neglectful of worship, unmindful of God, they go to
their ultimate home.   *[4*

Pious bathing and acts of charity, disciplined lives and endless rites; ||
Searching the scriptures, Hindu and Muslim; scanning the earth and the
heavens above; || Men who abstain from all food or from sex – ascetics
unnumbered I have seen and I know|| That though they be kings all their deeds
are in vain if their lives have no place for the praises of God.   *[5*

Seasoned troops in coats of mail, fearsome warriors with the strength to kill;||
Fiercely proud they stand their ground, steadfast in courage though
mountains take flight;|| Assailing their enemies, crushing their foes, humbling
the pride of their elephant hosts; || They too must finally rise and depart,
deprived of the grace of the Lord.   *[6*

Boundless in courage and matchless in strength, men who unflinching will
parry a sword; || Despoiling a country, slaying its people, its elephant armies
brought down to the dust; || Forts destroyed by the might of their arms, the
world subdued by the fear of their threats; || Yet all are humbled by the
Creator's power, beggars all in the presence of the Lord.   *[7*

Deities and demons, the divine,[6] the uncouth, repeating God's Name in the
future as the past,|| All the creatures of the earth and sea resigned to his will in
instant obedience;|| Praise for their virtue resounds afar, their evil deeds erased.
|| The devout go forth with joy in the world as their enemies cry in helpless
rage.   *[8*

Masters of men, commanders of elephants, powerful rulers who bestride the
world; || Endlessly bathing, prodigious in charity, sitting bedecked as their
marriages are made.[5] || All is futile, for even the gods,[8] however exalted, must
end in death. || Only the humble who touch God's feet shall finally sunder the
cycle of rebirth.   *[9*

What benefit comes from endless meditation, from sitting like cranes with
both eyes closed? || One may piously bathe in all seven oceans and yet lose
everything here and hereafter. || Some spend their lives deep in the jungle,
wasting their years in useless endeavour.|| Let all pay heed for I speak the truth:
only they who love God can find him.   *[10*

Some worship stones, borne on their heads; some hang lingams from their
necks.|| Some claim that God dwells in the south, whilst others bow to the West.
|| Some worship idols, foolishly ignorant; others put trust in the tombs of the
dead.|| All are astray, seduced by false ritual; none knows the secret of God. *[11*

5.2 THE EVENING PRAYER: SODAR RAHIRAS

The Sodar *order takes its name from the first word of its first hymn (1.2[5]). It is sung at sunset (4.5[8]).*   [1

5.2.1 Invocation

Pleasure seduces my mind from the Master; pain is the cure for this ill. || You are the Master, my Lord and Creator; I am as nothing, all worthless my deeds. || To you I offer this life as a sacrifice, infinite Lord, all-pervading, sublime.   [1

The light which is God shines in all that has life; each spirit is merged in that light. || You are the Master, our joy is to praise you; and he who adores you finds peace evermore. || Trusty and faithful, our Lord and Creator; he who supplies all our wants and our needs.[9]   [2

5.2.2 Sodar

By the grace of the Eternal One, the true Guru

Where, O Lord, is the place where you dwell, with its gate where you sit keeping watch over all, ||There where the music resounds to your glory, the heavenly strains of a host without number? || Boundless the range of your glorious harmony; infinite they who unite in your praise.   [1

The wind and the waters, the whole world of nature, unite in your praises and join in the song. || With them your scribe and his tireless attendants, praising your greatness while listing men's deeds. || Blest by your grace all the gods and their consorts, a mighty array singing hymns to your praise; || So too the Siddhs in their deep contemplation, and others of wisdom, austerities, strength. || They who are learned sing hymns to your glory, with rishis who study the scriptures of old. || Ravishing beauties add joy to the harmony, music in heaven, on earth and below. || Spirits most precious give voice to their gladness, their music resounding where piety dwells. || Heroes and warriors, famed for their victories, sing with creation one vast song of praise.   [2

They who enraptured lend voice to this harmony all win your love for the praises they sing. || Boundless, unnumbered, an infinite chorus, mighty assemblies which none may conceive. || Master eternal, our Lord and Creator, with Truth as your Name and unfailingly true, || All that exists in its forms and its colourings, all is your handiwork, all you sustain. || None may command you, none challenge your purpose, whatever you choose comes to pass. || You are the Master, our King all-prevailing, before whom all creatures must bow.[10]   [3

Told of your greatness men sagely describe it, yet only by seeing we know. || How can we measure a worth which is infinite? They who have glimpsed it are rapt in your praise.   [4

Refrain. Great is my Master, beyond comprehending, his virtues transcendent, divine. || None may encompass your might and magnificence; none may describe your true worth.   [5

Scholars assemble and ransack the scriptures, attempting to measure your worth; || Men of devotion, with gurus and teachers, yet never a jot can they show.   [6

Goodness and truth, all the strength of austerities, all that the Siddhs have achieved, || All is from you and without grace and mercy that union we seek is denied.   [7

Wondrous your storehouse, its rooms filled with treasure, a marvel which none may describe. || What need of aid when our Master supports us, the True One who comforts and guides.[11]   [8

I live by repeating the blest Name of God; if ever I cease I must die. || Hard is the way if one craves the true Name, yet the Name brings all pain to an end.   [9

Refrain. Mother of mine, let me never forget him. || True is my Master, his Name ever true.   [10

Those who would tell of the Name as they know it soon weary and fail in their task. || Let all strive together their effort is vain, for the Name far transcends all their claims.   [11

God does not die, there is no cause for mourning; his mercies unceasingly flow. || He alone is, with no other beside him, existing alone while eternity runs.   [12

Boundless his bounty for he too is infinite, he who makes night follow day. || Base is the wretch who forgets his true Master, vile if he scorns the true Name.[12]   [13

Hear my petition, true Guru and Lord, great and most wondrously wise. || Grant that this worm may receive your protection, the light of your glorious Name.   [14

Refrain. Guru and friend, grant the light of your Name, the guidance which prompts us to sing to your praise.   [15

Blessed are they who athirst for the Name nourish their faith in your grace, || Blest by your mercy they join with the faithful in virtuous deeds and in praise.   [16

Wretched are they who neglect the true Name, death is the fate they receive; || Never to join in the songs of the faithful, here and hereafter condemned.   [17

Some will be granted a place with the faithful, destined since time first began. || Blessed are they for the joy they obtain there, the joy of the glorious Name.[13]   [18

Why all these plans, why this care and disquiet when God watches over us all? || Even the life in the rocks and the boulders is given the succour it needs. [19

Refrain. Grant us release as we join with the faithful, restored like dry wood which has blossomed anew.   [20

No one supports you, no father nor mother; no son gives you aid, nor your wife. || Why should you fear when the Lord is your keeper, his help ever ready at hand. *[21*

Cranes mount aloft and depart for far places, leaving their chicks all alone.||
Who will then feed them, providing their sustenance; who shows them how to
survive? *[22*

All the earth's treasures are held in God's keeping, Master of strength and of
power.|| To you I offer my life as a sacrifice, infinite Master and Lord.[14] *[23*

5.2.3 So Purakh

By the grace of the Eternal One, the True Guru

To you the pure One free from stain, sublime and boundless Lord,|| To you
all hearts and minds are drawn, to you Creator God. || All that has life is your
possession, all owe that life to you. || They who adore him ponder the Lord, he
who relieves distress, || God is both Lord and one who serves, Nanak is lowly
dross. *[1*

Dwelling in every human heart, your light suffusing all;|| Some are givers,
others beggars, each in the role you choose. || You are the Giver, you receive,
and you alone I know.|| Infinite Master, boundless Lord, how can I praise your
worth?|| To those who humbly serve you, Lord, I sacrifice my all. *[2*

Peace dwells with those who turn to God, peace in this age of strife;|| Ponder
the Lord and freedom win, freedom from Death's grim net. || Turn to the Lord
who knows no fear and every fear shall flee;|| Serve him with faith and find true
bliss, merged in the being of God.|| For pious souls who turn to God I sacrifice
my all. *[3*

Brimful your treasure-house of praise, infinite gifts of joy; || Numberless
those who offer praise, endless ways to adore. || Countless the souls who speak
your Name, with penance harshly sore; || Endless the scriptures men recite,
deeds of devotion done. || Who are the truly blessed, Lord? They who receive
your grace. *[4*

Boundless Creator, Primal Lord, matchless your wondrous might; ||
Timeless, eternal, changeless, true, you are the One alone. || All that you
purpose comes to pass, all that you will must be.|| All that exists your hand has
made; all you will bring to dust.|| Sing to him, Nanak, hymns of praise; sing to
the Lord of all.[15] *[5*

Refrain. You are my Master, in truth the Creator,|| Absolute Lord, all I have
is from you. *[6*

To you the Creator all spirits are drawn, yet only by grace find the Name.||
That treasure awaits only those who obey; only they who obey are called. *[7*

You, Lord, are the river wherein all things dwell; apart from you nothing can
be. || All that has life owes that life to your purpose, some drawn to you, others
condemned. *[8*

Only those souls whom you choose to enlighten can know you and offer you
praise. || They who serve God find that peace without ending, their spirits
absorbed in the Name. *[9*

Wondrous Creator, the Maker of all things, apart from you nothing can be.||
Ever creating you scan your creation, revealed by the Guru's rich grace.[16]　*[10*

All have been cast in that lake which engulfs us, its waters exciting desire.||
How many souls have been snared in its marshes, their bodies dragged down in
its mire.　*[11*

Refrain. Who do I foolishly turn from my Master?|| Mindless of duty I waste
and decay.　*[12*

Rigorous discipline, virtue and learning, those merits which fools will
despise;|| Though I neglect them, my Lord and my Master, I pray for your
caring and grace.[17]　*[13*

Precious this life you receive as a human, and with it the chance to find God.||
Join with the pious and sing to God's praises, for no other deed will suffice.　*[14*

Refrain. Waiting to cross the dread ocean to freedom|| Why waste your life on
delights which must fade?　*[15*

Spurning my duty, the Name unrepeated, no disciplined path do I tread.||
No service I offer, my deeds mean and vile; in shame I seek shelter and
grace.[18]　*[16*

5.2.4 Benati Chaupai

Extend to me your guiding hand, grant this my heart's desire,|| That at your
feet, most gracious Lord, accepted I may dwell.　*[1*

Let all my foes be overcome, your hand my sure defence.|| Let all around me
live in peace, all those within my care.　*[2*

Your hand I crave, my rampart strong; destroy my foes this day.|| May sweet
success crown all my hopes, my praise for you endure.　*[3*

For you alone, Creator Lord, I follow and obey. || May all my people cross
life's sea; may all my foes be slain.　*[4*

Hold forth your hand when death draws near, let every fear depart.|| Sustain
me by your mighty strength, your sword the sign I bear.　*[5*

Protect me Master, be my shield, with all who hold you dear; || The poor
man's friend, the tyrant's foe, creation's only Lord.　*[6*

When you commanded Brahma rose, and Shivji came when called. || The
birth of Vishnu you ordained, for all is by your will.　*[7*

The Lord eternal fashioned Shiv, and Brahma, Vedic king. || The Lord
eternal fashioned all; to him I humbly bow.　*[8*

All worlds the Lord eternal made, all demons, gods and men.|| Since time
began he dwells alone, my Guru and my King.　*[9*

To him alone I humbly bow, to him Creator Lord.|| To those who serve him
grace and peace; to foes an instant death.　*[10*

He knows the thoughts of every heart, the woes of good and ill. || From
smallest ant to massive beast he watches over all.　*[11*

He suffers when the faithful grieve, rejoices in their joy.|| To him are known

the cares of all, the thoughts of every heart.   [12
The world we see reflects God's form; when God grows it grows too. || When
God contracts it needs must shrink, all drawn to him again.   [13
All nature's forms express God's truth, each in its special way. || Detached
from all he dwells apart, the truly learned know.   [14
The Formless One, eternal, pure, the uncreated Lord; || A fool alone would
dare describe a truth no scripture knows.   [15
The fool regards a stone as God, his mind immune to truth. || His
understanding weak and dim, he thinks that Shiv is God!   [16
Each in his own way sees you, Lord, and gives his own account; || Yet none
can know your boundless truth or how the world began.   [17
You are the One, the Lord supreme, here beggar, there a king. || From egg or
womb, from sweat or seed, all life is by your will.   [18
As Brahma clothed in might you sit, as Shiv the yogi's lord. || All nature joins
to sing your praise, our uncreated Lord.   [19
Your help I crave, sustain my Sikhs, the faithless overcome. || May all
oppressors meet the sword, the hosts of evil slain.   [20
Strike down the foes of all who seek your refuge and your aid. || Let those who
crave your mercy, Lord, be freed from every care.   [21
The man who turns to you but once is spared Death's waiting net. || His soul
secure while time shall run, all pain and fear at rest.   [22
Your gracious glance puts care to flight, an instant end to grief. || To such will
come life's greatest prize, from all their foes secure.   [23
And he who turns to you but once is spared the noose of Death. || He who with
faith repeats your Name is freed from every woe.   [24
Beneath your sword and banner, Lord, I seek a refuge sure. || In every place
stretch forth your arm and shield me from my foes.   [25

5.2.5 Savayya

Here at your feet I pledge my homage, no other lord I own. || Hindu and
Muslim gods and scriptures, infinite ways yet none are mine. || All that the
Hindu texts can offer, this I reject and spurn. || Lord of the Sword, I seek your
mercy; all is from you alone.   [1

5.2.6. Dohara

The only door I seek, O Lord, is that which leads to you alone. || Hear me and
keep me free from harm, save me your humble slave.[19]   [1

5.2.7 Anand

By the grace of the Eternal One, the true Guru
When the Guru comes, O mother, joyous bliss is mine; || Boundless blessing,
mystic rapture, rise within my soul. || Surging music, strains of glory, fill my
heart with joy; || Breaking forth in songs of gladness, praise to God within. ||
Comes the Guru, I have found him; joyous bliss is mine.   [1

Cling to God, my soul, for ever; safe within his care. || Hold him fast our sure Protector, he who heals all ills. || He will aid us by his mercy, sure support in need; || God the Master, Lord transcendent, he who governs all. || Hold him ever in remembrance, ever in his care. *[2*

True our Master, true his dwelling, store of all we need; || Life sustained by God's great bounty, source of all we own. || Sing his praises, sing for ever, guard his Name within; || Praise his Name, his Word our answer, mystic Word of grace. || True our Master, true his dwelling; all our needs fulfilled. *[3*

True his Name, that Name most sacred; on his Name I lean. || From his Name flows every mercy, every want fulfilled. || When the Name abides within us peace and joy it brings; || To the Guru, he who leads me, all I have I yield. || Hear me all who trust God's mercy; on his Name I lean. *[4*

Blest are they who hear within the mystic words of truth; || Happy hearts where God abiding speaks those words of joy. || Every evil thought surrendered, fear of death removed; || Marked by grace since time's beginning all who love God's Name. || They who hear the inner music know the peace it brings. *[5*

Blessed souls, I sing of joy, the joy of one fulfilled. || God himself has come to aid me; all my fears are stilled. || All my woes his voice has banished, sorrow, sickness, care; || By the perfect Guru's mercy pious souls find peace. || They who hear the Word are cleansed, the Guru's spirit theirs; || May they by the Guru's grace the mystic music hear.[20] *[6*

5.2.8 Mundavani

In this dish[21] three things are mingled — truth, contentment, deep reflection. || With them mixed the Master's Name, its nectar sweet sustaining all. || He who eats with lingering joy shall know the truth, his soul set free; || He who tastes will make this food his constant fare for evermore. || Darkness reigns yet they who trust the all-fulfilling grace of God, || Find beyond this sunless world God's all-pervading light.[22] *[1*

5.2.9 Shalok

Blind am I to all your deeds, my worth sustained by grace alone. || Base am I devoid of virtue; grant your pitying mercy, Lord. || Grace, O Lord, and tender mercy brought me to the Guru's feet. || Finding there the blessed Name, my spirit blooms in joyous bliss.[23] *[1*

5.3 KIRTAN SOHILA

Kirtan Sohila, *the late evening order, is described as follows in the Adi Granth commentary* Sabadarath Sri Guru Granth Sahib Ji. *[1*

The brief selection which constitutes *Sohila* is recited at night immediately before retiring and for this reason its length is restricted. At such a time the mind is weary and it would be unreasonable to prescribe works which require lengthy recitation or demanding reflection. The purpose is simply to free the mind from distraction, turning it away from life's myriad concerns to the oneness which is God. In order to assist the weary mind frequent use is made of metaphor. In one place we find the companions of a newly-wed bride pouring oil on her threshold before she crosses it for the first time. Elsewhere the contrast between the unity of God and his many manifestations is illustrated by contrasting the sun with the seasons, months, days and nights which derive from it. The metaphor of *arti* (worship which involves the waving of lamps before an idol) serves to express the ineffable radiance pervading the material world; and self-centred pride is depicted as a thorn which works ever deeper, progressively crippling the person who refuses to acknowledge the Guru.[24]   [2

The selection takes its name from the second line of the first hymn: 'Sing to his glory (sohila)'.   [3

When we are gathered to worship the Master sing to his praises and ponder his Name. || Sing to his glory, reflect on his wonders, he who is Lord and Creator of all.   [4

Refrain. Sing to his praises, our Lord who is fearless; || Humbly I bow for the song which brings joy.   [5

He who gives life is our constant Protector, watching and guarding us, safe in his care. || How can we judge all his goodness and mercies, how grasp the worth of his marvellous grace.   [6

God has determined the time for my nuptials; come pour the oil of joy at my door. || Bless me, my friends, that I find that sweet union, dwelling as one with my Master and Lord.   [7

All must receive their last call from the Master; daily he summons those souls who must go. || Hold in remembrance the Lord who will summon you; soon you will hear his command.[25]   [8

Six great traditions each with its master, six paths of doctrine and faith; || There is but One though his forms be unnumbered, Guru of gurus and Master of all.   [9

Refrain. If you would know how to gather true greatness, merit beyond compare, || Seek it where others sing hymns to their Maker, joining their praise to the Lord.   [10

Seconds and minutes, the hours, days and seasons, all own the one single source || Just as they spring from the sun their creator all that exists is of God.[26]   [11

The sky shall be our salver with its lamps the sun and moon, its pearls the host of stars which shine above. || Sweet sandalwood our incense, gently wafted by the breeze, and the plants which clothe the earth shall be our flowers.   [12

Refrain. Thus we offer worship to the Lord who stills our cares, thus we raise our lamps to offer praise. || The mystic Word within us is the drum we beat in praising him, that soundless Word which faith alone can hear.   [13

God's mystery must baffle us, a thousand eyes yet none; a thousand forms yet God can have no form. || A thousand feet of purest form though God must footless be, no fragrance yet a host of sweet perfumes.   *[14*

A splendour shines in every place, its light the light of God, a light which lightens every living soul; || Yet only by the Guru's grace that light can stand revealed, and pious lives alone can please our Lord.   *[15*

The dust your lotus feet let fall is sweetness to our souls; each day I seek the joy my spirit craves. || As cuckoos thirst for drops of rain I long to sip God's grace and find the joy his Name alone can bring.[27]   *[16*

Though my heart be filled with evil yet grace conquers and subdues. || Fate decreed the Guru's coming, he who leads my soul to God.   *[17*

Refrain. Raise your hands and praise the Guru, merit thus we gain. || Humbly prostrate lie before him, great the merit earned.   *[18*

Worldly souls who scorn God's sweetness suffer pain from self-conceit. || Deeper, deeper pricks the thorn as Death prepares to strike.   *[19*

They who love God's sacred Name shall break the bonds of birth and death. || Thus they find the Lord eternal; thus they win supreme renown.   *[20*

Poor am I and humble, Lord; save and keep me, God most high. || Grant the aid your Name can bring me, grant its peace and joy.[28]   *[21*

Hear me friends, the time has come to serve all those who love the Lord. || Thus we lodge that wealth with God which brings eternal peace.   *[22*

Refrain. Day and night our end draws nearer. || Seek the Guru; be prepared!   *[23*

Fear and evil rule the world, and only he who knows is saved. || Only he whom God has wakened tastes the Name and knows the truth.   *[24*

Purchase that for which you came; the Guru's grace will lead you on. || God will dwell within your heart and end the weary round.   *[25*

All-perceiving God who made us, grant this dearest wish I pray; || Grant your slave the joy of serving all who praise the Name.[29]   *[26*

5.4 ARDAS: THE SIKH PRAYER

Ardas or 'Petition' is a formal prayer recited at the conclusion of most Sikh rituals. When the appointed recitation or kirtan draws to its close a portion of Guru Amar Das' Anand Sahib is read (5.2.7). Ardas is recited, a concluding hymn from the Guru Granth Sahib is read, and the service concludes with the distribution of karah prasad to all who are present. Ardas is also recited at the conclusion of early-morning and early-evening devotions.   [1

The prayer consists of three parts. The first section, an invocation extolling the ten Gurus, comprises the introductory lines of Guru Gobind Singh's Chandi di Var supplemented by later references to Guru Gobind

Singh himself and to the Guru Granth Sahib. The second section recalls past trials and triumphs of the Panth. These are grouped in clusters, each punctuated by a fervent 'Vahiguru'.[30] The final section is the actual prayer of petition.   [2

Although these three sections are clearly defined the actual wording of Ardas has never been definitively fixed. Only the first eight lines and the concluding couplet are unalterable. Different versions of the second section are current in printed form, and personal or panthic intercessions are commonly introduced into the third section during the actual reciting of the prayer. An approved text of Ardas has been published in the authoritative Sikh Rahit Maryada (4.5), but the right of individuals to vary the wording is specifically acknowledged. The translation given below follows the Sikh Rahit Maryada text.   [3

Victory to the Lord, the Eternal One
May Almighty God[31] assist us
The Tenth Master's Ode to Almighty God   [4

Having first remembered God, turn your thoughts to Guru Nanak; ||
Angad Guru, Amar Das, each with Ram Das grant us aid. || Arjan and Hargobind, think of them and Hari Rai. || Dwell on Siri Hari Krishan, he whose sight dispels all pain. || Think of Guru Tegh Bahadur; thus shall every treasure come. || May they grant their gracious guidance, help and strength in every place.[32]   [5

May the tenth Master, the revered Guru Gobind Singh, also grant us 'help and strength in every place'. The light which shone from each of the ten Masters shines now from the sacred pages of the Guru Granth Sahib. Turn your thoughts to its message and call on God, saying, *Vahiguru!*   [6

The Cherished Five,[33] the Master's four sons,[34] and the Forty Liberated;[35] all who were resolute, devout and strict in their self-denial; they who were faithful in their remembrance of the divine Name and generous to others; they who were noble both in battle and in the practice of charity; they who magnanimously pardoned the faults of others: reflect on the merits of these faithful servants, O Khalsa, and call on God, saying, *Vahiguru!*   [7

Those loyal members of the Khalsa who gave their heads for their faith; who were hacked limb from limb, scalped, broken on the wheel, or sawn asunder; who sacrificed their lives for the protection of hallowed gurdwaras never forsaking their faith; and who were steadfast in their loyalty to the uncut hair of the true Sikh: reflect on their merits, O Khalsa, and call on God, saying, *Vahiguru!*   [8

[36] Remember the five *takhts*[37] and all other gurdwaras. Reflect on their glory and call on God, saying, *Vahiguru!*   [9

This is the first and foremost petition of the Khalsa, that God (*Vahiguru*) may dwell eternally in the thoughts of the entire Khalsa, and that by this remembrance all may be blessed with joyous peace. May God's favour and protection be extended to the Khalsa wherever its members may be found. Sustain it in battle, uphold it in the exercise of charity, and grant it victory in all its undertakings. May its name be exalted and may its enemies be subdued by the might of the sword. Call on God again, O Khalsa, repeating, *Vahiguru! [10*

Grant to your Sikhs a true knowledge of their faith, the blessing of uncut hair, guidance in conduct, spiritual perception, patient trust, abiding faith, and the supreme gift of the divine Name. May all bathe in the sacred waters of Amritsar. May your blessing eternally repose on all who sing your praises, on the banners which proclaim your presence, on all places which provide shelter and sustenance to your people. Let us praise the way of truth and call on God, saying, *Vahiguru!* *[11*

[38] May Sikhs be humble of heart yet sublime in understanding, their belief and honour committed to your care. O God, eternal Lord and Protector of the Panth, grant to the Khalsa continuing access to Nankana Sahib and to other gurdwaras from which it has been separated.[39] Grant to its members the right to behold these sacred places and to care for them in the service of love. Merciful Lord, pride of the humble, strength of the weak, defence of the helpless, our true Father and our God, we come before you praying that . . .[Refer here in appropriate words to the purpose for which the gathering or congregation has assembled.] Forgive us for any errors committed during the reading of the sacred scripture, and grant to all the fulfilment of their due tasks and responsibilities. *[12*

Bring us into the company of those devout souls whose presence inspires remembrance of your divine Name. *[13*

Nanak prays that the Name may be magnified; || By your grace may all be blest. *[14*

Vahiguru ji ka Khalsa! Vahiguru ji ki fateh!
Sat Sri Akal![40] *[15*

5.5 ASA KI VAR

One of the distinctive forms of the Adi Granth is the var, *a lengthy sequence of verses which was evidently adapted from an earlier model. The original Punjabi* var *was a heroic ballad recounting the exploits of some famous warrior. In the Adi Granth version God takes the place of the folk hero, and the exploits which it proclaims are strictly spiritual.* *[1*

The basis of the standard Adi Granth var *is a sequence of stanzas* (pauri) *composed by one of the Gurus. Each of these stanzas is preceded by supplementary verses* (shalok), *varying both in number and in length. Although the pauri sequence is the work of a single author this is not the case with the intervening shaloks. These may be drawn from the author's own works or from the compositions of one of the other contributors to the Adi*

Granth. Most pauris are preceded by two or three shaloks. The general theme of the var is carried by the pauri sequence, with the shaloks adding further detail and comment. [2

All the vars are written to be sung and each is recorded in the scripture *under its appropriate raga. The Adi Granth contains a total of twenty-two, all but two of them following the standard format. The exceptions are the brief var in* Basant *raga and a var in* Ramkali *raga by the bards Balvand and Satta.* Basant ki Var *consists of three stanzas by Guru Arjan with no attached shaloks.*[41] *The* Ramkali *var, a hymn of praise to the line of Gurus, is a double exception. Like* Basant ki Var *it presents an unbroken sequence of stanzas, and alone amongst the Adi Granth vars its stanza sequence is not by one of the Gurus.*[42] *The vars of Bhai Gurdas also consist exclusively of stanzas (1.4, 3.3.1).* [3

The best known of the vars is undoubtedly the one which appears in the *Adi Granth under* Asa *raga.*[43] *The twenty-four stanzas which provide the basic sequence for* Asa ki Var *are by Guru Nanak, and likewise forty-four of its fifty-nine shaloks. The remaining fifteen shaloks are by Guru Angad.* Asa ki Var *is regularly sung in gurdwaras early in the morning, daily in the case of large gurdwaras and weekly or as occasion demands in smaller centres.*[44] [4

Guru Nanak. I praise and adore my Guru a hundred times a day, || He who lifts men to the ranks of the gods, swiftly, without delay. (1.1)[45] [5

Guru Angad. If the heavens should hold a hundred moons, if a thousand suns should shine, || Without the Guru their light would be dim in a darkness dismal and cold. (1.2) [6

Guru Nanak. He who fails to remember the Guru || Is like sterile seed which is cast aside. || Left in the field for all to gather, || It may flower and fruit yet its end is dust. (1.3) [7

God the self-created, Maker of the Name, || Pervades his own creation, viewing it with joy. || God sustains his universe, supported by his grace. || Omniscient Lord, he gives us life and takes it back again, || Pervading all he looks with joy on all his hand has made. (1) [8

Guru Angad. The world is the place where the True One lives, this world which is his abode || Some by his order are brought to his presence; others are cast away. || Some he delivers if such be his will; others remain ensnared. || None can explain his mysterious ways, why some should be brought to the light. || He who is led by the Guru shall know when knowledge awakens within. (2.3) [9

Guru Nanak. Creating life and revealing the Name, the Master published his sacred law, || That law upholding truth alone, which sets all sinnners apart; || The false condemned, their faces shamed, despatched to the anguish of hell. || Victory to those who follow the Name, defeat to all who deceive! || In revealing the Name God published his law. (2) [10

The end must come for the frivolous soul as he leaves his life in ashes. || He who was once acclaimed by all is chained and marched away. || His record is read, the balance cast; || His fate is sealed and his cries unheard; || For the blind are condemned, their lives a waste. (3)   [11

When God bestows his gracious glance we enter the Guru's presence, || And souls which have wandered through endless births hear at last his Word of deliverance. || Let this message be heard by all who will hear, that the Giver supreme is the Guru. || Truth is the gift conferred by the Guru on all who abandon self-will. || To them shall the truth be revealed. (4)   [12

None can know God or come to him if he lacks the Guru's aid, || For God abides in the Guru's being, speaking a common voice. || Meeting the Guru brings total deliverance to those who abandon desire. || The greatest good one can ever achieve is to turn one's thoughts to his truth, || For thus one shall find the Giver of life. (6)   [13

In the first of the shaloks attached to the seventh pauri Guru Nanak expounds the distinctive meaning which he attaches to the words hau *and* haumai. *His distinctive usage is one which infuses profound ethical meaning into two simple pronouns. Both* hau *and* mai(n) *are first person singular pronouns meaning 'I' and the awkward expression 'I-ness' might well be regarded as a literal translation. When used in appropriate contexts both words designate that most basic of all human failings, man's congenital willingness to trust his own instincts and judgements rather than the divine guidance of the Guru. Because no satisfactory English equivalent is available the translation which follows is a free one. In the original Punjabi version the shalok has eighteen lines, all but four of them beginning with either* hau *or* haumai.[46]   [14

Without the Guru man wanders astray, foolishly trusting his own conceit, || Imbued with pride he enters the world and retaining his pride he departs. ||All that he gives and all that he takes is controlled by his selfish desire; || All that he gains and all he discards he ascribes to his own skill and power. || Sometimes truthful, sometimes false, virtuous now, then sinful; || Destined for hell or hoping for heaven he remains in the grip of self-centred pride.   [15

Thus he laughs and thus he cries, soils himself and washes clean; || Renounces gifts conferred by birth, sometimes stupid, sometimes wise. || Failing to find the path to deliverance, seduced by the world, assailed by doubt, || Trusting himself he transmigrates, lacking the knowledge which sets men free. || Devoid of wisdom he argues in vain, his future inscribed by God's command. || Such is the fate of self-centred man, blind to the purpose of God. (7.1)   [16

Guru Angad. Self-centred pride is the mark we bear, determining all that we do || Self-centred pride keeps us firmly bound, tied to the round of rebirth || How is it born and how destroyed, how can we loosen its grip? || It works in accord with God's divine will, created by deeds which are past. || Self-centred pride is a loathsome disease yet one which is subject to cure. || Grace is the balm, if God so will, wrought by the Guru's Word. || Let Nanak's cry be heard by all for thus is our malady cured. (7.2)   [17

Guru Nanak. You, O Lord, are the True One; truth is the message you bring;

|| He whom you choose receives the truth and lives as truth decrees. || Meeting the Guru we find the truth, lodged within our hearts. || Fools can never discover the truth, self-willed they squander their lives. || Why did they ever come into this world? (8)   [18

Peace descends when one meets the Guru; || The Name of God lives in our hearts. || We meet the Guru if God shows grace, || Set free by the Word, all pride consumed. (9.2)   [19

Falsehood prevails in place of truth; in the Age of Darkness men become ghouls. || All honour to those who planted the seed, but how can split lentils sprout?[47] || The seed must be whole and the season kind; || Raw cloth must be treated if dye is to cling. || Let my body be boiled in the fear of God and imbued with humble submission. || Dye it deep in devotion to God, for thus is falsehood purged. (11.1)   [20

Pain is the cure if ease should infect me, driving you far from my thoughts. || You are the Master, I am as nothing, my deeds all worthless and wasted. (12.1)   [21

Refrain. Your presence pervading all · creation, vast beyond power of comprehending, || Humbly I bow to you.[48]   [22

Your light in all, in all diffused, a radiance shed with artless art; || You are the truth, your praise sublime, the path to sure deliverance. || All that we need we receive from your hand, from the hand of the Lord our Creator. (12.2)   [23

Departing this life we leave behind us those outward forms which feed our pride. || Our deeds alone can earn reward, the evil and the good. || Narrow the path a man must follow, however vast his earthly powers; || Gruesome the sight the wretch presents as naked he creeps to hell, || There to repent his sins. (14)[24

He who receives the grace of God is guided in all his deeds; || He who walks in the ways of God faithfully serves his Lord. || He who walks in the ways of God may enter his Master's home. || If his Lord is pleased he receives his reward, all that his heart desires, || With honour robed in his Master's court.(15)   [25

God remembers every creature, watching over all; || Some he honours with fame and greatness, guiding the deeds of all. || Greatest of all in this vast creation, he assigns to each his appointed task. || If ever he turns his gaze in anger kings are reduced to straw, || To wretches who vainly beg for alms. (16)   [26

They who believe in pollution should know that pollution is everywhere. || Insects live in the dung which is burnt; they also live in wood. || Life exists in wheat and corn, a separate life in every grain. || Water itself is filled with life, for without it nothing can live. || How then can one avoid pollution whenever one turns to preparing food? || Such foolish notions are futile, Nanak; only true knowledge can cleanse. (18.1)   [27

Greed is the mind's pollution, falsehood pollutes the tongue; || Eyes are polluted whenever they stray to another's wife or his worldly wealth. || Ears are polluted by slanderous tales, by malice and wilful spite. || He who was pure is enslaved by such sins and delivered in chains to hell. (18.2)   [28

Foolish is he who believes in pollution; that which pollutes is our carnal desire, || Destined to lead in the order of God to the endless cycle of death and rebirth. || Pure is our food and pure our drink, both of them given by God. || Pure the devout who perceive this reality; none may declare them unclean. (18.3) *[29*

Praise and extol the one true Guru, fount of all virtue and good. || He who by grace is brought to the Guru is witness to this truth. || If it pleases God to show us grace the truth is enshrined in our hearts and minds. || Our fate is inscribed by the order of God, all evil expelled from within. || If the Master is pleased we are granted a share of the bounteous wealth he bestows. (18)   *[30*

From women born, shaped in the womb, to women betrothed and wed, || We are bound to women by ties of affection; on women man's future depends. || If a woman dies we seek another, source of society's order and strength. || Why then should one speak evil of women, they who give birth to kings? || Women also are born from women, as are all who have life and breath. || God alone is excepted, Nanak, the one true Master and Lord. || Blessed are they, both men and women, who endlessly praise their Lord. || Blessed are they in the court of God; there shall their faces shine. (19.2)   *[31*

Creation, O Lord, is the work of your hands, sustained by your art alone, || Everything under your watching and caring, men who are evil and men who are good. || All who are born must pass away, each as his turn shall come. || Each has received his life as your gift; why should he ever forget? || Each must acknowledge a duty to follow the way which his Master desires. (20)   *[32*

Let us remember our Lord and our Master, he whose service is perfect joy. || If all our deeds bring their certain reward why would we ever do harm? || Spurn all those deeds which are evil and hurtful, look to the future and what it will bring. || Follow the course which the Master approves, the way which our Master desires. || Follow the course which the Master approves; follow the course which wins. (21)   *[33*

Guru Angad. If one should serve his Master in a spirit of arrogant pride, Whatever the words he may utter the Master will never approve. || So purge your pride and labour with zeal for thus is honour won. || He who is loyal in all his deeds is he who shall win renown. (22.1)   *[34*

Guru Nanak. God is infinite, boundless, Nanak; none can discern his end. || He it is who fashions creation; he it is who destroys. || One may be shackled, chained by the neck; another rides proud-stepping mares. || All that occurs is the purpose of God; to whom can I cry for aid? || He who has fashioned the whole of creation holds all that exists in his care. (23)   *[35*

God it is who shapes the vessels, God who gives them final form. || Some are filled with cooling milk, others endure the fire. || Some find rest on pleasant beds, others are watched and confined. || They who receive God's gracious glance find all their needs fulfilled. (24.1)   *[36*

Guru Angad. All that exists is God's creation, all by God sustained. || All that has life is his creation, set on earth and carried away. || To God alone can we cry, O Nanak, Maker and Lord of all. (24.2)   *[37*

Guru Nanak. Who can recount his wondrous glory, his greatness vast beyond telling. || Creator Lord, supreme yet gracious, giving to each his daily bread. || All must perform their appointed tasks, assigned by God when time began. || Serve him, Nanak, serve him alone; work to fulfil his plan. (24)   *[38*

5.6 SUKHMANI

The theme of Guru Arjan's Sukhmani *is the grandeur of the divine Name. In lyrical poetry of sustained quality it extols the beauty of the Name, repeatedly declaring its crucial importance in man's quest for liberation. The title of the work incorporates a pun in that* mani *can mean either 'pearl' or 'mind'. It can thus be translated either as 'The Pearl of Peace' or as 'Peace of Mind'.*   *[1*

The complete poem, which runs to almost 2,000 lines, is divided into twenty-four parts.[49] *Each part comprises an introductory couplet (shalok) and a sequence of eight stanzas (an* astapadi *or octave). The only variation to this pattern occurs in the first section which is preceded by a four-line shalok in place of the usual couplet, and which includes an additional couplet between the first and second stanzas. This inserted couplet is regarded as an epitome of the entire poem.*   *[2*

The Name of God is sweet ambrosia, source of all inner peace and joy. || The Name of God brings blissful peace to the hearts of the truly devout.   *[3*

According to tradition the poem was composed by Guru Arjan beside the sacred pool of Ramsar in Amritsar. The date of its composition is not known, but it must have been before 1604 as the text appears in the Adi Granth. A date shortly before 1604 seems likely, for Sukhmani *is obviously a work of great maturity. It is also a work which inevitably suffers serious injury in translation. No rendering in English can hope to capture the skill of Guru Arjan's epigrammatic style or the beauty of his language.*   *[4*

Sukhmani commands a notable popularity. Although it is not a part of the regular Nit-nem many Sikhs include it in their early morning devotions. Many Punjabi Hindus also recite it regularly. Following an invocation to the eternal Guru the poem states its theme in the opening stanza.   *[5*

Turn to the Lord in contemplation; in his remembrance find peace. || Thus is our inner turmoil stilled, all anguish driven away. || Behold the glory of the earth's Sustainer, numberless those who repeat his Name. || The hallowed pages of sacred scripture are but a fragment of all it contains. || He who receives a glimpse of its meaning will earn a glory which none may describe. || With those who seek that glimpse, O God, your servant Nanak finds release. (1.1)[50]   *[6*

The first octave proceeds to develop the theme of nam simaran, listing the many blessings which accrue to those who devote themselves to regular remembrance of the divine Name. The second stanza is typical of the entire octave.   *[7*

Through remembrance of the Lord one is freed from rebirth. || Through remembrance of the Lord death's messenger flees. || Through remembrance of the Lord death itself succumbs. || Through remembrance of the Lord all enemies are scattered. || Through remembrance of the Lord all barriers fall. || Through remembrance of the Lord one remains alert. || Through remembrance of the Lord our fears are dispelled. || Through remembrance of the Lord all pain is relieved. || Through remembrance of the Lord one is numbered with the devout. || Steeped in remembrance of God's divine Name we gather all the treasures which his grace supplies. (2.1)   [8

The introductory shalok announces the theme of the second octave.   [9

Solace of all in need or anguish, Help of the helpless, dwelling within. || Remain with me for ever, O Lord, for I cast myself on your grace.   [10

The second octave raises the problem of suffering and announces its remedy. The sure and certain panacea is the divine Name.   [11

When the time comes to leave this life, bereft of parents, sons and friends, || The Name of God goes with us, our comfort and support. || When Death's dread messengers hover near, seeking to capture and destroy, || The Name alone stays by our side, our only sure protection. || When grievous problems weigh us down the Name of God brings instant help. || Futile our acts of expiation; only the Name can cancel sin. || Repeat the Name as the Guru directs, for this is the means to abundant joy. (1.2)   [12

Octave 3 contrasts the liberating power of the divine Name with the inadequacy of the ancient scriptures and the futility of conventional religious practices.   [13

So many scriptures, I have searched them all. || None can compare to the priceless Name of God.   [14

Alms and oblations, sacrifice and renunciation, ritual bathing and austerities – all are useless. Only the Name can bring a person to deliverance. The octave concludes: [15

Better by far then any other way[51] is the act of repeating the perfect Name of God. || Better by far than any other rite is the cleansing of one's heart in the company of the devout. || Better by far than any other skill is endlessly to utter the wondrous Name of God. || Better by far than any sacred text is hearing and repeating the praises of the Lord. || Better by far than any other place is the heart wherein abides that most precious Name of God. (8.3)   [16

In octaves 4–6 Guru Arjan contrasts God's greatness with man's infirmity. Apart from God and the Guru's guidance man is a creature of vicious desires. To outward appearances he may appear to be a person of great piety. Inwardly, however, he nurtures falsehood, lust, greed, deceit, and a host of other sins. Seduced by the attractions of the ephemeral world he ignores the divine Name, spurning thereby the peace and joy which God proffers to all. Let him turn again to God for only thus can he achieve the bliss of deliverance.   [17

This insistent claim raises the question of how one is to find God. The shalok which introduces octave 7 acknowledges the problem and enunciates an essential part of the answer. [18

God is infinite, beyond all comprehending, || Yet he who repeats the Name will find himself set free. || Hear me, my friend, for I long to hear || The tale which is told in the company of the saved. [19

All who seek deliverance must seek it in the company of others dedicated to the same objective. The concept is fundamental to the teaching of the Gurus and nowhere does it receive a more insistent emphasis than in the seventh octave of Sukhmani. The terms normally used for this feature of the Gurus' teaching are sangat *(assembly),* satsang *(the assembly of those who have found the truth), and* sadhsang *(the assembly of those who have brought their minds and instincts under control).*[52] *All three, together with other variant forms, express the same basic feature of the Gurus' message. Guru Arjan spells it out in detail.* [20

Faces shine in the company of the faithful; || There, in their midst, sin's filth is washed away. || Pride is conquered in the company of the faithful; || There, in their midst, God's wisdom stands revealed. || God dwells near in the company of the faithful; || In the calmness of their presence all doubt is laid to rest. || There one obtains that precious jewel, the Name, || And striving by their aid one finds that blissful peace with God. || Who can hope to utter the wonder of their glory, || The glory of the pure and true in union with the Lord. (1.7) [21

Subsequent stanzas expand this description of the Guru's fellowship, stressing the qualities bestowed on all who join it. Octave 8 and 9 shift the focus, directing attention instead to a definition of the braham-giani. *The* braham-giani *is he who possesses an understanding of God's wisdom, the person who has found enlightenment in the company of the devout. Such a person acquires thereby an impressive range of virtues, some involving his relationship with men and others his relationship with God. The former include such qualities as purity, humility, patience, kindness, and detachment. The latter pre-eminently requires remembrance of the divine Name. He who devotes himself to the discharge of these obligations attains deliverance for himself and the power to confer it on others by means of word and example. Men teach and observe various beliefs concerning the means of deliverance. All should realise that there is but one way. Evil is universally proscribed and the Name is accessible to all.* [22

Octaves 10 and 11 bring us back to the infinite greatness of God and the absolute nature of his power. The infinity of the creation bears witness to its Maker and over its boundless span countless creatures join to honour him in their various ways. He who brought this creation into being reigns supreme, determining by his unfettered will all that takes place. Man, in contrast, powerless except for the strength conferred by grace. His birth and status, his understanding and actions, his hope of deliverance – all are dependent on the absolute will of God. [23

Man has no power to work his will, for power resides in God alone. || Helpless he follows as God directs; what pleases God must come to pass. || At times exalted, at times abased; now plunged in sorrow then raised to joy.|| Sometimes led to slander and blame; lifted to heaven and then cast down. || Sometimes blessed with wisdom divine, man comes to God in God's own time. (5.11)   *[24*

Foolish men fail to recognise God's authority and the next two octaves describe the fate which awaits them. The perverse will be punished, the proud brought low. They who put their trust in riches, worldly power, or outward piety will be disappointed. He who denigrates the truly pious will suffer all manner of retribution and by his churlish behaviour will bind himself more firmly to the round of transmigration. Octave 14 follows this catalogue of sinful deeds with an appeal to all who so foolishly commit them. All men should abandon wordly concerns and turn to God. Trust in him; remember the Name; walk in his way. [25*

By the Guru's grace he perceives his nature, and in that knowledge sheds all desire. || He praises God in the company of the faithful and sets himself free from the body's ills. || Singing God's praises by day and by night he keeps himself pure though he lives with his family.[53]|| He who puts trust in God alone shall tear the net which Death has laid;|| And he who craves the presence of God shall find all suffering stilled. (4.14)   *[26*

Octaves 15–17 continue the theme of God's greatness and of the rewards to be secured by those who put their trust in him. [27*

Tell of his glory day and night, for the power to praise is the gift of God.|| They who love him with ardent devotion dwell rapt in the mystic presence divine.|| Putting behind them all that is past they strive in the present to honour his will. || Who can hope to recount his glory? The least of his wonders must shame our art! || Fulfilled are they who day and night eternally dwell in the presence of the Lord. (7.17)   *[28*

The presence of God is signified by the divine Name and man's duty is devout contemplation of the Name. There remains, however, the problem of how man can recognise the Name and follow the contemplative discipline which will enable him to appropriate its benefits. The answer is the Guru, God's mediator here on earth. [29*

The Guru leads and instructs his disciple, freely bestowing his grace; || Cleansing his mind of the refuse of falsehood, teaching him how to repeat the Name.|| By the Guru's grace his bonds are severed; set free he renounces all that defiles.|| The wealth of the Name is the gift of the Guru, and he who receives it is wondrously blessed. || Saved by the Guru both here and hereafter, he dwells with his Guide and Protector for ever. (1.18)   *[30*

The remaining octaves return again to the Name, the source of true bliss and the essential means of deliverance. Octave 24 summarises the message of Sukhmani. [31*

Give heed to the words of the perfect Guru; see God ever-present and near at hand.|| Repeat God's Name with every breath, for thus shall your cares depart.|| Turn from the world of transient desire, seek the blessing the faithful bestow.||

Abandon pride, put your trust in God, find the peace which their company brings.|| Gather the treasures which God bestows and honour the perfect Guru. (1.24) *[32*

He who nurtures the Name within will find the Lord ever present there. || Gone for ever the pain of rebirth, his precious soul in an instant freed.|| Noble his actions, gracious his speech; his spirit merged in the blessed Name. || All suffering ended, all doubts, all fears; renowned for his faith and his virtuous deeds. || Raised to honour, wondrous his fame! Priceless the pearl, God's glorious Name! (8.24) *[33*

5.7 SCRIPTURAL PASSAGES FOR SPECIAL OCCASIONS

Apart from the three Nit-nem selections (5.1–3) there are very few hymns or other portions of scripture formally appointed for particular occasions.[54] *This does not mean, however, that the practice of reciting appropriate scripture is discouraged. The sacred scripture is central to the life of the Sikh and it is entirely natural that certain hymns should acquire widespread acceptance as contributions to particular occasions. Suggested hymns or extracts for various occasions are to be found in the widely used style of breviary known as a* gutka *or* Sundar Gutka. *Each* gutka *contains the complete Nit-nem text together with a selection of scriptural passages for particular occasions.* *[1*

5.7.1 Petitions for blessing on a forthcoming undertaking

Kahn Singh offers a justification for petitionary prayer and describes the manner in which it should be performed.

The Guru has decreed that petitionary prayer should be offered for the fulfilment of worthy ambitions; for the forgiveness of transgressions (both of omission and of commission); for deliverance from acts of pride and arrogance; and for dedication of oneself to the will of God . . . The sacred scripture clearly states that prayers of petition are to be offered only to God, and that one should stand with palms joined while reciting a prayer . . . He who violates the fundamental principle by offering prayers of petition to gods, goddesses, temples, or any other feature of God's creation, justifying his error by appealing to some spurious authority, is ignorant of the precepts of Sikhism . . . There is no particular direction which one should face while offering prayer, and one may do so in a sitting or lying position if suffering from any disability . . . One should not pray with head uncovered. Shoes should be removed, except when actually|| travelling or if offering prayer while on horseback.[55] *[1*

The Sundar Gutka *supplies the following suggestions for such occasions.*

Lean on the only trusty support, spurn any other aid.|| Hold the true Name in unceasing remembrance and all your endeavours will thrive.[56] *[2*

If you have need of a task to be done speak to the merciful Lord. || All that you ask shall be surely accomplished, performed by the grace of the Guru. || Treasure is found where the faithful assemble; seek the ambrosial Name. || Quieten my fears, keep me safe gracious Lord, ever safe in your caring protection. || Lord, you are infinite, far beyond wisdom, yet they who sing praises can know.[57]   [3

Lord most high, of boundless greatness, who can hope to sing your praise? || Singing hymns and hearing praises, thus can we redeem our sins. || All may seek the grace you offer, beast and spirit, fools set free. || Humbly Nanak begs for shelter, gladly yielding all to you.[58]   [4

5.7.2 The conception of a child

God has laid his protecting hand on my head, on my brow, on my body. || My spirit too is in his keeping, safe at his blessed feet. || Merciful Guru, keep and protect me, banish all fear and distress. || Friend of the faithful, Lord of the humble, ever my refuge and aid.[59]   [1

From grief and disease, from the perils of water, he saves and protects us in numberless ways. || Foes may assail us with pitiless fury, yet all of their blows are astray. || His outstretched hand is our sure protection, safe from the hordes of sin. || His mercy extends to the child yet unborn; what tribute of praise can we bring?[60]   [2

Safe from the heat of the searing wind, in God's protecting care, || Within the line which the Master has drawn,[61] safe from all grief and pain.   [3
Refrain. All is the work of the perfect Guru, he who has come to my aid. || The wondrous Name cures all my ills, blending my spirit in God's.   [4
Divine Protector, by your aid all pain is wiped away. || All who are granted the grace of the Master receive his kindly care.[62]   [5

5.7.3 The birth of a child (4.5[15])

God has broken every barrier, pain and sorrow swept away. || Blissful joy to all who know him, all to whom he gives his grace.   [1
Refrain. Joy abounds in all creation, praise him you who love your Lord, || God Almighty, perfect Master, all-pervading, everywhere.   [2
God's eternal word has reached us, chasing far our grief and care. || God is gracious, filled with mercy, Nanak thus proclaims this truth.[63]   [3

God has sent this wondrous gift; conceived by grace may his years be long. || Boundless the joy of his mother's heart when the child appeared in her womb. [4
Refrain. Born our son, born to adore, faithful disciple of God. || His fate inscribed since time began, now given for all to see.   [5
Ten months carried then given by God; all sorrows flee as joy descends. || His

mother's friends sang songs of praise, songs which delight the Master's heart. /6
The mighty vine has seeded again, for God ensures that his truth remains. ||
The Guru has granted my heart's desire; my spirit stilled, at one with God.   [7
A father earns his child's respect, and thus I speak as the Guru bids. || No
mystery dims these words of mine; this child is the gift of the Guru's grace.[64]   [8

5.7.4 The amrit ceremony (Khalsa initiation) (4.5[34])

Grant me protection, merciful Lord, prostrate here at your door; || Guard me
and keep me, Friend of the humble, weary from wandering far. || You love the
devout and recover the sinful; to you alone I address this prayer: || Take me and
hold me, merciful Lord, carry me safely to joy.[65]   [1

Friend of the humble, hear my prayer, my Lord, my God, my King. || The
refuge of your Name I crave, repeating it evermore. || Friend of the faithful,
shield me from shame, for such is the love you bear. || Nanak has claimed your
protection, Lord, the saving power of your Name.[66]   [2

All I had heard of the Guru's grace I have seen and know to be true, || How he
brings lost souls to the presence divine, our friend in the court of God. || He gives
us the message of God's true Name, purging our hearts of pride. || Our fate
which was written when time began decrees that we come to God.[67]   [3

Refrain. Who can compare to our wonderful Lord, what other can equal his
grace? || Friend of the poor, my Master divine, Giver of honour and fame!   [4
Those whose touch is held to defile[68] are under your gracious care. || Fearless
our Master, merciful Lord, exalting the lowly and weak.   [5
Namdev and Kabir, Trilochan and Sadhana, saved by your mercy, together
with Sain.[69] || Ravidas has declared: let the faithful pay heed that the Lord does
whatever he wills.[70]   [6

5.7.5 Betrothal

With the Guru's aid I searched for God, and searching found him within. ||
Precious this body, this earthly abode, built as the fortress of God. || Sharp as a
diamond, finely honed, God is the jewel which pierces us through. || Blest be my
destiny, God I have found; blest be the rapture he brings.[71]   [1

Happy the girl, now awakened to love, when the match-maker comes with his
news.[72] || Thus she shall enter the sacred assembly, there to sing praises to God. ||
Joyfully singing the words of the Guru she finds in their midst perfect peace. ||
Purged from her spirit all false worldly longing, all evil and doubt put to flight. ||
Deep the contentment, pride's anguish supplanted, all sickness for ever
dispelled. || By the grace of the Guru she comes to know God, the Master of
infinite worth.[73]   [2

5.7.6 Marriage (4.5[25–7])
5.7.6.1 Introduction
Here I begin as the Guru directs me, turning my steps where he leads. || The Guru has taught me the words I must utter; I live by repeating the Name.   *[1*

Refrain. Humbly I fall at the feet of the Master, my doubts and my fears all destroyed. || Blest by God's grace, by his infinite goodness; blest by his message of truth.   *[2*

Grasping my hand he has graciously led me, showing the way he approves. || The gift which he gives us, the grace he confers, is the means of true greatness, true fame.   *[3*

Let us for ever sing praise to the Master, ever repeating his Name. || The vow which I made to obey his commandment the Lord by his grace has sustained. *[4*

Sing to the Name, sing its wonder and glory, joy which the Guru bestows. || We are his hawkers, we trade in his merchandise, serving our infinite Lord.[74] *[5*

5.7.6.2 The approach of the bridegroom
The Master has come to bring joy to my home and I have been led to his presence. || God in his love has brought peace beyond telling, my mind and my body subdued. || The prize which I treasure is now in my keeping, that prize which my heart so desired. || He comes every day and my joy overflows, his temple he makes in my heart. || The Master has come to bring joy to my home as the mystical music resounds.[75]   *[1*

Come divine Friend, for I long to behold you, deep the desire as I gaze from my home. || Lord, hear the prayer which proceeds from my longing, source of my hope and my trust. || Let me but see you for thus we find freedom, ending the wearisome round of rebirth. || By your light you are known, by the light all-pervading; your love brings us close to your side, || I offer my life to my Lord in submission; he comes when one lives by the truth.[76]   *[2*

The Lord has come, he dwells within; I sing to his praise with joyful heart; || Eternal joy with the peace it brings as I hymn God's praise, my hunger stilled. || He who adores the Name of God is praised and revered by all around. || God draws us near or drives us far; the only Lord, he has entered my heart.[77]   *[3*

5.7.6.3 Advice to the groom and his bride (4.5[27])
When husband and wife sit side by side why should we treat them as two? || Outwardly separate, their bodies distinct, yet inwardly joined as one.[78]   *[1*

Comply with whatever your Lord may desire, never resisting, spurning deceit. . . . || Obey his commands in total surrender; this is the fragrance to bring. . . . || Abandon self-will and your Lord will draw near; all else is futile cunning.[79]   *[2*

Be humble in manner and practise restraint, let sweetness of speech be your prayer. || If these are the garments adorning a bride the husband she seeks will be found.[80]   [3

Sweet is her speech, approved by her Lord; grant that her joy may endure evermore.[81]   [4

Filled with the spirit of truth and contentment, her family's pride and joy.|| She who is constant in goodness and virtue is cherished and loved by her Lord.[82]   [5

Behind closed doors and a forest of curtains he lies with another's wife. || When the angels of Death shall demand your account how then can the truth be concealed?[83]   [6

This is the message the Guru has brought; let this be your vow while your body has breath. || Bestow your affection on none save your wife; spurning temptation, avoid other beds,|| Watchful, untainted, even in dreams.[84]   [7

5.7.6.4 Before commencing the *lavan*[85]

God aids his faithful in all their endeavours, crowning their deeds with success. || Blessed this land and the lake which adorns it; blessed the water it holds.[86]|| The lake fills with water, our labours are over, sustained by the mercy of God. || Joyous the cries as we sing to our triumph; all struggle and suffering done.|| Wonderful Master, of glory eternal, hymned by the scriptures of old.[87]|| Lord of all mercies, eternally constant, with gladness we ponder your Name.[88]   [1

By the Guru's grace I am wed to God in a marriage which God has himself arranged.|| By the Guru's grace he has come to claim me, filled with love for his waiting bride. || In the midst of the faithful I sing God's praises, decked and adorned by my Master divine. || Wondrous the escort which comes with the bridegroom, gods with their minstrels and beings unknown. || Free from the cycle of death and rebirth is the Lord who has made me his bride.[89]   [2

5.7.6.5 The bride grasps the groom's hem (4.5[27])

Praise is empty, slander void; each I despise and spurn. || Vain the delights which the world can give; I cling to your hem alone.[90]   [1

This precious robe I receive from you to cover my shame and preserve my respect.|| Mighty Lord, all-wise, all-seeing, how can we know your worth?[91] [2

5.7.6.6 The lavan (4.5[27])

The first time round is the time for toil, for work in the world as the Lord may decree;|| The Word of the Guru the text which we follow,[92] confirming our faith and destroying our sin. || Be firm in believing and ponder God's Name, as prescribed by the scriptures of old.[93]|| Give to the Guru devout adoration, renouncing all evil and wrong.|| Blessed is she who adores the Lord's Name, for its praises bring radiant bliss. || Nanak declares that the first of our rounds marks the start of our marriage with God. [1

The second time round is the time for our meeting, the meeting which comes with our only True Lord. || Fear is dispelled and our spirits are cleansed from the filth of our self-centred pride. || The fear we retain is our fear of the Lord as we sing to his praise and perceive him in all; || The Master is present in all his creation, his being pervading whatever we see. || Within and without he is ever our comrade; come join with his faithful and sing to his praise. || The mystical music resounds in our hearts as we follow the second round. [2

The third time round is the time for detachment, for freeing our minds from all wordly desire. || Blessed is she who unites with the faithful, for thus she is brought to her Lord. || She who finds God will sing hymns to his glory, the words which she utters inspired by her Lord. || Blessed is she who is found with the faithful, who utters the words of ineffable truth. || God's Name shall resound in the depths of her spirit, the Name we repeat if our fate so decrees. || The third round progresses, God rises within us, and cleanses our minds from all pride and desire. [3

Our spirits find peace as the fourth round commences, for God comes to dwell in our hearts and our minds. || By the grace of the Guru we know he is present, his sweetness pervading our bodies and souls. || This sweetness flows forth from the love which God nurtures for all who are rapt in his infinite bliss. || Desires they have treasured find precious reward at the sound of his glorious Name. || The bride who is chosen to marry her Lord knows that wonderful Name as it surges within. || Nanak declares that the fourth of our rounds brings our ultimate union with God.[94] [4

That joy, my friend, so long desired is a joy I now possess; || For the Lord whom I sought to be my own has come and my heart is blest. || Wondrous the joy my Husband brings, ever-renewed his grace; || Blessed am I that the Guru has shown me God's presence amidst the devout. || In the midst of the faithful my hopes are fulfilled, my spirit at one with my Lord. || My prayers are all answered, joy I have found; joy by the Guru's grace.[95] [5

I am joyously wed, O Father, having found my Lord by the Guru's grace. || Gone is the darkness of ignorant doubt, for the Guru has shown me his light. || The darkness flees as his light shines forth, the light which reveals my Lord. || The sickness of selfish conceit is cured, all pride consumed by his grace. || I have found my Lord, my immortal King, he who is free from the bondage of death. || I am joyously wed, O Father, having found my Lord by the Guru's grace.[96] [6

All my hopes are fulfilled, O Lord, all my intentions achieved. || Worthless am I and helpless Master; virtue is yours alone. || All merit is yours alone, O Lord, what words can render you praise? || Remembering neither my virtue nor failings you offer immediate grace. || The treasure is mine, my heart leaps with joy, the mystical music resounds. || I have found my way to my Husband's home;

my sorrows have vanished and gone.[97]   [7

5.7.7 Death

At the time of his death the Guru said, || 'When I am gone sing only those hymns which will lead the devout to blissful deliverance.'[98]   [1

Each day that dawns must reach its end; || All must depart, for none may stay. || Our friends take leave, we too must go. || Death is our fate, our journey far.   [2
Refrain. Heedless one, awake! awake! || This life is transient, doomed to end   [3
God gives us life and with it food, || His love dispensed to every soul. || Let God be praised, let pride be purged; || And bless his Name within your heart.   [4
Life's end is near, its tasks undone, || And darkness falls as night draws on. || Let fools be warned by Ravidas: || This mortal life must end in death.[99]   [5

Refrain. This is a lesson to learn, my friend, this we must surely know. || That each pays heed to his own concerns, sparing no thought for another.   [6
When you are prosperous all will come, eager to be at your side. || When troubles assail you all depart, not one prepared to stay.   [7
She whom you wed, your loving companion, remains for as long as your life shall run; || But when at the end your spirit takes flight she will call you a ghost and flee.   [8
This is the way of the world, my friend, our way with those whom we love. || None shall remain when your life is done, none save the Lord your God.[100]   [9

Refrain. Death must sunder all family ties, with parents and brothers, with wife and with sons. || All must be severed at death.   [10
As soon as your spirit has taken its leave your death is proclaimed by all; || Your body is banished, despatched from the house, no thought for respect or delay.   [11
This world is unreal, a deceitful mirage; reflect on this truth in your heart. || Sing praises to God for his gift of salvation; for ever exalt his Name.[101]   [12

Refrain. Awake, my soul, from heedless sleep. || No man can retain the body God gave.   [13
They whom you love while here on earth, your parents, your sons, your kin, || Will consign your remains to the funeral fire when your spirit takes leave and goes.   [14
The world pays heed to a man while alive, observing his presence while life remains. || Yet all is a dream, save only God; sing praise to his glorious Name.[102]   [15

Refrain. Worldly affections are transient, false. || All seek your love for their own selfish ends.   [16

All will possess you vowing their love, claiming to be your friend.|| At the end they desert you, bereft and alone, for such is the way of the world.   *[17*

Slow-witted mind, will you never perceive, though I teach you by day and by night,|| That only the faithful who sing the Lord's song can be saved from life's turbulent sea.[103]   *[18*

Refrain. They who adore him will witness God's greatness, seeing the marvels their Lord has performed. || No one has fathomed that wonder of wonders, why death comes to one while another is spared.   *[19*

Caught in the grip of his lust and impatience, seduced by desire he forgets his true Lord. || This body, he thinks, will remain his for ever; this flesh which dissolves like a transient dream.   *[20*

All that we see must pass on and be gone from us, slipping away like the shadow of clouds. || Such is the world, a mere vision that perishes, leaving the Lord our sole refuge and friend.[104]   *[21*

6 DIVERSITY WITHIN THE PANTH

6.1 THE NIRANKARI SIKHS

Adherents of the Nirankari movement have always maintained that the purpose of their founder Baba Dayal was to recall Sikhs to their original loyalty. Military triumph under Maharaja Ranjit Singh had deflected many from Guru Nanak's stress on the divine Name and Baba Dayal's preaching was directed to the recovering of that message (1.8[1]). Because the Nirankaris acknowledge a line of Gurus descending from Baba Dayal their orthodoxy has been questioned. The Nirankaris themselves respond by insisting that they are the truly orthodox, repeatedly emphasising their claim that the present observance of the Anand marriage rite derives from Nirankari example.   [1

The movement includes both amrit-dhari *and* sahaj-dhari *Sikhs, and to outward appearances they are indistinguishable from most other Sikhs. The one substantial point of difference remains the Nirankari recognition of a continuing line of personal Gurus. Nirankaris do not dispute the traditional belief in the line of ten Gurus beginning with Nanak and concluding with Gobind Singh, nor do they reject the doctrine of the Guru eternally present in the sacred scripture. Their belief is that Baba Dayal represents renewal. The Panth had strayed from its duty and Baba Dayal was despatched by God to recall it to obedience.   [2*

6.1.1 A summary account of Nirankari history

The reform brought about in the Sikh religion by the Nirankari Satguru Baba Dayal and [his successor] Satguru Darbara Singh beggars description. Yet what trials these supremely devoted men had to face from their own caste and family as a result of their desire to reveal the truth and establish the authentic Sikh code of conduct (*gur-maryada*). They suffered agonising exclusion from their own caste brotherhood and from normal intercourse with others; they were banned from the use of wells and cremation grounds; they were deprived of traditional ceremonies, and much more. Repeated efforts were made, in all ways and by all means, to persecute these loyal teachers of the Nirankari faith. *[1*

Satguru Baba Dayal [1783–1855] was a contemporary of Maharaja Ranjit Singh, the Lion of the Punjab. He was born three years later than Ranjit Singh and continued to preach for fifteen more years after the Maharaja's death. Although it is claimed that Sikh rule had been established in the Punjab, traditional [Hindu] practices were being observed at Sikh shrines. Idols were being worshipped, gods and goddesses were being venerated. Within the precincts of such sacred places as Darbar Sahib Amritsar and Darbar Sahib Tarn Taran images of the eight-armed Durga and Bhagauti had been installed. [Because of his opposition to such practices] Satguru Dayal had to suffer much hardship and distress from his contemporaries, both Sikhs and Hindus. *[2*

Satguru Dayal perceived that the people were reading Gurbani without paying heed to its meaning and that the Sikhs had begun to treat their sacred scripture as if it were a collection of Sanskrit mantras, believing that they would acquire merit merely by chanting its words. When he realised that this was happening he immediately began a campaign to banish the darkness of superstition and let the light of Gurbani shine once again in its full glory. Like a trusty hero he declared for the truth and contested all that denied it. He was afraid neither of those who served at the Sikh shrines nor of the families descended from the Gurus, and he was intimidated by neither Brahman nor Muslim. Fearlessly he stood forth as the champion of Gurmat. *[3*

As he read verses of Gurbani to Sikhs and other people Satguru Baba Dayal told them of the great gulf which separated their way of life from the sacred scripture, and he explained to them what this meant. He thus began a powerful movement and his successor, Satguru Darbara Singh, raised the Red Flag (the Nirankari *nishan sahib*) as a symbol of the revolution which was to free the Sikhs from Brahman clutches. Satguru Darbara Singh [1855–70] was a spirited man of great courage, one whose words carried enormous influence. He set about the task of preaching, carrying his message to hundreds of Sikhs as he travelled from village to village. For transport he took with him several camels and horses, together with palanquins flying the *nishan sahib*.[1] Wherever he went, wherever he pitched his marquee and preached, his presence was proclaimed afar by the red Nirankari flag waving over his camp. *[4*

Satguru Darbara Singh could see that the Sikhs had been ensnared by false beliefs. Throughout his entire life he laboured to have all rituals celebrated in accordance with the principles of Gurmat. In the rich district of Pothohar and the Chhachh area[2] he established religious centres (*bire*), each under a supervisor called a *biredar*. Each centre received a manual of conduct[3] and a red Nirankari flag dedicated to Satguru Dayal, and an annual gathering was held to mark the anniversary of the Satguru's death. At the Nirankari Darbar in Rawalpindi this great festival was celebrated by groups of Sikhs from all over the district, each led by its *biredar*. On that day, 19 Magh, hundreds of red Nirankari pennants were to be seen. At Dayalsar,[4] amidst the beating of drums and the clash of cymbals, Satguru Dayal was commemorated by the reading and singing of passages from the scriptures. Ninety-two of these annual assemblies were held in Rawalpindi prior to Partition, and they continue to be held each year in India.[5]   [5

For fifteen years Satguru Darbara Singh fearlessly preached his message, and gradually the earlier hostility abated. He died at the age of fifty-six, having entrusted the reins of responsibility to his younger brother, Sahib Rattaji [1870–1909].   [6

During the time of Satguru Sahib Rattaji several more Nirankari centres were established and Nirankari teachings began to spread far and wide. Sikh preachers from further east began to visit the Nirankari Darbar, there to learn about Nirankari rituals from Sahib Rattaji and his followers. Over a period of some years Giani Dit Singh and Giani Thakur Singh went up to Rawalpindi from Amritsar several times and shared in worship with Satguru Sahib Rattaji's sangat. In response to the encouragement which they received from Bhai Manna Singh they founded the Singh Sabha in Amritsar and Lahore; and with the assistance of Nirankari preachers whom they repeatedly invited they introduced the Anand marriage ceremony into their own districts. The first marriage to be celebrated in Lahore according to the Anand rite was that of the daughter of Sardar Jawahar Singh Kapur, Chief Secretary of Khalsa College. This marriage was conducted by the Nirankari preacher Bhai Manna Singh, who came down from Rawalpindi for the purpuse . . . Maharaja Hira Singh of Nabha visited the Nirankari Darbar in order to pay homage to Satguru Sahib Rattaji and acting on his encouragement succeeded, against massive opposition, in having the Anand Marriage Act passed by the government of India in 1909. Baba Ram Singh [the Namdhari leader] (6.2.1[8–10]) had earlier visited Satguru Darbara Singh at the Nirankari Darbar and he too had been urged to promulgate the Guru's version of the marriage ceremony among his followers . . .   [7

In S. 1964 [1907 A.C.] Satguru Sahib Rattaji summoned a large assembly and announced that Satguru Gurdit Singh would succeed him. Fourteen months later he died [early in 1909]. It was Sahib Gurdit Singh [1909–47] who refaced the exterior of the Nirankari Darbar in Rawalpindi with beautiful marble. His present successor is the noble Sahib Hara Singh,[6] to whom has fallen the task of establishing new centres in various places and reuniting his followers after the shattering experience of Partition.[7]   [8

6.1.2 The Nirankari Hukam-nama

Sri Satguru Dayal once visited the realm of God (*Nirankar*). There he found an assembly in session, attended by Guru Nanak and the nine Gurus who succeeded him. The assembly stood and God issued his command: 'Man of God, go forth and preach the Rahit to all Sikhs. All who acknowledge the authority of the ten Gurus are now entrusted to your care.' Satguru Dayal humbly replied: 'My Lord, what strength have I to perform this task?' God reassured him, saying, 'He who obeys you will attain deliverance and find a dwelling-place in heaven (*sach khand*). The Brahmans have been misdirecting everyone along the path which leads to hell. Show them to path of the divine Name.' Having thus received his orders from God himself Satguru Dayal returned to the world of men.   [1

Once Sri Satguru Darbar Singh was sitting in a religious assembly. While the scriptural discourse was in progress a Sikh arrived from the Punjab. Entering the assembly, he said, 'My Lord, the Brahmans have entangled us in a net of futile rituals and ceremonies. Please explain to us the scriptural ceremonies for birth, death and marriage. Tell us what the Guru has commanded.' The Satguru addressed the sangat, saying, 'There is but one answer for all Sikhs and it is that all should repeat the Name of God. If anyone should deny this refer him to God's sacred scripture where at the very beginning it is recorded in *Japji Sahib*: "God's ultimate dwelling is the Realm of Truth, the ineffable home of eternal bliss. There the Creator keeps watch over all, imparting grace, bestowing joy." . . .   [2

'In the presence of the assembled congregation of Sikhs who acknowledge Satguru Baba Dayal and the Guru Granth Sahib, in its presence say, "Glory, glory be to God!" (*dhan dhan nirankar*). Repeat these words again and again: "Glory be to God!"   [3

'There now follow the usages decreed by the Guru Granth Sahib.   [4

'Whenever a child is born, whether it be a son or a daughter, we sing the Guru's hymns. When the birth takes place we distribute the Guru's karah prasad (4.5[12]). Do not believe that the mother should be regarded as polluted following childbirth . . . After fifteen days the mother should bring the child into the presence of the Guru Granth Sahib and the Guru's karah prasad should there be offered. A name taken from the Guru Granth Sahib is then bestowed on the child. This is the ritual to be observed following a birth.   [5

'The child is betrothed when it is old enough to understand what is taking place . . . When the marriage is to take place the Guru's blessing is invoked by singing his hymn. Women as well as men sing the third Guru's *Anand* in *Ramkali* raga (5.2.7) . . . We should never invite a Brahman to conduct a marriage. Brahmans encourage superstition in order to satisfy their own greed . . .   [6

'Celebrations should be held in the house during the course of the ten days preceding the departure of the marriage party . . . When the marriage party sets out the Guru Granth Sahib should be carried in a palanquin, protected by a canopy and by the use of a whisk. . . . When the party reaches the bride's house with the Guru Granth Sahib a carpet is spread on the ground, a canopy is suspended above it, and a screen erected around it. The Guru Granth Sahib is then set within the enclosure on a stool. After *Ardas* (5.4) has been recited the ends [of the sashes worn by the bride and groom] are tied to each other and the couple walk four times round the Guru Granth Sahib while we recite Guru Arjan's hymn in *Suhi* raga (5.7.6.4[1]). . . . After the couple have been seated the *lavan* are recited.[8] . . . We then sing more hymns and then after reciting *Anand Sahib* we serve karah prasad in the presence of the Guru Granth Sahib. The couple then proceed to their home, escorted by others singing hymns. We do not demand a dowry, brother, as this is forbidden by the Guru. . . .   [7

'We sing the Guru's hymns or listen to them during the course of our daily round, brother. Whenever a Sikh is about to begin an [important] task he offers *Ardas* before the Guru Granth Sahib. He then prostrates himself and [as a token of humble submission] cleans the shoes [of others who have assembled before the Guru Granth Sahib]. It is not our custom to ascertain auspicious times for such activities. . . . All the years, months, and days given by the Guru are suitable, brother. The Tenth Master, Guru Gobind Singh, tells us that a Gursikh should simply invoke the Guru's name and set about his business even though all the omens may appear bad. Even tasks which seem impossible can be performed with the Guru's aid. Such is the power of the divine Name.   [8

'When by God's grace a life draws to its end, when the call comes and a Sikh departs this life, we cover the corpse with a white shroud and either cremate it or commit it directly to flowing waters, singing hymns as we do so. We do not weep and wail. Whether the deceased be a child, a young person or one advanced in years we simply wrap him in a white shroud. . . . When we cremate a Sikh we recite *Anand* and *Kirtan Sohila* (5.2.7, 5.3). We then serve karah prasad and fried cakes (*luchi*) as our means afford, and return to the Guru Granth Sahib, reciting hymns antiphonally as we go. When we arrive we inaugurate a reading of the complete scripture. This is Guru Nanak's rite, brother, restored again by Satguru Dayal. It is the scriptural rite and Sikhs should observe it. . . .   [9

'When Brahmans conduct the *shradh* ceremony commemorating a death, brother, they claim that the ancestors of Khatris have become crows, dogs, snakes, cows and frogs! They also insist on being given feasts. Gursikhs should have nothing to do with such practices. For them the only path is the divine Word. Do not engage in mourning for a deceased person, brother. . . . When anyone departs for the realm of God, brother, then, humbly submitting to the will of the eternal Satguru, we clothe ourselves in pure white garments and go about our normal business. We do not spread [mourning] mats. The only other thing we do is gather the bones and ashes after five days and commit them to flowing water. As we do this we sing hymns. . . .   [10

'The traditional rituals and ceremonies are all spurious. What you should do, brother, is repeat the divine Name. Take no account of astrological predictions. "A host of suns shine when the Name is repeated, banishing the darkness of ignorance." This hypocrisy, brother, is entirely due to the greed of the Brahmans. What difference can it make if a star is ascending or declining! . . . [11

'Attend the sangat, joining with others in the presence of the Guru Granth Sahib, and [acknowledge your submission to the sangat by humbly] washing their feet. We already observe the practice of signifying our submission to God by cleaning the shoes of those who assemble in the presence of the Guru Granth Sahib. This we do because Guru Nanak has told us to do it. . . . [12

'There are three other precepts to be observed, all of them taught by the immortal Guru Nanak and by Satguru Dayal. 1. Sing songs of praise to God. 2. Serve your parents. 3. In obedience to God live by your own labours and renounce all evil. As Kabir says in shalok 233: "He who consumes bhang, fish, or liquor shall surely go to hell, regardless of all his pilgrimages, fasts, and disciplines." The purpose of these three precepts is as follows. We sing God's praises in order to bring the round of transmigration to an end. We should serve our parents because a mother carries the child in her womb for ten months and once God has brought it to birth the parents must assume complete responsibility for it. And we should earn our own keep because one should not be dependent on others. Do not believe anyone who violates any of these three principles. They have been delivered by Satguru Nanak himself and by Satguru Dayal. . . .' [13

The Sikh who received this homily [from Satguru Darbara Singh] fell at this feet and asked to be initiated as a disciple. He was told that his prime duty must be to worship none save the Guru's divine Word and to devoutly repeat the name of God (*Nirankar*).[9] [14

6.2 THE NAMDHARI SIKHS

The Namdhari or Kuka movement originated in the same circumstances as the Nirankari. Both emerged in the north-western corner of Ranjit Singh's kingdom and both did so in response to a growing conviction that all was not well with the Panth (1.8[1]). In terms of subsequent development, however, the two groups followed widely divergent paths. The Nirankari strength remained concentrated in the north-west until the 1947 partition of India, and the general acceptance by orthodox Sikhs of the Anand marriage order settled a major issue as far as the Nirankaris were concerned. The Namdharis meanwhile developed a rural base in eastern central Punjab, an outward appearance which clearly distinguishes them from the orthodox, a distinctive ritual, and a belief concerning the succession of Gurus which the orthodox vehemently reject. [1

Namdhari Sikhs are easily recognised by their practice of wearing white homespun clothing and by their method of tying the turban horizontally across the forehead. Around their necks they wear a white woollen cord (mala), *woven as a series of 108 knots and serving as a rosary. Their distinctive rituals include the fire ceremony* (havan) *which is described below and the practice of circumambulating a fire during the course of their wedding ceremony. The orthodox belief that the line of personal Gurus ended with the death of Guru Gobind Singh is denied by the Namdharis. They insist that the tenth Guru lived for many years after 1708, eventually bestowing the succession on Balak Singh of Hazro.*[10] *The Namdhari Sikhs are strict vegetarians and vigorous protectors of the cow. They attach equal importance to the Adi Granth and Dasam Granth, and they include the Dasam Granth composition* Chandi di Var *in their daily nit-nem.* [2

6.2.1. The history and doctrines of the Namdhari Sikhs

The historical evidence enables us to affirm categorically that in Nander Guru Gobind Singh repeated in a more dramatic way the stratagem which he had earlier used when escaping from Chamkaur.[11] It is clear from the evidence that the Guru did not die in Nander (2.2.8[16]) but that he was able by means of a ruse, to escape under cover of darkness. . . . [1

But why did the Guru decide to depart alone and under such mysterious circumstances? The reason was that the Mughals were pursuing him. According to Lala Daulat Rai. . . . Bahadur Shah [the Mughal emperor], hoping to sweep all obstacles from his path, had hatched a plan to attack Guru Gobind Singh. Prompted by intuition the Guru was able to foresee the Emperor's evil design and realising what was afoot he slipped away from Nander during the night. There is no reliable historical work which suggests (a) that the Guru died in the presence of his Sikhs; (b) that the Sikhs placed his corpse on the funeral pyre; or (c) that the Sikhs actually performed his cremation by setting light to the pyre. What history does tell us is that the Guru, still alive, sat on the pyre and then ordered his Sikhs to leave the enclosure which had been constructed by placing screens around the pyre. Indeed, he went even further than this. He sternly commanded them to stand with their backs to the enclosure after they had left it. What was the point of having a screened enclosure erected and then insisting that his Sikhs, having left it, should stand with their backs to it? There can be no doubt that it was because the Guru wanted to slip away as he had done at Chamkaur; and that he wanted to do this in order that he might thereafter live in disguise. . . . [2

What actually happened was that after his mysterious disappearance from Nander the Guru continued to move around the country. Until he finally departed this life in S. 1869 [1812 A.C.] he continued, as previously, to assist his Sikhs in whatever trials they might encounter. The first indication which the histories offer of his activities after leaving Nander concerns the two Rajput chieftains Rustam Rao and Bala Rao. Heeding their prayers for assistance the

Guru carried them safely out of the Satara fort, each clinging to one of his stirrups. He then took them back to their own area. . . .   [3

After freeing Rustam Rao and Bala Rao the Guru helped the Rajput ruler of Bhadra.[12] He remained in Bhadra until S. 1812 [1755 A.C.] and then moved to Jind, staying there until S. 1818 [1761 A.C.]. From Jind he proceeded to Patiala where he resided for twelve years and then made preparations to shift to Nabha. In the month of Magh S. 1830 [January/February 1774 A.C.] he moved to Nabha and established his residence there in a grove of trees. This remained his home base until his death in S. 1869 [1812 A.C.]. He lived out the remainder of his life under the name of Baba Ajapal Singh and during those chaotic years continued to aid his Sikhs in times of distress[13] . . .   [4

Once during this Nabha period, and under this guise, the Guru visited the Attock area. There lived in that area Balak Singh, son of Dayal Singh of Hazro. Ever since his early childhood Balak Singh had been absorbed in the worship of God, but although he had led a saintly life he still felt the need of finding a guru who could provide him with spiritual satisfaction. At that time he was still only twelve years old. His father had a shop in the village of Chhoi and Balak Singh was frequently required to make the journey from Sarvala to Chhoi. Early one morning he set out for Chhoi, following the road which would lead him past the place where the Haro stream joins the Indus river. Sant Indar Singh Chakravarti takes up the story: [5

> This is a supremely peaceful spot, a delightful place of great beauty. Ahead lies a magnificent view of Mount Chhoi, a marvellous scene for anyone who appreciates the splendour of nature. In such a setting the restless mind is stilled and one's spirit is irresistibly drawn to the praise and worship of God. It was mid-morning by the time the devout Guru Balak Singh approached this place. As he came down to the river his mind was concentrated on the blessed feet of the Guru and while he was thus rapt in meditation he beheld Guru Gobind Singh riding a horse in the company of five Sikhs. He immediately grasped the reins and the Guru, having dismounted took the seat which was offered to him. Perceiving in his countenance features associated with the Tenth Guru, Balak Singh questioned him. Knowing full well what was in his mind, the Guru declared, 'Until now I have kept my identity a secret as it was felt better not to reveal it. . . .'   [6

Thus did the Tenth Master confer on Balak Singh the praise and adoration due to one divinely endowed. He proceeded to designate him his successor as Guru, laying five copper coins and a coconut before him and then prostrating himself. . . .   [7

Giani Gyan Singh relates the birth of Satguru Ram Singh (the twelfth Guru) in a particularly beautiful passage. . . . According to Gyan Singh he was born in the village of Bhaini Raian, Ludhiana District, on the fifth day of the waxing moon in the month of Magh, S. 1872 [1816 A.C.]. The birth took place in the house of his parents Jassa Singh and Sada Kaur.   [8

Following a childhood notable for its marvellous achievements the youthful Ram Singh enlisted in the army of Maharaja Ranjit Singh. Together with his brother-in-law Kabal Singh he joined the Naunihal Regiment and remained in the army until the first Anglo-Sikh war [1845–46]. While serving as a soldier he devoted his spare time to singing God's praise, with the result that his unit came to be known as the 'Bhagat's Regiment'. Sant Nidhan Singh Alam describes how in 1841 Satguru Ram Singh happened to be quartered in Hazro while marching with his platoon to Peshawar on some official business. At that time Guru Balak Singh was delivering the divine discourses which were winning worldly souls to true happiness. While conferring the succession on him Guru Gobind Singh had told him that he would himself return as the twelfth Guru and reclaim it from him.   *[9*

When Satguru Ram Singh visited Guru Balak Singh to pay his respects the latter was engaged in interpreting the hymn 'I have come for your protection, Master.'[14] When Satguru Ram Singh prostrated himself in the usual way Guru Balak Singh said, 'Come, my Lord and Master! I have awaited your coming for a long time.' Joyfully he arose (he had been sitting behind the Granth Sahib) and lovingly embraced Satguru Ram Singh. He then introduced him to the assembled congregation and [initiated him by] whispering the divine mantra in his ear. . . . Guru Balak Singh then commissioned him with the sacred duty of preaching the message of deliverance to all who dwell in ignorance. Placing five copper coins and a coconut before him he entrusted him with the divine responsibility of serving as Guru. . . .   *[10*

Thus the Guru's succession which had extended from S. 1526 to S. 1765 [1469–1708 A.C.][15] did not come to an end. . . . It continued to run, the inheritance passing from Guru Gobind Singh through Guru Balak Singh to Satguru Ram Singh.[16]   *[11*

6.2.2 The Namdhari Rahit-nama

The Rahit-nama
issued by the Twelfth Master

By the grace of the Eternal One, the True Guru.

From Ram Singh and the Khalsa of Bhaini to all members of the Khalsa. Accept our greeting: 'Vahiguru ji ka Khalsa, Sri Vahiguru ji ki fateh' (4.5[20]). This rahit-nama has been written for the benefit of all sangats and has been issued from Bhaini.   *[1*

Rise during the last watch of the night and taking a pot of water [for cleansing] go out into the fields to relieve nature. When you return scour the pot twice, remove the clothes which you were wearing while in the fields, clean your teeth, bathe, and recite [the prescribed portions of] sacred scripture. If you do not already know these by heart you should learn them. Everyone should do this, including women both old and young. Commit both *Japji* and *Jap* to memory, and also *Shabad Hazare*.   *[2*

You must also learn *Rahiras* and *Arti Sohila*[17] by heart. All should lead a life of restraint and contentment. Offer praise to the Guru, [the Lord] of Truth, throughout the day and the night.   *[3*

Respect the daughter or the sister of another man as you would your own. The Guru has told us how we should regard the rights of others.

Violating another's rights, Nanak, should be treated with the same abhorrence as a Muslim would feel for eating a pig or a Hindu would feel for killing a cow.[18]

He who fails to take initiation from the Guru and who utters the Guru's mantra without first receiving it from him shall have his face blackened in this world and the next.   *[4*

Let no one speak maliciously of another. Be forgiving towards others, taking no account of what they may say about you. Even the person who strikes you must be forgiven. The Guru is your Protector.   *[5*

Always conceal your own good deeds from others. Gather to sing the sacred hymns regularly. Sing passages from the scriptures daily.   *[6*

When a *jag* (*yajna*) is to be performed purify the place where it is to be held [the *jag* square] by plastering it.[19] Bring earthen vessels which have not previously been used and wash your feet before entering the *jag* square. There perform the *havan*, or *hom* [ritual fire ceremony]. Use wood from either the *patas* or the *ber* tree. Do not [fan the fire by] blowing it with human breath. During the course of the ritual fire service [five officiants] should read the following from copies of the scriptures: *Chaupai, Japji, Jap, Chandi Charitra* and *Akal Ustat*.* A sixth officiant should meanwhile pour incense[22] [on the fire] and a seventh should [intermittently] sprinkle a few drops of water on it.   *[7*

Do not admit to religious assemblies anyone who commits an evil deed such as adultery or theft. If the culprit happens to be a powerful person all should pray that he will be rendered unable to enter the congregation.   *[8*

But my understanding is limited. You yourselves know all that one needs to know. Let all stand reverently before God with palms joined and pray, 'Sustain our faith, O Lord.'   *[9*

Always wear the approved breeches (*kachh*) (4.5[36]). When taking off a *kachh* withdraw one leg and put it in the leg hole of another pair before withdrawing the second leg. Never conceal an evil deed committed by another person. Do not sell or barter a daughter or a sister. Constantly repeat the Guru's name. Never eat meat or drink alcoholic liquor. Continue always in the fear of God.[23]   *[10*

6.2.3 The Namdhari Ardas

Ardas
in the name of the Twelfth Master

Having first remembered God turn your thoughts to Guru Nanak; Angad

---

* Sri Satguru Hari Singh commanded that *Chandi di Var*[20] and *Ugar-danti*[21] should also be read during the ritual fire service. [Footnote to original text.]

Guru, Amar Das, each with Ram Das, grant us aid. Arjan and Hargobind, think of them and Hari Rai. Dwell on Guru Hari Krishan, he whose sight dispels all pain. Think of Guru Tegh Bahadur; thus shall every treasure come. May Guru Gobind Singh grant us help and strength in every place.[24] Remember Guru Balak Singh, he who has shown us the way to truth. Remember Satguru Ram Singh, Master of our faith and he who directs our worldly actions, he who knows our inmost thoughts, God himself who sets us free from the grip of death. Remember Guru Hari Singh, light incarnate, he who heals and restores; and Satguru Pratap Singh who in this present Age of Darkness has preached perfect piety, purity, the practice of repeating the divine Name and recitation of the scriptures. May they grant us help and strength in every place.   [1

Remember the Master's four sons, the Cherished Five, and the Forty Liberated (5.4[7]). Remember all martyrs to the faith; they who were faithful in their remembrance of the divine Name and generous to others; they who gave their heads for their faith, steadfast in their loyalty to the true teachings of Sikhism and defending their uncut hair to their last breath; they who fearlessly spoke the truth; they who for their faith wielded the sword and shared their sustenance with others; they who were blown away from guns,[25] condemned to the horrors of transportation,[26] or to hanging, and who yet clung to their faith in the Satgurus. Meditate on the greatness of these stalwart disciples and call to mind the divine Name.   [2

Guru and Master, we who are miserable sinners, having heard how you wondrously raise the fallen, cast ourselves at your door. Bestow on us, by your grace, the blessing of the Guru's teachings. Grant that we may be found only in the company of your faithful servants, never with the proud and worldly. May the commandments which as Guru you give in the Granth Sahib always be obeyed. Grant me the gift of faith in your commandments wherever I may be. Save me, Lord, from wavering in my faith. Grant that my love may be bestowed on none save only you. Preserve me ever, O Lord, from loss of faith in you.   [3

All in this assembly pray that you will mercifully reveal yourself in all your glory. Bring to an end the killing of the poor and the cow, extend the true faith over the earth, free all who are imprisoned, destroy those who are evil, and exalt your True Khalsa (*sant khalsa*).   [4

Our sins, O Lord, are many. Regard not our sins but mercifully bring us into your care and protection.   [5

In your name we pray, and in the trust that we may behold your presence. Forgive the shortcomings of our prayer. Dwell within all our hearts that we may continue to sing your praises to eternity. May your Sikhs be victorious in all places and may they who have heard and sung your praises be sustained in all their deeds. Grant that we may behold your most sacred presence. May the name of Satguru Ram Singh be magnified and by your grace may all be blessed.[27]   [6

6.3 THE NIHANGS

The Nihangs constitute a distinctive order within the Khalsa. Ardent in their loyalty to the Khalsa they regard themselves as an elite corps dedicated to its defence and the advancement of its martial ideals. They first appeared during the eighteenth century as a particularly warlike element within the militant Khalsa of the misl period (1.7[2]). Ranjit Singh, recognising their value as a fighting force, incorporated them in his army as a colourful if turbulent brigade of reckless infantry. During this early period of their existence they were known as Akalis.[28] [1

The Nihangs are organised as four 'armies' (dal) *but share a sense of common discipline and purpose. Most Nihangs are unmarried, their belief being that as soldiers of the Khalsa they must be unencumbered by family ties. For part of the year they remain in their 'camps'* (dera) *attending to cultivation and cropping. At other times they roam the Punjab on horseback, conspicuously visible in their blue garments and for the range of steel weapons which they carry.* [2

The Nihangs are a sect of Khalsa Sikhs [recognisable by their distinctive appearance]. On their heads they wear a high turban known as a *damala*, surmounted by a piece of cloth called a *pharhara* ('standard' or 'flag'). [In their turbans they wear] steel quoits, and they carry other weapons such as a cannon-match, two-edged sword, kirpan, etc. Their garments are always blue. Because they have renounced all fear of death Nihangs are always ready to die for their faith. They also renounce worldly concerns, which is what their name, *nih-ang*, means. . . . [3

Many Nihangs claim that the practice of wearing the high turban and symbolic *pharhara* was instituted by Guru Gobind Singh. According to Vivek Singh of Amritsar, however, it was Baba Naina Singh [a military leader of the mid-eighteenth century] who began it. He did so by attaching his standard to a high turban worn by his standard-bearer, the intention being that the standard-bearer should be able to lead with the flag while still having his hands free to use his weapons. [4

Baba Naina Singh's pupil Akali Phula Singh became a famous general in the Sikh army [of Maharaja Ranjit Singh]. Because they are devotees of Akal [Purakh] and because they observe the devotional discipline of repeating the word 'Akal' Nihangs are also known as Akalis.[29] [5

Nihangs are rigorous in their observance of the Rahit. They live austere lives, distinguished by their love for the scriptures, their fearless acceptance of God's will, and their generosity of spirit. During the time of the twelve misls and subsequently in the reign of Maharaja Ranjit Singh they rendered notable service as defenders of the Panth and as exemplars of its discipline. If the Nihangs would give up cannabis and opium, and if they could be persuaded to develop an interest in education, their services to the Panth would be of enormous value.[30]

[6

7 MODERN WORKS

Modern Sikh scholarship is deeply indebted to the Singh Sabha movement (1.9). Most of the important writers of the early twentieth century were associated with it and its influence is still plainly evident in much of the material produced within the Panth today. The Singh Sabha was a reformist movement, one which endeavoured to introduce critical reasoning without sacrificing traditional loyalties. The five writers who appear in this concluding section all represent the characteristic Singh Sabha approach to Sikh history and religion

[1

7.1 THE SIKH RELIGION

Religion is the pathway revealed by saints and sages for the fulfilment of mankind's deepest longings. There are in fact several religions and of these one is supreme. This is the way revealed by the ten Gurus, beginning with Guru Nanak and continuing through to Guru Gobind Singh. It is known as the Sikh religion and its basic doctrinal position may be described as follows.   *[1*

The fundamental purpose of religion is not to provide men with a means of access to heaven or any such place. It is rather to bring them to everlasting union with God, to that mystical merging in the divine which alone can bring the transmigratory round of death and rebirth to an end. God (*Vahiguru*) is described in the following terms:

There is one Supreme Being, the Eternal Reality. He is the Creator, without fear and devoid of enmity. He is immortal, never incarnated, self-existent, known by the grace of the Guru. (5.1.1[1])   *[2*

This means that God is one and unique, that he is immune from death and destruction, that he is the creator of all things, and that he dwells immanent within his creation. Unlike the gods [of popular imagination] he neither fears nor does he provoke fear. His condition is one of endless bliss, never involved in the process of birth and death. Creator of all things he is himself created by none. With the blessing of his grace all things are possible.   *[3*

In order to know God one must know the Guru. The Guru was manifested in the ten personal Gurus and is now eternally manifest in the Guru Granth Sahib.   *[4*

Devoted disciples who understand the meaning of the Guru's teachings and the deeper mysteries of religion should be accepted as supremely enlightened guides. By associating with such exemplary believers we can acquire the same exalted character which they themselves possess. The pattern of behaviour which this involves has two aspects, personal and corporate. The principal requirements of the personal aspect are as follows: [5

1. Each of us must seek mystical union with God through the discipline of 'remembering the divine Name' (*nam simaran*).   [6
2. Each day one should read from the Guru Granth Sahib and study its teachings.   [7
3. All other people should be regarded as brothers. Discrimination based on caste and nationality must be replaced by love and selfless service.   [8
4. The duties of one's religious faith should be discharged in the context of regular family life, [not by renouncing the world].   [9
5. One must live according to the Guru's teachings (*gurmat*), not in accordance with misconceived notions of untouchability, sorcery, idol worship, or superstition.   [10

Corporate or panthic obligations include the following:

1. Having submitted to the [Khalsa] discipline one must strictly observe its code of conduct (*rahit*).   [11
2. Acknowledging the Panth as a manifestation of the Guru one must render it loyal and dedicated service.   [12
3. Gurmat must be publicly preached and disseminated.   [13
4. All who profess devotion to Guru Nanak should be regarded as Sikhs regardless of their outward appearance,[1] and they should receive the affection due to fellow Sikhs. One must always strive for the welfare of all.   [14
5. Gurdwaras and other places of religious significance should be administered in accordance with the Gurus' commands.   [15

Kahn Singh Nabha, *Gurusabad Ratanakar Mahan Kos*,
vol. 1 (Amritsar, 1930), pp. 576–7

7.2 'WE ARE NOT HINDUS'

Dear Member of the Khalsa: You may be surprised when you read what I have written. You will ask why there should be any need of such a work as *We Are Not Hindus* when it is perfectly obvious that the Khalsa is indeed distinct from Hindu society. Or you may want to know why, if such a work is to be written, there should not be books which show that we are not Muslims or Christians or Buddhists. In answering these questions let me acknowledge that such a work is certainly not needed by those who already believe implicitly in the Gurus, who live in accordance with their teachings, and possess a sound understanding of the principles of the Khalsa tradition. This book has not been written for their benefit. It has been produced for the benefit of those brethren to whom the following historical parable applies. The tale, briefly, is as follows.   [1

Guru Gobind Singh once covered a donkey with a lionskin and set it loose in the wasteland. Men as well as cattle thought it was a lion and were so frightened of it that none dared approach it. Released from the misery of carrying burdens and free to graze fields to its heart's content the donkey grew plump and strong. It spent its days happily roaming the area around Anandpur. One day, however, it was attracted by the braying of a mare from its old stable. The donkey cantered to the house of the potter who owned it and stood outside the stable. There it was recognised by the potter who removed the lion skin, replaced its pannier-bags, and once again began whipping it to make it work. [2

The Guru used this parable to teach his Sikhs an important lesson. 'My dear sons,' he said, 'I have not involved you in a mere pantomime, as in the case of this donkey. I have freed you, wholly and completely, from the bondage of caste. You have become my sons and Sahib Kaur has become your mother (4.5 [42]). Do not follow the foolish example of the donkey and return to your old caste allegiance. If forgetting my words and abandoning the sacred faith of the Khalsa you return to your various castes your fate will be that of the donkey. Your courage will desert you and you will have lived your lives in vain.' [3

Many of our brethren are in fact neglecting this aspect of the Guru's teaching. Although they regard themselves as Sikhs of the Khalsa they accept the Hindu tradition. They imagine that it is actually harmful to observe the teachings of Gurbani by acknowledging that the Sikh religion is both distinct from the Hindu religion and superior to it. The reason for this is that they have neither read their own scriptures with care nor studied the historical past. Instead they have spent their time browsing through erroneous material and listening to the deceitful words of the self-seeking. The tragedy is that these brethren are falling away from the Khalsa. They forget the benefits which the Almighty Father has bestowed on them – how he has exalted the lowly, raised paupers to be kings, turned jackals into lions and sparrows into hawks. Seduced by those who oppose the Gurus' teachings they are ensnared by deceit and thereby forfeit the chance of deliverance which this human existence confers. [4

This book is restricted to the difference between Hindu tradition and the Khalsa because our brethren are already aware that they do not belong to other religions. This much they know, yet they mistakenly regard the Khalsa as a Hindu sect. I am confident that my erring brethren will return to their own tradition when they read this book. Realising that they are indeed the children of Guru Nanak and of all ten Gurus they will stand forth as members of the Khalsa, firmly convinced that *we are not Hindus*. [5

The bulk of Ham Hindu Nahin *consists largely of proof texts drawn from the Sikh scriptures and presented as evidence that Khalsa faith and conduct differ from Hindu tradition to such an extent that the Khalsa must be regarded as a separate religious system, distinct and autonomous in its own right. The proof-texts are grouped under such headings as religious texts, caste, avatars, gods and goddesses, idol worship, etc. Having thus pressed its vigorous claims to a separate Sikh identity the book concludes on an irenic note.* [6

Our country will flourish when people of all religions are loyal to their own traditions yet willing to accept other Indians as members of the same family, when they recognise that harming one means harming the nation, and when religious differences are no longer an occasion for discord. Let us practise our religion in the harmonious spirit of Guru Nanak, for thus we shall ensure that mutual envy and hatred do not spread. [7

Beloved brothers in the Panth of Guru Nanak, I am fully persuaded that having read the discussion recorded above you will recognise your separate identity as the Sikh community and that you will know beyond all doubt that *we are not Hindus.* At the same time you will grow in affection for all your fellow countrymen, recognising all who inhabit this country of India as one with yourself. [8

Kahn Singh Nabha, *Ham Hindu Nahin*
(Amritsar, 4th edition, 1914), pp. 4–9, 244–5.

7.3 THE NATURE OF GURMAT

God. The Being who brought the entire world, visible and invisible into existence is known as *Akal Purakh*, the Eternal One. Guru Nanak has described him in the following words: 'There is one Supreme Being, the Eternal Reality. He is the Creator, without fear and devoid of enmity. He is immortal, never incarnated, self-existent, known by the grace of the Guru.' (5.1.1[1]) [1

What these words mean is that this Being is one and alone. He is eternal; he is immanent in all that exists; and he is the Sustainer of all. Creator of all, he permeates that which he has created. He fears nothing and bears enmity towards none. Time has no influence upon him and he is free from the cycle of birth and death. He is himself responsible for his own manifestation, and by the Guru's grace he is made known to men. [2

These attributes are further enunciated and clearly explained in the sacred scriptures. Some philosophers maintain that 'spirit' (*purusa*) and 'matter' (*prakriti*) are the two eternal realities and that the world is the product of their fusion. Many add a third reality called 'god' (*isvar*), claiming that it too is eternal and that the entire universe derives from all three. Others say that *maya* is an entity, both real and illusory which exists apart from God (*brahma*) and has been used as a means of constituting the created world. The Guru, however, affirms that there is but one Reality, that eternal Reality which is the first cause of all. . . . [3

Many have recorded the belief that the creation was brought into being by gods such as Brahma. The Guru declares that Brahma, Visnu, Shiva, the ten avatars and all other divinities were themselves created by Akal Purakh. . . . Akal Purakh is exalted far beyond such divinities, none of whom may comprehend his greatness. . . . [4

Some philosophers believe that the Supreme God (*par-braham*) is inactive and that the creation derives from the activity of matter or *maya*. The Guru disagrees. Akal Purakh is the Creator and from this single Being the entire creation proceeds. . . . He dwells within all things, and all things owe their existence to him. Having created all that exists he continues to sustain the whole of creation, and to maintain its order and regularity. . . . Immanent and eternal, Akal Purakh is also conscious and sentient. He sees, he reasons, and he comprehends, for he possesses perfect intelligence. . . . [5

All are within the constraints of his divine Order (*hukam*), but the actual results produced by the divine Order depend on the deeds which one performs.[2] The transmigratory round of birth and death is determined by the divine Order. . . . [6

He himself is created by none. He cannot be represented by any material image and it is futile to worship him in the form of idols. . . . [7

He does not reveal himself only by his deeds. Because he is supremely gracious Akal Purakh restores erring humanity to the path from which it has strayed. . . . [8

At this point it may be asked whether such a Being really does exist. Could he not be a rational hypothesis devised in order to explain the riddle of the universe, or perhaps a product of the imagination? In response the Guru explains that this Being is not separate and distinct from us. The basis of what we call the 'self' is in fact the divine presence. We cannot perceive God in the manner we comprehend something which is truly separate from us. Yet he is, in fact, real. He is neither a rational hypothesis, nor is he imaginary. Just as we can know that we ourselves exist so, in the same way, we can be aware of his existence within our own inner spirits. . . . In what form does he manifest himself to our awareness? He is manifested by his indwelling presence in all creation, a creation which functions and develops as God directs. [9

Creation. According to some systems of belief the universe is a continuous never-ending process. In other words, the universe has always existed and will continue to exist through eternity. It has neither beginning nor end. This is not a doctrine which we find in Gurmat. The Gurus affirm in their works that there was once a time when the universe did not exist, a time when there was only God. . . . [10

When was it created, and how? The Guru replies that only the Creator knows. Man cannot know. When, in the *Siddh Gost*, the Siddhs question Guru Nanak concerning the beginning of the created world and the location of God's dwelling place he answers that to reflect upon such questions can merely induce awe.[3] Pondering first causes will produce nothing but wonder. And God's dwelling place is everywhere, for he is immanent in all creation. . . . We cannot know how creation was first brought into being. . . . The Gurus do, however, believe that creation is the product of the will of God. . . . [11

But what of that feature of our existence which is variously called *maya*, illusion, encumbrance or sin? Why was it created? Physical strength develops as a result of overcoming material obstacles. Similarly, virtue grows from resisting temptation. We progress spiritually as we triumph over lust, anger, avarice, worldly attachment, and pride; over those evil impulses which appeal to the self-centred human nature.[4] According to the Guru's teachings these obstacles have been set before us in order that we may make spiritual progress, for it is in resisting them that we develop spiritual strength.He who contends with them in obedience to the principles of Gurmat will have grasped the chance conferred by human life, whereas he who succumbs to them squanders his opportunity.   [12

The Eternal Guru. A few writers on Sikh history and religion have claimed that the importance of the Satguru for spiritual growth was emphasised only by those Gurus who came after Guru Nanak. This seems to me to be a mistake. In the Basic Credal Statement (*mul mantra*) which introduces *Japji Sahib* (5.1.1 [1]) Guru Nanak makes it clear that God is known *gur prasadi*, 'by the Guru's grace'. In *Asa ki Var* he tells us that when the transmigrating soul receives God's mercy it does so by encountering the eternal Guru. . . . From these extracts it is perfectly evident that Guru Nanak also affirmed the same doctrine of the eternal Guru. . . .   [13

The first question to arise is why man cannot obtain deliverance simply through the exercise of his own reason. Why should he need a preceptor? We mistakenly believe that man is a rational being and that he always behaves in accordance with reason. Modern psychology has shown that theory to be wholly erroneous. Man acts in accordance with his instincts, not his reason. People use their reason to refine their instinctive behaviour. In order words, they cloak with reason deeds which fundamentally derive from the evil impulses within them.   [14

A second difficulty is that a man's reason can extend no further than his experience. This is illustrated by the famous story of the swan and the frog. A swan from Lake Manasa came to a well in which there lived a frog. The frog wanted to know how big Lake Manasa was and the swan replied that it was very large. 'As big as this?' asked the frog jumping half-way across the well. 'Much bigger,' replied the swan. With a supreme effort the frog leapt right across the well. 'As big as that?' he asked. 'No, much bigger,' answered the swan. 'Be off, you liar!' said the frog. 'How can there possibly be a pool larger than this one?'   [15

A man's understanding necessarily depends on the circumstances in which he spends his life and we cannot escape from the ruts which we wear. Usually a man cannot comprehend anything that lies beyond the constricted limits of his own experience. What is required is that he should be confronted by a being who has found spiritual peace. Thus confronted he must trust in that being and act as he directs. In Sikh terminology it is expressed in terms of abandoning *manmat* (one's own self-willed impulses) and turning to *gurmat*. A new life is thereby begun. Gradually a man renounces his earlier way of life and its conventions, a life-style which was instinctively developed and which held him in its grip. At the same time he grows ever stronger in the new nature which he has acquired until eventually he reaches full stature. No other method can succeed. *[16*

Before the Guru's teachings were delivered it was believed in India that whenever ignorance spread and men disobeyed their sacred duty God assumed the form of an incarnation (*avatar*) to restore men to the path of truth. According to Gurmat God is never incarnated. The Sikh belief is that at such a time it is the Guru who appears. Bhai Gurdas tells us in stanzas 22 and 23 of *Var* 1 how darkness spread as obedience dwindled. Hearing mankind's anguished cry God sent Guru Nanak, and Guru Nanak once again revealed the truth to men (3.3.1[6]). . . . *[17*

From these examples it is evident that in Sikh usage the word 'guru' assumes those meanings which were originally associated with 'avatar'. As such it refers to those special beings sent by God to reveal the path of truth again. It does not possess the same meaning as ordinary Hindus attached to the word 'guru' prior to the coming of the Sikh faith. In order that he might develop spiritually each Hindu would attach himself to some worthy person whom he regarded as his guru. Within a single family (not to mention the country as a whole) there might be several preceptors. Such people did not claim to have been specially sent by God. Failure to realise this difference has led some Sikhs astray. *[18*

One other point must be understood. The gurus who roam around nowadays have all taken instruction from some person or other. Guru Nanak, however, did not have a man as his Guru. In the janam-sakhi account of the Vein river incident it is clearly stated that Guru Nanak received the 'cup of the Name' directly from God himself (2.1.2[5]). *[19*

God (*Niranjan*) is the essence of all and his light shines in all places. All is God and nothing is separate from him. He who is the infinite, supreme God is the Guru whom Nanak has met.[5] *[20*

The tenth Guru has also declared: 'Know that the eternal and incarnate One is my Guru.'[6] *[21*

There are, of course, many who claim to have been sent into the world by God, each indicating a different way to him. The result is that the ordinary person is confused. Mercifully the True Guru has himself enumerated in the sacred scriptures the criteria which enable the ordinary person to recognise the Guru. The first of these is that the Guru who would lead the disciple to union with God must himself have attained that perfect union. . . . He must also be one who preaches his message and seeks to lead others to the divine Name without any concern for his own gain. . . . And he must be free from all enmity. These are the qualities which enable a disciple to recognise the Guru as a true representation of God. And his words are God's words. Because the Guru is spiritually one with God his message communicates the divine wisdom of

God. . . . [22

It is by means of the Word alone that the disciple is made one with the Guru. By means of the Word (that which he utters) the Guru expresses his own experiences and so by means of the Word he indicates the way of truth. . . . Only by heeding the Guru's Word can one obtain the divine Name. . . . the Guru's Word is the same as the Gurus' utterances [as recorded in the scriptures]. . . . And so the scripture which incorporates the utterances of the succession of personal Gurus is in fact the Guru. [23

The divine Name. The noun which we use to designate any person, place or thing is called its 'name'. Every name represents something. But the name which is given to any particular thing is of no assistance to a person who has not actually seen whatever it designates. Whenever this happens we endeavour to explain it by describing its attributes. In order to explain the nature of God the Gurus use many names. At the same time they describe God's attributes in order to overcome misconceptions based on any of these contrived 'names'. [24

In the words of the Gurus, however, the word 'Name' (*nam*) bears a sense and a meaning much larger than any ordinary noun or name. . . . *Nam* designates an omnipresent power, immanent everywhere and manifest within every human heart. In its scriptural sense it is not a mere 'name' of God, for if this were so it would be fatuous to claim that the Name can be apprehended only with the assistance of the Guru. Anyone can know a mere name. People daily utter innumerable names of God, but only with the aid of the Guru can the immanence of the Name be revealed. . . . [25

To comprehend the immanent and all-sustaining nature of the divine Name is the supreme purpose of human life, for it is in achieving this objective that the human spirit finds mystical union with God. . . . The means whereby this immanence is realised are repetition of sacred words or texts (*jap*), meditation (*simaran*) and singing God's praises (*kirtan*). Observance of these three practices is therefore held up as the highest of ideals. . . . [26

The divine Name dwells within every person, but without the Guru's aid it cannot be discerned. This is precisely because it is an indwelling power and not a mere word. By means of a particular code of conduct (*rahit*), the words of sacred scripture (*bani*), and meditation (*simaran*) the Guru cleanses us from the filth of self-centred pride (*haumai*), thereby enabling us to apprehend the Name. The Guru enjoins a discipline which ensures that meditation will have its intended effect. It therefore follows that no one can lay hold of the divine Name until he heeds the teachings of the Guru and strives to bring his life into conformity with them. . . . [27

The practice of 'repeating a name' is also enjoined, [for one of the methods of apprehending the divine Name is to repeat with intense devotion one of the names by which God is known]. . . . But which name should be repeated? The Gurus have given us many names which illuminate the nature of God. There is, however, one particular name which is widely used in Sikh sangats and which has been commended by those such as Bhai Gurdas who have described the practice. This is 'Vahiguru'. The Tenth Guru himself invoked this particular name when he promulgated the greeting: *Vahiguru ji ka Khalsa, Sri Vahiguru ji ki fateh.* [28

Jodh Singh, *Gurmati Niranay*, chs. 1, 2, 6 and 8, *passim*

7.4 THE DIVINE NAME

There is one, and only one, way to worship God. It is to extol him, to glorify him, to sing his praises, to 'take the Name', believe in the Name, repeat the Name. But what is this Name? The word is used in several ways in the works of the Gurus. [1

(1) God may be 'nameless and placeless' but as Guru Nanak indicates in the nineteenth stanza of *Japji* (5.1.1[21]) certain names must be applied to him if error and misunderstanding are to be overcome. It is entirely proper to do this in whatever language or with whatever words one normally uses when speaking of him. For this reason the Guru himself includes in his works names for God drawn from the current usage of Hindus, Muslims, Naths, Vaisnavas and Saivites. At the same time he is anxious to ensure that no single name, with its inevitable bias, should acquire dominant favour amongst his Sikhs. To prevent this from happening he often refers to God simply as 'the Name'. In such instances the meaning of 'Name' is simply 'God', he who is made manifest in a way which no ordinary word can possibly express. The actual being or existence of God is thus called 'the Name'. What other word could the Guru have produced in order to express his meaning? In the same sense Kabir says: 'Hindus believe that the Name dwells in an idol, each identified with the other.'[7] What he means is that according to Hindu belief God dwells in an idol, that God and the idol are one and the same. No one would want to suggest that a word formed from letters could ever make its home within an idol! [2

(2) Kabir adds, however, that 'none may comprehend his glory'.[8] In other words, it is impossible for man to comprehend God in his fullness. 'Only he who matches his height can ever aspire to understanding.'[9] The most that we can ever hope to achieve is a partial revelation of God. This is the second sense in which 'Name' is used with reference to God. It refers in this to the revelation of God which a man may actually perceive. When reference is made in *Asa ki Var* to 'his lofty greatness, the mighty Name', the meaning of 'name' in this context is 'the revelation of God's attributes'. The same sense applies to the reference in *Japji*: 'Whatever he has made gives form to his Name'. [3

(3) This revelation of God is to be found in the works of the Gurus, recorded in the sacred scriptures. As the third Guru says, 'Recognise the true Word as the true Name.'[10] ... The contents of the sacred scriptures (*bani*) are frequently called 'the Name'. The third Guru also says: 'The Guru's Word is nectar sweet; daily recite the Name of God.'[11] By reciting the nectar-sweet Word of the Guru

one recites the Name of God. . . .   *[4*

(4) What then is meant by 'repeating the Name' (*nam japan*)? The Guru condemns this practice and also commends it. The difference lies in what the term is actually understood to mean. Before the time of Guru Nanak 'repeating the Name' meant repeating a particular word without focusing one's mind on the deity whom it was supposed to represent. This practice was dismissed out of hand by the Guru. To claim that *jap* can only mean 'repetition' is incorrect, for the word is also used in a sense which assumes concentrated attention or meditation. According to Sikh belief *nam japan* means to focus one's attention on God as revealed in the works of the Gurus, and to do so repeatedly.   *[5*

When one is engaged in praising God by singing or reading the scriptures one may be transported by the wonder of God's greatness, and in such a condition one may reflect with profound thankfulness on the blessed grace of the Guru who has revealed God's glory to us. At such times one may feel moved to murmur 'Vahiguru, Vahiguru'. This is actually a composite term expressing total surrender to the Guru (the visible form of God), but because it is typically uttered while one is in the presence of God it has come to be applied to God himself. From the earliest days of the Panth the experience of religious fervour has prompted Sikhs to repeat 'Guru, Guru', to cry 'Vah! Vah!',[12] or to join the two and say 'Vahiguru! Vahiguru!' In the janam-sakhis we read of how this person or that would come to Guru Nanak and how having been converted to belief in the divine Name, 'he began to repeat "Guru, Guru".' When during *Ardas* the sacrifices performed by loyal Sikhs are paraded before our eyes then too the words 'Vahiguru, Vahiguru' are uttered as a response (5.4[2]). As we enter into the spirit of their experiences we repeat the names of those devout and dedicated souls. In the same way we 'repeat the divine Name'. When we meditate with heart and mind enraptured, transported by that sense of ineffable joy we give praise to the Guru for the blessings he has bestowed, saying, 'Vahiguru! Vahiguru!! Vahiguru!!!' When the spirit is wholly absorbed words cease and we are silent, having reached the condition which is known as 'soundless repetition' (*ajapa jap*).   *[6*

Teja Singh, *Asa di Var da bhav prakasani tika*
(Amritsar, 1952), pp. 24–8

7.5 WORLDLY TEMPTATION: A COMMENTARY ON GURU NANAK'S HYMN SIRI RAGU 1

Guru Arjan begins [the Adi Granth] with *Japji, Sodar Rahiras*, and *Sohila* (1.2[4–6]). Having recorded these three portions, which together constitute the daily order (*nit-nem*), he turns to the ragas. As the first of these he chose *Siri Raga* and he opens with this shabad by Guru Nanak, a hymn which introduces the grand theme of deliverance according to Gurmat (3.1.1[2–6]). The specific point which it makes is that the Sikh who desires deliverance should actively seek to find God. This should be his goal, and apart from finding God he should have no other ambition. *[1*

In ordinary circumstances ambition takes one of four forms. (1) The desire to obtain worldly goods. (2) Sexual desire. (3) The quest for superhuman powers. (4) A craving for worldly power. These four varieties of ambition or desire are each described in the four stanzas of the shabad. Each is shown to be transient, unpredictable as the wind, and altogether futile as a means of obtaining eternal peace. *[2*

In the shabad's refrain we are told that the soul which remains separated from God is doomed to burn. One must labour to achieve any worldly ambition. It requires strenuous effort and even when it is secured it still has to be protected. If it is lost or destroyed the result is agony and distress, and it must certainly be lost when one dies, for no such possession can accompany the soul at death. The spirit remains troubled and after death must wander in anguish, bitterly regretting its sins. This is what the Guru means when he speaks of the soul 'burning'. Elsewhere he describes worldly desire as 'fire'. 'Assailed by worldly temptation they burn in the fire of inward desire.'[13] *[3*

According to Gurmat the route to God is the divine Name. This shabad warns us that we must not fall a prey to those desires which lead us astray and turn us from remembrance of God to careless neglect. Such desires will surely prove to be obstacles in the path of those who are seeking to reach God. . . . *[4*

The psychological effect produced by the pursuit of sensual pleasures must be to distract and soil the mind, whereas the influence of the divine Name concentrates it and confers authentic pleasure. The divine Name draws one's attention towards God and holds it there, with the result that there develops in the mind a sense and awareness of the divine presence. The effect of sensual pleasures, on the other hand, is to direct one's attention to external interests and thus to banish any sense of God's presence. One's thoughts are invaded by a desire for sensual gratification, turning them firmly away from God. *[5*

The antidote for these four varieties of avarice is, we are told, supplied by faith in the divine Name and thus by finding God. But there is an irony implicit in this explanation. Whenever anyone who has taken up the discipline of the Name achieves that mystical union with God he naturally acquires something of a reputation. Worldly goods come his way and people want to become his disciples. His mental powers are greatly increased by the discipline and by their exercise he acquires power. When the seeker gets caught in this process he effectively plants obstacles in his own path to God. All four temptations will assail the person who practises the discipline of the Name and he must be on his guard. He must anticipate them and he must resist them. *[6*

The first two stanzas of the shabad concern the seeking and enjoying of physical desires. The third stanza involves mental effort and attainment, and so too does the fourth. In the case of the fourth, however, the rewards are perceived as greater, for as popular opinion would have it 'the practice of austerities will earn the right to rule'. . . . There are thus two different kinds of effort and attainment covered by the two pairs of stanzas, both of them shown to be transient, unstable, and searing to the soul. The cure is to find God, and the means of doing so is provided by the divine Name. Thus does the human spirit find eternal peace.   [7

Nothing in the shabad suggests that devotion to the divine Name necessarily requires anyone to renounce ordinary married life and become an ascetic. What is required is that one should live a life of piety in ordinary circumstances; that one should resist all temptations to succumb to worldly desires; and that one should never abandon the practice of remembering the divine Name. Guru Nanak elsewhere declares:

> As the lotus dwells in water or the duck swims free on the stream,
> So do we cross the dread ocean of life by accepting the Word, by repeating the
> Name.[14]   [8

Vir Singh, *Santhya Sri Guru Granth Sahib*,
vol. 1 (Amritsar, 1958), pp. 221–3

7.6 THE FUNDAMENTALS OF SIKH BELIEF

7.6.1 The essence of Japji (5.1.1)

Question. How can man's separation from God be overcome?   [1

Answer. By obeying the will of God and by merging one's individual self in the divine being of God. It is like the relationship between a father and his son. If the son obeys his father neither is alienated from the other. Traditional methods of bridging the gap cannot succeed. Such practices as giving charity, bathing at pilgrimage centres, or protracting one's life by means of yogic breath control are all futile. (Stanzas 1–7)   [2

Question. How is the will of God to be obeyed?   [3

Answer. The more a person follows the Guru's instructions and devotes himself to praising God the more appealing he will find God's will. In order to obey the will of God one must therefore apply oneself to his praise and adoration. This should be done with a persistence which leads to total dependence on God, the mind never wholly disengaged from the practice of worship. (Stanzas 8–15)   [4

This persistence in devotion does not mean, however, that a man may fully comprehend God or his creation. God is infinite and so too are his manifold works. The one result which does follow from persistent devotion is that the devotee is confirmed in his submission to God's will. (Stanzas 16–27)   [5

Charity, pious bathing, breath-control, and Upanishadic theories of creation are all doomed to failure as a means of overcoming man's separation from God. The same also applies to the ear-rings and patched quilts of the yogis. Regular disciplined remembrance of God is the one and only method. When a person receives God's grace he abandons all selfish concern for his own pride and interests, turning instead to the practice of *simaran*. Thus is the separation overcome. It is ended by this method and this method alone. (Stanzas 28–33) *[6*

Raised from his lowly status by the grace of God the devotee initially perceives that he has been brought into the world in order to discharge a particular duty. Transcending his earlier concern for narrow family interests he realises that the entire creation comprises a single family with God as its Father; and realising this he applies himself to its service. As he devotes himself to both remembrance of the Creator and the service of humanity his vision progressively expands; and as it expands the door of grace opens ever wider to reveal God's immanent presence in all. As a goldsmith heats gold in his crucible and beats it on his anvil, so too does the devotee shape his inner self in the mint of *simaran* . . . (Stanzas 34–38) *[7*

Question. Why is this composition called *Japji*? Why did Guru Arjan place it at the very beginning of the Guru Granth Sahib? Why should it be recited daily? *[8*

Answer. (1) The first stanza of this composition poses the question of how man's separation from God is to be overcome, and it replies that the solution lies in submission to the will of God. What makes the will of God attractive? It is the practice of *simaran* or 'remembrance of God' which achieves this end. By following this discipline one learns to love God; and in loving God one is attracted to all that he has created. Thus does his will seem sweet. The practice of *simaran* or *jap* is the only means whereby man's separation from God can be overcome. The whole point of this composition is that every other means of bridging the gulf is futile, whether it be charity, pilgrimage, breath control, cosmological theory, or the blanket and ear-rings of the yogi. *Simaran* is the one and only means of reaching God, and it is *simaran* which is enunciated in this composition. This explains why it has been called *Japji*. The word *jap* means the same thing as *simaran*. it means remembrance of God, worship of God, prayer and praise to God. *[9*

(2) If one reads through the entire contents of the Guru Granth Sahib carefully it will be observed that within each raga or metrical subdivision the works of Guru Nanak are recorded first. After his compositions come those of Guru Amar Das, then Guru Ram Das, Guru Arjan, and finally Guru Tegh Bahadur. . . . This means that the Guru Granth Sahib had to begin with a work by Guru Nanak. Moreover, it was entirely appropriate that this initial contribution should concern the practice of *simaran*, for *simaran* is the fundamental feature of Sikh belief. *Simaran* is like a foundation stone on which is erected the entire structure of that belief. It was thus fitting that the Guru Granth Sahib should begin with a work which so clearly enunciated this central principle. Of all the compositions by Guru Nanak dealing with this particular subject *Japji* is the one best suited to the need. Guru Arjan accordingly placed it at the beginning of the Guru Granth Sahib. *[10*

(3) Notwithstanding the many gifts received from God a man remains miserable if separated from the source of true happiness, God himself. How is

this separation to be overcome? By obeying the will of God and by merging one's own nature in God's divine nature. Contact can be established with the divine nature if one constantly remembers God and unites with him in bonds of love. This is a vital question, one which must be regularly pondered if misery and desire are to be banished. The issue is discussed with unique clarity in Guru Nanak's *Japji* and for this reason the Guru has directed that it should be recited daily. This ensures that each Sikh is daily reminded that there exists a way of overcoming man's separation from God. The method is *simaran*, the devotional practice which comprises remembrance of the divine Name and the reciting of God's praises.   [11

Sahib Singh, *Sri Guru Granth Sahib Darapan*, vol. 1
(Jalandhar, 1962), pp, 35–8

7.6.2 Grace and the divine Name: the theme of Asa ki Var (5.5)

God created the universe out of his own being, and dwelling immanent within it he observes the never-ending drama which it presents. Man has been created in order that he may apprehend the truth and offer worship to the Lord of Truth. Unfortunately he has chosen to squander his opportunity on worldly desires.   [1

God's grace supplies the answer to this need. He who by grace finds the Guru empties himself of all pride and self-centred conceit. In accordance with the Guru's instruction he undertakes the discipline of remembering the divine Name, as a result of which all pain and anguish depart. Without the Guru's aid this gift can never be obtained. Only the Guru's eye can perceive the all-pervading presence of God.   [2

What then are the benefits to be derived from remembrance of the divine Name? The benefits of the divine Name include a life of quiet contentment; God's permanent presence within one's heart; the joy of singing with his devout disciples; and freedom from the need to rely on one's own infirm understanding. Instead of relying on his own limited strength [enlightened man] puts his trust in the grace of the Guru, renouncing all intellectual pride and overweening arrogance. Aided by the Guru he crushes his self-centred pride and lives thereafter a life of pious deeds, a life which reflects his total obedience to God./3

Worldly fame is spurious, for true greatness is bestowed by God alone. If one should seek to grasp power and reputation, though he be a king he will be reduced to beggary. It is a terrible mistake to let oneself be seduced by worldly power and riches, and to waste one's life on wanton pleasure. Spiritual virtue is the noblest form of wealth and this wealth one receives only from the Guru. Let not avarice or vanity lead to evil company or to the kind of behaviour which injures others. Live a virtuous life and remember God, for one cannot remain here for ever. Our own actions bring us either pleasure or pain so why follow the path of wickedness when retribution must surely follow? Seeking the counterfeit fame and authority offered by the world can only bring humiliation. To some God gives pleasure and on others he bestows pain. He alone directs our lives. He alone supports and sustains us. *[4*

God has created man in order that man may find the truth and devote himself to *nam simaran*. Instead of doing this, however, he wastes his life on worldly pleasures. He to whom God shows grace will find the Guru and with the Guru's aid will come to a knowledge of the divine Name. As a result he will be exalted to true greatness. He will realise that worldly renown is false and he will discover that God is his only refuge. *[5*

Sahib Singh, *Sri Guru Granth Sahib Darapan*, vol. 3
(Jalandhar, 1963), pp. 608–9

In this dish three things are mingled – truth, contentment, deep reflection.
With them mixed the Master's Name, its nectar sweet sustaining all.
He who eats with lingering joy shall know the truth, his soul set free;
He who tastes will make this food his constant fare for evermore.
Darkness reigns yet they who trust the all-fulfilling grace of God,
Find beyond this sunless world God's all-pervading light.

Blind am I to all your deeds, my worth sustained by grace alone.
Base am I devoid of virtue; grant your pitying mercy, Lord.
Grace, O Lord, and tender mercy brought me to the Guru's feet.
Finding there the blessed Name, my spirit blooms in joyous bliss.

NOTES

ABBREVIATIONS

AG. The Adi Granth (1.2)
B40. *The B40 Janam-Sakhi*, translated with introduction and annotations by W. H. McLeod, Amritsar, 1980 (1.5[4])
BN. Guru Gobind Singh's *Bachitar Natak* (1.3[3], 3.2.3)
DG. The Dasam Granth (1.3)
EST. W. H. McLeod, *Early Sikh Tradition: a study of the janam-sakhis*, Oxford, 1980
ESC. W. H. McLeod, *The Evolution of the Sikh Community*, Delhi, 1975, Oxford, 1976
GNSR. W. H. McLeod, *Guru Nanak and the Sikh Religion*, Oxford, 1968; Delhi, 1976

MK. Kahn Singh Nabha, *Gurusabad Ratanakar Mahan Kos*, 2nd edition revised with addendum, Patiala, 1960 (1.9[5])

1 THE LITERATURE OF THE SIKHS

1. *ESC.*, pp. 60–1.
2. For a description and discussion of the three versions see *ESC.*, pp. 73–9.
3. For an expanded version of this description of the structure of the Adi Granth see *EST.*, pp. 286–8. See also *ESC.*, pp. 70–3.
4. For a note on the languages of the Adi Granth see *ESC.*, pp. 69–70. For a

detailed examination see three articles by C. Shackle in the *Bulletin of the School of Oriental and African Studies*, vol. XL, part 1 (1977), pp. 36–50; and vol. XLI, parts 1 and 2 (1978), pp. 73–96, 297–313.

5. A complete text of the Persian originals of all Nand Lal's works, together with a clear Punjabi translation, is given in Ganda Singh (ed.), *Bhai Nand Lal Granthavali* (Malacca, 1968).

6. This particular janam-sakhi has been translated into English. W. H. McLeod (trans.), *The B40 Janam-sahhi* (Amritsar, 1980). For brief descriptions of the various janam-sakhi traditions see *EST.*, ch. 3.

7. A detailed study of the janam-sakhis is provided in *EST*. For a summary account see *ESC.*, ch. 2.

8. Surjit Singh Hans, 'Historical analysis of Sikh literature (A.D. 1500–1850)' (unpublished Ph.D. thesis, Guru Nanak Dev University, Amritsar, 1980), p. 504. Chapters 9 and 10 of this thesis provide the best available treatment of the *gur-bilas* tradition.

9. *Ibid.*, pp. 429–30, 440–1.

10. The actual contents of the poem date from a much earlier period in the author's lifetime. Ratan Singh Bhangu was a Sikh of distinguished lineage who aided early British attempts to compile information concerning the Sikhs. In 1809 the British moved troops up to Ludhiana and it was there that Ratan Singh offered his services as instructor to Captain William Murray. He subsequently recorded his material in Punjabi verse, completing the work in 1841.

11. The Nirankaris who follow Baba Dayal and his successors must be clearly distinguished from the so-called Sant Nirankaris, members of the Sant Nirankari Mandal of New Delhi. During recent years there has been considerable feeling within the Khalsa against the Sant Nirankaris. This enmity does not extend to the older group descended from Baba Dayal and his followers. For an account of the older group see John C. B. Webster, *The Nirankari Sikhs* (Delhi, 1979). For a summary history of the sect see pp. 122–4).

12. Webster, p. 4.

13. For a brief account of the Namdharis see W. H. McLeod, 'The Kukas: a millenarian sect of the Punjab' in G. A. Wood and P. S. O'Connor (ed.), *W. P. Morrell: a Tribute* (Dunedin, 1973), pp. 85–103, 272–6.

14. For a summary account of the Singh Sabha movement and its literary achievement see the introduction to N. G. Barrier, *The Sikhs and their Literature* (Delhi, 1970). See also the special Singh Sabha issue of *The Panjab Past and Present*, VII.1 (April 1973).

15. Vir Singh was a versatile and prolific writer who left a particularly deep impression on Punjabi literature. In addition to his commentary his published output included novels, poems, drama, biographies of the Gurus, a three-volume dictionary of the Adi Granth, pamphlets and newspaper articles.

2 THE GURUS

1. The village, now known as Nankana Sahib, lies forty miles south-west of Lahore.

2. *Janam-sakhi Sri Guru Nanak Dev Ji* (the *B40 Janam-sakhi*), ed. Piar Singh (Amritsar, 1974), pp. 33–7.

3. The three-hour period from 3 a.m. until 6 a.m.

4. Ganda Singh (ed.), *Sources on the Life and Teachings of Guru Nanak* (Patiala, 1969), Punjabi section, p. 36.

5. *Puratan Janam-sakhi*, ed. Vir Singh (Amritsar, 5th ed., 1959), pp. 14–16.

6. Ganda Singh, p. 36.

7. *Janam-sakhi Sri Guru Nanak Dev Ji* (the *B40 Janam-sakhi*), pp. 73–4.

8. *Bhai Bale-vali Janam-sakhi*, sakhi 147. The location came to be known as

Panja Sahib, 'the sacred hand-print'. For an analysis of the anecdote see *EST.*, pp. 92–3.

9. *Puratan Janam-sakhi*, pp. 111–15.

10. Literally, 'He repeated, "Guru, Guru." ' The formula recurs frequently in the janam-sakhis and was obviously a widely used devotional practice. Those who observe it today would normally repeat the word 'Vahiguru'. Another popular choice for simple repetition (*nam japan*) is 'Satnam'.

11. *Puratan Janam-sakhi*, pp. 106–7.

12. Gorakhnath was the reputed founder of the Nath sect of yogis. Although he died long before the birth of Guru Nanak he frequently appears as an interlocutor in janam-sakhi anecdotes. *EST.*, pp. 66–70.

13. *Puratan Janam-sakhi*, pp. 107–8.

14. Kirpal Das Bhalla, *Mahima Prakas Varatak*. Khalsa College manuscript no. 2308, ff. 21b–22b.

15. The word *amrit* (deathless) is used in the sense of 'nectar', the fluid which confers immortality (deliverance from the transmigratory cycle) on whoever drinks it or bathes in it. The water which fills the pool is described as *amrit* because it possesses this liberating power, and the pool which contains it is thus known as *amrit-sar*. The town surrounding the pool was originally known as Chak Guru and then as Ramdaspur. The central importance of the pool and its temple (Harimandir) eventually led to its name being transferred to the town. Ramdaspur thus became Amritsar.

16. Sarup Das Bhalla, *Mahima Prakas Kavita*, anecdotes concerning the fourth Guru, no. 5, Gobind Singh Lamba and Khazan Singh (ed.), *Mahima Prakas*, vol. 2 (Patiala, 1971), pp. 291–4.

17. Prithi Chand, the elder brother of Guru Arjan and his rival for the title of Guru. The followers of Prithi Chand and of his son Miharban came to be known as Minas. See 3.1.5[30], 4.5

[33].

18. *AG.*, pp. 432–4. The composition by Guru Nanak entitled *Patti* or 'The writing slate' is a series of thirty-five couplets, each beginning with a different letter of the Gurmukhi alphabet.

19. Santokh Singh, *Suraj Prakas*, III.33.6–17 and III.41.2–6. Vir Singh edition, vol. 6 (Amritsar, 1963), pp. 2045–6, 2083.

20. Gian Singh, *Tavarikh Guru Khalsa* (Patiala, 1970), pp. 699–701, 731–2, 733.

21. *Ibid.*, pp. 856–61.

22. Sainapati, *Sri Gur Sobha*, XVIII:8–20, 32–7, 40–3. Ganda Singh edition (Patiala, 1967), pp. 124–9.

3 THE SCRIPTURES

1. *Siri Ragu* 1, *AG.*, p. 14.

2. For a more detailed exposition of *nam* see *GNSR.*, especially pp. 195–6.

3. *GNSR.*, pp. 214–19.

4. *GNSR.*, pp. 196–9. *ESC.*, pp. 46–50.

5. *GNSR.*, pp. 191–4. The word is pronounced 'shubud' in Punjabi.

6. *GNSR.*, pp. 199–203.

7. *nirankar*, 'the Formless One'.

8. *Siri Ragu* 2, *AG.*, pp. 14–15.

9. Literally, 'the Provider and the Consumer', a metaphor expressing God's immanence in his created world. The doctrine is restated in the second and fifth couplets.

10. *Sorath* 11, *AG.*, pp. 598–9.

11. *B40*, pp. 5–9.

12. *Siri Ragu* 6, *AG.*, p. 16.

13. *Var Majh* 7:1, *AG.*, pp. 140–1.

14. For a brief description of the Naths and their *hatha-yoga* discipline see *EST.*, pp. 66–70, and *B40*, p. 97. See also 3.3.1[27] and footnote.

15. *sahaj yog nidhi*: the jewel of *sahaj*. *GNSR.*, pp. 224–5.

16. Whereas yogis smear their bodies with ashes Nanak covers himself with an awareness of God's all-pervading presence.

17. Yogis practise asceticism; Nanak follows the teachings of the divine Guru (God).
18. Raja Bharathri, a celebrated Nath yogi.
19. *Asa* 37, *AG.*, pp. 359–60.
20. Two lotus metaphors are widely used in Indian devotional literature. The simpler of the two treats the lotus as a figure representing the human spirit. Although the lotus has its roots in slime it produces a perfect flower. Similarly a man who dwells in the midst of the world's filth can bloom spiritually. The more complex metaphor treats the lotus as a representation of the divine Name present within the gross material world. Just as frogs are unaware of the lotus which shares their pool so too are many people blind to the immanent presence of God. The black bee, however, is irresistibly drawn to the lotus, and like the black bee each faithful soul is drawn to the divine Name.
21. *Siri Ragu* 27, *AG.*, pp. 23–4.
22. *EST.*, pp. 122–4. For one of these stories see *B40*, pp. 42–5.
23. Literally, 'it dwells in a *tirath*'. A *tirath* is a place of pilgrimage where devotees bathe.
24. Bathing at a *tirath* (or performing any other external ritual) is no proof of true piety.
25. The *simmal* or silk-cotton tree has an attractive appearance but is otherwise useless.
26. *Suhi* 3, *AG.*, p. 729. The 'chains' are the attitudes and actions which bind men to the round of transmigration.
27. For a description of the *Babar-vani* and a discussion of Guru Nanak's experience of the Mughal invasion see *GNSR.*, pp. 132–8. See also *B40*, pp. 70–80.
28. A custom believed to confer blessing.
29. A *lakh* (a hundred thousand). Coins were offered to the bride and groom during the course of their marriage ceremony, the amount determined by the status and affluence of their families.

30. The Lodi rulers of the Delhi Sultanate.
31. 'One [the Muslim] is deprived of his time [for *namaz*] and the other [the Hindu] his attendance at *puja*.'
32. Ram is a Hindu name for God, Khuda a Muslim name.
33. *Asa astapadi* 11, *AG.*, p. 417.
34. *EST.*, pp. 286–8.
35. Each day is divided into eight watches, four for the period of actual day and four for the night. Each watch is three hours in duration.
36. The fourth watch of the night (3 a.m. to 6 a.m.).
37. *Majh ki Var* 18:1, *AG.*, p. 146.
38. *hukam:* the divine Order. See *GNSR.*, pp. 199–203.
39. *Gauri* 1, *AG.*, pp. 157–8.
40. M. A. Macauliffe, *The Sikh Religion*, vol. 2 (Oxford, 1909), pp. 134–5.
41. *man.* The word recurs in this shabad and is variously translated as 'spirit', 'nature', 'mind' and 'heart'. See *GNSR.*, pp. 178–81.
42. Literally, 'There will be no more shouting of the Shastras and the Vedas.'
43. *Malar* 10, *AG.*, p. 1261.
44. Literally *haumai* and *maya*. See p. 107.
45. *duja:* 'the other', viz. anything other than God; that which conflicts with the truth.
46. *Vadahans Chhant* 5, *AG.*, pp. 570–1.
47. *manmukh:* the person who follows his own perverse will, as opposed to the *gurmukh* who follows the Guru.
48. *Asa* 1, *AG.*, p. 365.
49. Literally, 'Let him wash [his body] and let him bathe in the lake of *amrit*.' Having first washed his body he should engage in *nam simaran*.
50. *Gauri ki Var Mahalla 4* 11:2, *AG.*, pp. 305–6.
51. A selection from *Sarang ki Var*, pauris 1, 4, 13–15, 18, *AG.*, pp. 1237–44.
52. *panje:* the 'five impulses', viz. lust, anger, covetousness, attachment and pride. *GNSR.*, pp. 184–5.
53. *Basant ki Var, AG.*, p. 1193. This *var* is exceptional in that it comprises only

three pauris and no shaloks.
54. *Gauri* 118, *AG.*, p. 204.
55. *Sorath* 87, *AG.*, p. 630
56. *Sorath* 88, *AG.*, p. 630.
57. *Gauri* 164, *AG.*, p. 216.
58. *Maru* 14, *AG.*, pp. 1002–3.
59. Literally, 'Let that which proceeds from your heart be as the dust from pious feet.' Touching the feet of a pious person, or smearing one's forehead with dust which his feet have touched, signifies reverence for his piety and secures a blessing from it.
60. *Asa* 36, *AG.*, p. 379.
61. *Bhairau* 9, *AG.*, p. 1137.
62. *Sorath* 49, *AG.*, pp. 620–1.
63. *Asa* 15, *AG.*, p. 479.
64. *Sorath* 8, *AG.*, p. 656.
65. *Gujari* 1, *AG.*, p. 525.
66. *Sorath* 7, *AG.*, p. 659.
67. *Shalok Farid* 19 and 81, *AG.*, pp. 1378, 1382.
68. *ESC.*, p. 75.
69. This is a reference to a story from the *Bhagavata Purana*. A celestial musician (*gandharva*), cursed to be an elephant, was seized by a crocodile while bathing. His cry for help brought divine assistance. *MK.*, p. 293.
70. There is an old Sikh tradition which affirms that shalok 54 is the work of the tenth Guru, not the ninth. According to this tradition Guru Tegh Bahadur composed shalok 53 while imprisoned in Delhi and sent it to his son at Anandpur in order to test the strength of his resolve. Gobind returned shalok 54 as his reply. Tradition also associates shaloks 55–7 with the ninth Guru's confinement in Delhi, Fauja Singh and G. S. Talib, *Guru Tegh Bahadur* (Patiala, 1975), pp. 195–203.
71. *Shalok Mahala* 9, 1–10 and 51–7, *AG.*, pp. 1426, 1428–9.
72. *Chandi charitra* 231, *DG.*, p. 99.
73. This invocation is unusually difficult to translate unless one adopts the cryptic brevity of the original text. A literal translation would read: 'The protection of the One beyond Time is mine‖The protection of the All-Steel is

mine‖The protection of the All-Death is mine‖The everlasting protection of the All-Steel is mine.'
74. *yaksh.* Kuber is the god of wealth in Hindu mythology.
75. *DG.*, p. 11.
76. This canto, which consists of the so-called *Ten Savayyas*, is recited as a part of the order for early morning prayer. *DG.*, pp. 13–15. See 5.1.3.
77. The warbler's cry resembles the words *tu hi*, 'Thee only'.
78. Literally, 'Karta (Hindu: Creator) and Karim (Muslim: the Gracious One) are the same, as are Rajak (Hindu: Lord) and Rahim (Muslim: the Merciful One).' The word *rajak* may also be construed as *raziq* (Muslim: the Sustainer).
79. *Akal Ustat*, 14:84–20:90, *DG.*, pp. 19–20.
80. *Ibid.*, 19:199–20:200, *DG.*, p. 30.
81. *DG.*, p. 39.
82. *BN.*, 1:37–38, *DG.*, p. 41.
83. *BN.*, 1:101, *DG.*, p. 46.
84. For a fuller description of the Khatri caste and its sub-castes see *ESC.*, pp. 87–90.
85. This refers to the tradition that Guru Tegh Bahadur's decision to face death in Delhi was prompted by a deputation of Brahmans from Kashmir (2.2.7 [1–6]).
86. The Guru possessed the power to escape death by performing a miracle. This he refused to do, choosing instead the martyrdom which was to inspire the overthrow of Mughal tyranny.
87. *BN.*, 5:1–16, *DG.*, pp. 53–4.
88. *BN.*, 6:1–5, *DG.*, pp. 54–5.
89. *BN.*, 6:29–33, *DG.*, p. 57.
90. *tribeni:* the threefold confluence of the visible Ganga and Yamuna rivers, and the invisible Sarasvati. The latter is believed to ascend from underground to join the other two rivers at their point of confluence. At the confluence is situated the city of Prayag, generally known as Allahabad.
91. *BN.*, 7:1–3, *DG.*, p. 59.
92. The Guru left Makhowal (later to be

called Anandpur) and travelling east entered the Shivalik hills. There he settled at Paunta (or Paonta), a small town on the banks of the upper Yamuna (Kalindri).

93. *BN.*, 8: 1–3, *DG.*, p. 60.

94. *BN.*, 8:31–8, *DG.*, p. 62.

95. *EST.*, pp. 43–5.

96. *satnam*, the 'True Name'.

97. Life in this world is conventionally represented as a passage across an awesome, treacherous ocean (the 'Ocean of Existence' or the 'Ocean of Fear'). Those who fail to live virtuous lives or neglect to discharge their proper duties are drowned in the ocean. In the Adi Granth the Guru is represented as a vessel which will infallibly succeed in crossing the ocean. One must therefore put one's trust in the Guru. He who delivers himself into the Guru's keeping will be safely ferried over life's sea.

98. *nam dan isnan*, 'the divine Name, charity, and bathing'. *B40*, p. 110n.

99. The frontal mark (designating sectarian allegiance) and the sacred thread.

100. The mythical bull which, according to the Puranas, supports the earth.

101. Literally, 'He performed the ritual of washing his feet and administered the water to his disciples to drink.' In other words, he performed the traditional *charan-amrit* ('foot-nectar') rite of initiation whereby prospective disciples are formally admitted to the following of a Guru by sipping water in which his toe has been dipped.

102. Janam-sakhi accounts of the life of Guru Nanak include a tradition that for several years he subsisted on a daily diet of a handful of sank and an *ak* pod. The pod of the *ak* shrub (*Calatropis gigantea*) is poisonous. *B40*, pp. 83, 115, 192.

103. For summary versions of these stories see *GNSR.*, pp. 34–6.

104. Literally, 'He sat on a *manji*.' The *manji* is a small string bed. In the villages of the Punjab acknowledged

leaders, spiritual and temporal, would commonly receive their followers seated on a *manji*.

105. *Sach Khand* (5.1.1[37]).

106. The Nath sect of yogis commanded considerable influence during the time of the Gurus. 'Nath' means 'master' and the *Adinath* or 'Primal Master' was generally believed to have been Shiva. In addition to the Adinath there were believed to have been nine other Naths, master yogis who had attained immortality through the practice of hatha-yoga and who were supposed to be living far back in the fastnesses of the Himalayas. According to some traditions Shiva was one of the nine, but the leadership was generally accorded to Gorakhnath.

107. The three-hour period from 3 a.m. to 6 a.m. Normally Bhai Gurdas uses the term *amrit vela* (the 'ambrosial hour'), a picturesque expression introduced by Guru Nanak in *Japji* 4 (5.1.1[6]). In the Bhai Gurdas translations it is rendered by such forms as 'the peace of early morning' (26:4) or 'as night draws near to dawn' (40:11).

108. *AG.*, pp. 305–6.

109. *AG.*, p. 83. For further examples of Guru Nanak's view and that of his successors see *ESC.*, pp. 85–6.

110. Although *varna* designates each of the four major caste groupings (Brahman, Kshatriya, Vaish and Shudra) its literal meaning is actually 'colour'. The betel leaf is green, but the wad made with betel leaf, betel nut and paste turns red when masticated.

111. *Ved Kateb:* the Hindu and Muslim scriptures.

112. *Zindagi-nama* 1–20.

4 KHALSA AND RAHIT

1. A potion prepared from raw sugar and other ingredients which is administered to an infant immediately after its birth. *MK.*, p. 318.

2. Guru Gobind Singh's fortress of

Anandpur was situated on the fringe of the Shivalik hills in northern Punjab. The territories on either side of Anandpur and in the hilly tract behind it were controlled by petty Hindu rulers known as the hill chiefs or hill rajas.

3. Baptism with water in which the Guru has dipped his toe.
4. Ratan Singh Bhangu, *Prachin Panth Prakas* 16:1–36. Vir Singh edition (Amritsar, 1962), pp. 40–2.
5. Sikhs who revere the Gurus and practise *nam simran* but do not seek membership of the Khalsa are known as *sahaj-dhari* Sikhs. *ESC.*, p. 92n. A third term in common usage is *kes-dhari*, 'one who retains his hair (*kes*) uncut'. Uncut hair is mandatory in the case of Khalsa Sikhs and for this reason *kes-dhari* is often used as a synonym for *amrit-dhari*. There is, however, a possibility of confusion with regard to the meaning of *kes-dhari*. Many Sikhs observe the requirement concerning the *kes* without receiving formal initiation as a member of the Khalsa. Strictly speaking they are thus *kes-dhari* but not *amrit-dhari*. Although it would be impossible to offer any accurate estimate of the number of uninitiated *kes-dhari* Sikhs it is evident that they constitute a substantial portion of the total community.
6. *sir-gum:* those who accept initiation and then subsequently cut their hair.
7. The five proscribed groups with whom members of the Khalsa can have no dealings (4.5[46]).
8. Sainapati, *Sri Gur Sobha* V, ed. Ganda Singh (Patiala, 1967), stanzas 6.122, 8.124, 14.130, 19.135, 21.137, 24.140, 25.141, 26.142, and 30.146, pp. 20–4 *passim*.
9. Piara Singh Padam (ed.), *Rahit-name* (Patiala, 1974), pp. 73–86 *passim*.
10. This is the third manifestation as originally enunciated.
11. *Bhai Nand Lal Granthavali*, ed. Ganda Singh (Malacca, 1968), pp. 191–4.
12. *Ibid.*, p. 195.

13. *Ibid.*, pp. 196–7.
14. *Ibid.*, p. 199.
15. *Ibid.*
16. Piara Singh Padam (ed.), *Rahit-name*, p. 53.
17. *Ibid.*, p. 55.
18. *Pothi Rahit-nama te Tanakhah-nama Sri Guru Gobind Singh ji Patsahi 10 ka* (Amritsar, 1922), p. 6.
19. *Ibid.*, p. 9. The designation 'Khalsa' can be applied to individual members as well as to the order as a whole.
20. The Shiromani Gurdwara Parbandhak Committee (commonly known as the SGPC) is an elective body responsible for the administration of the principal gurdwaras in the Punjab.
21. The current edition is the fourteenth (Amritsar, 1979). Two English translations are available, both entitled *Rehat Maryada: a Guide to the Sikh Way of Life* (London, 1971, and Amritsar, 1978).
22. *AG.*, pp. 773–4. See 5.7.6.6[1–4].
23. These are the 'Five Ks'. The *kangha* is a wooden comb which is used to hold the topknot of the *kes* in place.
24. 'Taking a *hukam* (order)' means opening the Guru Granth Sahib at random and reading the shabad which appears at the top of the left-hand page.
25. *bir-asan*. The right knee is laid on the ground with the body's weight on the right foot. The left knee is held upright.
26. Sahib Kaur was the third of Guru Gobind Singh's three wives.
27. The gurdwara at Anandpur Sahib which commemorates the founding of the Khalsa.
28. The Minas, Dhir-malias, and Ramraias were schismatic groups which emerged during the late sixteenth and seventeenth centuries. The masands were territorial supervisors who had provided faithful service under earlier Gurus, but who had become arrogantly independent by the time of the tenth Guru (4.1[1–2]).

5 LITURGICAL TEXTS

1. The 'one without form'; God.
2. *AG.*, pp. 1–8.
3. Literally 'the garbless one', the one without clothing.
4. *Jap* 189–99, *DG.*, pp. 1, 10.
5. *DG.*, pp. 13–15. The 'Ten Savayyas' should not be confused with the 'Thirty-three Savayyas' (*DG.*, pp. 712–16).
6. *ses-nag:* the thousand-headed snake which supports and canopies Vishnu as he sleeps between periods of creation.
7. *svambar:* a ceremony at which a woman of high rank chose her husband from an assembly of suitors.
8. Brahma, Shiva, Vishnu and Indra.
9. Guru Nanak, *Asa ki Var* 12:1–2, *AG.*, p. 469.
10. Guru Nanak, *Asa Sodar*, *AG.*, pp. 6, 8–9, 347–8.
11. Guru Nanak, *Asa* 2, *AG.*, pp. 9, 348–9.
12. Guru Nanak, *Asa* 3, *AG.*, pp. 9–10, 349.
13. Guru Ram Das, *Gujari* 4, *AG.*, pp. 10, 492.
14. Guru Arjan, *Gujari* 5, *AG.*, pp. 10, 495.
15. Guru Ram Das, *Asa So Purakh*, *AG.*, pp. 10–11, 348. The hymn begins with the words *so purakh.*
16. Guru Ram Das, *Asa* 2, *AG.*, pp. 11–12, 365.
17. Guru Nanak, *Asa* 3, *AG.*, pp. 12, 357.
18. Guru Arjan, *Asa* 4, *AG.*, pp. 12, 378.
19. Guru Gobind Singh, *Benati Chaupai* with *savayya* and *dohara*, *DG.*, pp. 1386–8, 254.
20. Guru Amar Das, *Ramkali Anand*, stanzas 1–5 and 40, *AG.*, pp. 917, 922.
21. The 'dish' is variously interpreted as the heart of the believer and the sacred scripture.
22. Guru Arjan, *Mundavani*, *AG.*, p. 1429.
23. Guru Arjan, *Shalok*, *AG.*, p. 1429.
24. *Sabadarath Sri Guru Granth Sahib Ji*, vol. 1 (n.p., 1936), p. 12n.
25. Guru Nanak, *Sohila Rag Gauri*

Dipaki 1, *AG.*, pp. 12, 157.
26. Guru Nanak, *Asa* 2, *AG.*, pp. 12–13, 357.
27. Guru Nanak, *Dhanasari* 3, *AG.*, pp. 13, 663.
28. Guru Ram Das, *Gauri Purbi* 4, *AG.*, pp. 13, 171.
29. Guru Arjan, *Gauri Purbi* 5, *AG.*, pp. 13, 205.
30. Literally 'Praise to the Guru' but usually translated 'Wonderful Lord' (7.4[6]). Originally an ascription of praise the term is now used as a name for God. Vahiguru and Akal Purakh are the two favoured names for God in popular usage. *B40*, p. 45n.
31. The actual word used in the invocation, in the title of the hymn, and in the first line is *Bhagauti*, a name which normally designates the goddess Durga. Sikh tradition is, however, emphatic in its insistence that it here means *Akal Purakh*, Almighty God. *Bhagauti* can also mean 'sword'.
32. *Chandi di Var*, stanza 1, *DG*, p. 119.
33. The original *Panj Piare* or 'Five Loved Ones' were the five Sikhs who responded to Guru Gobind Singh's call for sacrifice at the founding of the Khalsa and who were accordingly initiated as its first members (2.2.8[6–8]). These are the *Panj Piare* who are remembered in *Ardas*. After they had been initiated Guru Gobind Singh himself received baptism from their hands and all subsequent initiation ceremonies have been conducted by groups of five Sikhs. All such groups are similarly known as *Panj Piare*, as are those which are chosen to conduct any ceremony or decide any issue. The latter includes any allegation concerning serious breaches of the Khalsa code of discipline (the Rahit). Such allegations are judged by *Panj Piare* who have authority to impose appropriate punishment if a charge is proved.
34. The four sons of Guru Gobind Singh are reverently remembered as martyrs to their father's faith. The two elder sons, Ajit Singh and Jujhar Singh, fell

at the battle of Chamkaur in 1705. The two younger sons, Zorawar Singh and Fateh Singh, were executed soon afterwards by the Mughal governor of Sirhind. Khushwant Singh, *A History of the Sikhs*, vol. 1 (London, 1963), pp. 91–3.

35. During the siege of Anandpur, which preceded the battle of Chamkaur, forty of the Guru's followers deserted and returned to their homes. Shamed by their women they rejoined the Guru's force prior to the battle of Khidrana (or Muktsar) later in 1705 and were all killed. In recognition of their restored loyalty and subsequent sacrifice the Guru declared them to be *mukte,* men who had attained deliverance. Teja Singh and Ganda Singh, *A Short History of the Sikhs* (Bombay, 1950), pp. 72, 75. Most works in English refer to them as the forty 'Saved Ones'.

36. Teja Singh's translation of *Ardas* inserts the following cluster prior to the prayer for *takhts* and gurdwaras: 'Those who, to purge the temples of long-standing evils, suffered themselves to be ruthlessly beaten or imprisoned, to be shot, cut up, or burnt alive with kerosene oil, but did not make any resistance or utter even a sigh of complaint: think of their patient faith and call on God!' Teja Singh, *Sikhism* (Calcutta, 1951), p. 123. His footnotes indicate that this addition commemorates the struggles for control of the gurdwaras which took place during the years 1921–25. Teja Singh's translation is reproduced in Kanwaljit Kaur and Indarjit Singh, *Rehat Maryada: a guide to the Sikh way of life* (London, 1971), pp. 2–3.

37. Five of the major gurdwaras are designated *takhts,* or 'thrones', signifying a seat of temporal authority within the Panth. The principal 'throne' is Akal Takht which stands opposite the gateway to the Golden Temple in Amritsar. Early editions of *Sikh Rahit Maryada* refer to only four *takhts,* the remaining three located in Patna,

Anandpur and Nander. In recent years, however, the SGPC has declared Damdama Sahib (near Bhatinda) to be a fifth takht. This is acknowledged in the current edition of *Sikh Rahit Maryada.*

38. The remainder of *Ardas* differs considerably in the Teja Singh version, *op. cit.,* pp. 125–6.

39. This petition refers to gurdwaras located in Pakistan. The partition of 1947 separated the Panth from all its sacred places in the new State of Pakistan.

40. God is true!

41. *AG.,* p. 1193 (3.1.5[1–3]).

42. *AG.,* pp. 966–8. Rai Balvand and Satta the Dum served as bards in the Gurus' entourage over a period extending from the second to the fifth Guru. Their composition, which comprises eight stanzas, extols the achievements of the first five Gurus. It is also known as *Tikke di Var,* or the 'Coronation Ode'.

43. *AG.,* pp. 462–75.

44. For a summary of the theme of *Asa ki Var* see 7.6.2.

45. When two numbers follow a particular verse the first number designates the pauri and the second the number of the shalok. If there is only one number it indicates that the verse is a pauri. Shaloks precede the pauris to which they are attached.

46. For a discussion of the meaning of *haumai* and a literal translation of the first six lines of the shalok see *GNSR.,* pp. 181–4.

47. Men have mutilated the truth, with the result that it must fail to produce its fruits of enlightenment and peace.

48. The inclusion of a refrain *(rahau)* at this point indicates that shaloks 1 and 2 of pauri 12 are actually a shabad.

49. *AG.,* pp. 262–96.

50. In its original form each stanza consists of ten short lines. In this and subsequent stanzas most couplets have been rendered as single lines.

51. *dharam (dharma):* religious obliga-

tion, pattern of religious observance determined by one's caste.

52. In this volume the term is normally translated as either 'the company of the faithful' or as 'the company of the devout'. The usual translation is 'the company of the saints'. The term 'saint' is inappropriate for Sikh texts and carries powerful Christian connotations. Unless one is alert to the differences which distinguish the Christian 'saint' from the Indian *sant* or *sadh* the former usage is liable to direct readers to a definition charged with Christian content. See also 3.3.1[20–1].

53. Traditional piety assumes that purity requires the renunciation of family ties. The Sikh view is that purity can be attained within the context of the family (7.1[9]).

54. Guru Ram Das's hymn *Suhi Chhant* 2 is an integral part of the Sikh marriage ceremony (5.7.6.6); portions of Nit-nem are recited during the order for Khalsa initiation (4.5[38]); *Kirtan Sohila* forms a part of the funeral service (4.5[29]); and several rituals include the traditional selection of six stanzas from Guru Amar Das's *Ramkali Anand* (5.2.7).

55. Kahn Singh, *Gurumat Martand* (Amritsar, 1962), pp. 36–8.

56. Guru Arjan, *Bavan Akhari* 35:1, *AG.*, p. 257.

57. Guru Ram Das, *Siri Rag ki Var* 20, *AG.*, p. 91.

58. Guru Arjan, *Bilaval* 4:4, *AG.*, p. 802.

59. Guru Arjan, *Salok Sahiskriti* 52, *AG.*, p. 1358.

60. Guru Gobind Singh, *Akal Ustat* 248, *DG.*, p. 35.

61. *ramkar:* Rama's line. This is a reference from the *Ramayana*. While Rama was hunting in the forest his wife Sita was forbidden, for her own protection, to cross a line drawn in front of their hut. In this Adi Granth context it evidently designates *ram-nam*, the Name of God.

62. Guru Arjan, *Bilaval* 79, *AG.*, p. 819.

63. Guru Arjan, *Sorath* 77, *AG.*, p. 628.

64. Guru Arjan, *Asa* 101, *AG.*, p. 396.

65. Guru Arjan, *Var Jaitasari* 16, *AG.*, p. 709.

66. Guru Ram Das, *Asa Chhant* 15(4), *AG.*, p. 449.

67. Guru Arjan, *Ramkali ki Var* 1:1, *AG.*, p. 957.

68. Ravidas, the author of this shabad, was an outcaste (1.2[8], 3.1.6.3).

69. These five bhagats, though not outcastes, all belonged to castes which were regarded as inferior. Hymns by all five appear in the Adi Granth.

70. Ravidas, *Maru* 1, *AG.*, p. 1106.

71. Guru Ram Das, *Asa Chhant* 16(1), *AG.*, p. 449.

72. Literally, 'She is filled with truth, contentment and love when the matchmaker comes to offer a betrothal; I sacrifice myself to you O God.' The Guru is the intermediary who brings to the devout seeker God's offer of mystical union.

73. Guru Ram Das, *Suhi Chhant* 1(2), *AG.*, p. 773.

74. Guru Arjan, *Asa* 115, *AG.*, p. 399.

75. Guru Nanak, *Suhi Chhant* 2(1), *AG.*, p. 764.

76. Guru Nanak, *Suhi Chhant* 3(1), *AG.*, pp. 764–5.

77. Guru Amar Das, *Suhi Chhant* 1(4), *AG.*, p. 768.

78. Guru Amar Das, *Var Suhi* 9:3, *AG.*, p. 788.

79. Guru Nanak, *Tilang* 4, *AG.*, p. 722.

80. Farid, *Salok* 127, *AG.*, p. 1384.

81. Guru Arjan, *Asa Chhant* 7(2), *AG.*, p. 457.

82. Guru Nanak, *Var Maru* 5:2, *AG.*, p. 1088.

83. Guru Arjan, *Sorath* 26, *AG.*, p. 616.

84. Guru Gobind Singh, *Pakhyan Charitra* 21:51, *DG.*, p. 842.

85. *lav* (pl. *lavan):* the reverent circumambulation of a sacred scripture or fire. During the course of a Sikh wedding ceremony the couple walk around the Guru Granth Sahib four times, each round accompanied by a verse from Guru Ram Das's *Suhi*

Chhant 2 (4.5[27]).

86. *amrit-jal:* ambrosial water. According to tradition this hymn was composed to mark the completion of the sacred pool of Amritsar. *Sabadarath Sri Guru Granth Sahib Ji* (n.p., 1939), p. 783n (2.2.3[7]). It can also be read allegorically, with 'land' construed as the believer's body, 'lake' as his heart, and 'ambrosial water' as the divine Name. Sahib Singh, *Sri Guru Granth Sahib Darapan*, vol. 5 (Jalandhar, 1963), p. 629.

87. *ved purani:* the Vedas and the Puranas.

88. Guru Arjan, *Suhi Chhant* 10(1), *AG.*, p. 783.

89. Guru Ram Das, *Suhi Chhant* 3(4), *AG.*, p. 775.

90. Guru Arjan, *Ramkali ki Var Mahalla 5* 14:1, *AG.*, p. 963. During the course of the four *lavan* the bride holds the hem of the groom's garment (commonly a scarf or sash). The expression 'to grasp the hem' is also used to signify the trusting believer's total dependence on God.

91. Guru Arjan, *Gujari ki Var* 8:2, *AG.*, p. 520.

92. Literally, 'The utterances [of the Guru] are Brahma and the Veda.'

93. The Smritis.

94. Guru Ram Das, *Suhi Chhant* 2, *AG.*, pp. 773–4.

95. Guru Arjan, *Jaitasari Chhant* 1(4), *AG.*, p. 704.

96. Guru Ram Das, *Siri Ragu Chhant* 1(2), *AG.*, p. 78.

97. Guru Arjan, *Vadhans Chhant* 1(4), *AG.*, p. 577.

98. Sundar, *Ramkali Sadu* 5, *AG.*, p. 923.

99. Ravidas, *Suhi* 2, *AG.*, pp. 793–4.

100. Guru Tegh Bahadur, *Sorath* 12, *AG.*, p. 634.

101. Guru Tegh Bahadur, *Devagandhari* 2, *AG.*, p. 536.

102. Guru Tegh Bahadur, *Tilang* 2, *AG.*, pp. 726–7.

103. Guru Tegh Bahadur, *Devagandhari* 3, *AG.*, p. 536.

104. Guru Tegh Bahadur, *Gauri* 2, *AG.*,

p. 219.

6 DIVERSITY WITHIN THE PANTH

1. As a mark of respect the Guru Granth Sahib is either carried on the head of a bearer or in a palanquin (*palki*).

2. Pothohar is the area around Rawalpindi. Chhachh designates a portion of Attock District bordering the Indus river.

3. The Nirankari hukam-nama (6.1.2).

4. The central shrine (the Nirankari Darbar) was located within Rawalpindi. Outside the city a second shrine marked the spot where Baba Dayal's body had been consigned to the Lei stream. This was Dayalsar. It served as the Nirankari cremation ground until India was partitioned in 1947.

5. The central Nirankari shrine is now located in Chandigarh.

6. Sahib Hara Singh died on 15 January 1971 and was succeeded as Guru by his elder son Baba Gurbakhsh Singh. His younger son, Dr Man Singh Nirankari of Amritsar, also continues to occupy a prominent position in Nirankari affairs.

7. *Nirankari Gurmati Prarambhata*, ed. Baba Surindar Singh Nirankari (Amritsar, 1951), introduction, pp. 4–6.

8. This is the one point at which the Nirankari marriage ceremony differs from the standard order promulgated by the Singh Sabha reformers (4.5[27]).

9. *Nirankari Gurmati Prarambhata*, pp. 157–69. For a complete and more literal translation of the *Hukam-nama* see John C. B. Webster, *The Nirankaris* (Delhi, 1979), pp. 83–99. Dr Webster's translation includes the numerous proof texts incorporated in the *Hukam-nama*.

10. For an orthodox criticism of the Namdhari doctrine of the Guru see Ganda Singh, *Guru Gobind Singh's Death at Nanded* (Faridkot, 1972). The

Namdharis would, of course, reject the suggestion that they are unorthodox.

11. In 1705 Guru Gobind Singh, having evacuated Anandpur, was besieged with a small force in the village of Chamkaur. The traditional account of his escape from Chamkaur relates that a Sikh called Sant Singh donned the Guru's apparel in order to mislead the Mughal attackers. While a small remnant remained in the tiny fortress, pretending that they were a much larger force, the Guru slipped out while it was dark and evaded his pursuers.

12. A small town situated in northern Rajasthan, a short distance from the Haryana border.

13. A person called Ajapal Singh certainly moved from Bhadra to Nabha during the period indicated by this account, and eventually died in Nabha in 1812. *MK.*, p. 35. Needless to say, orthodox Sikhs dismiss the Namdhari claim that this was Guru Gobind Singh travelling incognito. Ganda Singh examines the claim at length in his *Guru Gobind Singh's Death at Nanded.*

14. Guru Arjan, *Sarang* 74, *AG.*, p. 1218.

15. From the birth of Guru Nanak to the death of Guru Gobind Singh.

16. Swaran Singh Sanehi, introduction to *Namdhari Nitnem* (Namdhari Darbar, Sri Bhaini Sahib, S. 2035 = 1978 A.C.) pp. 51–2, 55–6, 57–8, 61, 63–4, 69–71, 72.

17. *Kirtan Sohila*, 5.3.

18. Guru Nanak, *Var Majh* 7:2, *AG.*, p. 141.

19. A *jag* or *havan jag* is a purification ceremony designed to cleanse all evil thoughts from the minds of participants and replace them with a spirit of true piety. The ceremony consists of burning a sacred fire on which ghee and incense are cast to the accompaniment of prescribed passages from the Sikh scriptures.

20. *DG.*, pp. 119–27.

21. This work does not appear in the authorised version of the Dasam Granth, only in some manuscript copies. The text is given in *Namdhari Nitnem*, pp. 617–40.

22. This consists of 'a mixture of saffron, musk, sandalwood powder, sugar, ghee and about fifteen other such things'. Swaran Singh Sanehi, 'Kukas as they live', in John C. B. Webster (ed.), *Popular Religion in the Punjab Today* (Delhi, 1974), p. 34.

23. *Namdhari Nitnem*, introduction, pp. 113–17. The Namdhari rahit-nama was evidently circulated among the followers of Ram Singh in 1866. Nahar Singh, *Gooroo Ram Singh and the Kuka Sikhs* (New Delhi, 1965), p. 26.

24. The invocation in the Namdhari version of Ardas corresponds to the orthodox Sikh version (5.4[5]), thus honouring the requirement that this portion must never be changed. The last couplet is also the same as the orthodox version, with the significant difference that the name of Ram Singh is substituted for Nanak.

25. This refers to an incident in 1872 when a group of Kukas (Namdharis) were executed at Malerkotla after attacking a small fort in Ludhiana District. Forty-nine were executed without trial by the British official in charge of the district, and another sixteen were subsequently executed after a summary trial by his superior from Ambala. The executions were conducted by lashing each prisoner to a gun and then firing the gun.

26. Following the Malerkotla executions the government of India decided to crush the Kuka movement by transporting its leader Ram Singh and several of his followers.

27. *Namdhari Nitnem*, pp. 671–3.

28. For a vivid contemporary description of Ranjit Singh's Akali (Nihang) soldiers see W. G. Osborne, *The Court and Camp of Runjeet Singh* (London, 1840), pp. 143–7. The word 'Akali' now designates a member of the Sikh political party, the Akali Dal. It is seldom applied to Nihangs today.

29. *MK.*, p. 527.

30. Kahn Singh, *Gurumat Martand* (Amritsar, 1962), pp. 29–30. See also J. S. Badyal, 'The Nihang Singhs', in John C. B. Webster (ed.), *Popular Religion in the Punjab Today* (Delhi, 1974), pp. 40–5.

7 MODERN WORKS

1. This refers to the so-called Sahaj-dhari Sikhs, those who profess loyalty to the Gurus but do not seek initiation into the Khalsa. *ESC.*, p. 92n.

2. For a discussion of the doctrine of the *hukam* see *GNSR.*, pp. 199–203.
3. *AG.*, p. 940.
4. *GNSR.*, p. 184.
5. Guru Nanak, *Sorath* 11, *AG.*, p. 599.
6. *DG.*, p. 1387.
7. *AG.*, p. 1349.
8. *AG.*, p. 340.
9. *AG.*, p. 5.
10. *AG.*, p. 832.
11. *AG.*, p. 1057.
12. 'Praise! Praise!' or 'Wonderful! Marvellous!'
13. *AG.*, p. 14.
14. *AG.*, p. 938.

BIBLIOGRAPHY

TRANSLATIONS

Asa di Var, trans. Teja Singh, Amritsar, 1957.
The B40 Janam-Sakhi, trans. W. H. McLeod, Amritsar, 1980.
Bani of Sri Guru Amar Das, trans. Gurbachan Singh Talib, New Delhi, 1979.
Bhagat bani. Translations included in Jodh Singh, *Kabir* (Patiala, 1971), Charlotte Vaudeville, *Kabir* (Oxford, 1974), and Prabhakar Machwe, *Namdev* (Patiala, 1968).
Bhai Vir Singh: Poet of the Sikhs, trans. Gurbachan Singh Talib and Harbans Singh, with Yann Lovelock, Delhi, 1976.
The Epistle of Victory (Zafarnama), trans. Gursharn Singh Bedi, Amritsar, 1960.
Gospel of Guru Nanak in his own words, trans. Jodh Singh, Patiala, 1969.
Guru Gobind Singh's the Jap, trans. Trilochan Singh, Delhi, 1968.
Guru Granth Ratnavali (translations of selections from the Adi Granth into Hindi and English), Patiala, n.d.
Holy Nit-nem, trans. Rajinder Singh Vidyarthi, Singapore, n.d.

Hymns of Guru Nanak, trans. Khushwant Singh, New Delhi, 1969.
Hymns of Guru Tegh Bahadur, trans. Trilochan Singh, Delhi, 1975.
Japji. Translations of *Japji* include those by Teja Singh (Lahore, 1920), Jodh Singh (Amritsar, 1956), Khushwant Singh (London, n.d.), Harnam Singh (New Delhi, 1957), Gurdip Singh Randhawa and Charanjit Singh (New Delhi, 1970), Gursaran Singh (Delhi, 1972), Gurbachan Singh Talib (New Delhi, 1977) and Parkash Singh (Amritsar, 1978). Sohan Singh's *The Seeker's Path* (Calcutta, 1959) is a commentary on *Japji*.
The Psalm of Peace (Sukhmani), trans. Teja Singh, Madras, 1938.
Rehat Maryada: a guide to the Sikh way of life, trans. Kanwaljit Kaur and Indarjit Singh, London, 1971.
Rehat Maryada: a guide to the Sikh way of life, trans. anon., Amritsar, 1978.
Sacred Nitnem, trans. Harbans Singh Doabia, Amritsar, rev. ed., 1976.
Sacred Sukhmani, trans. Harbans Singh Doabia, Amritsar, 1979.
Selections from the Holy Granth, trans. Gurbachan Singh Talib, Delhi, 1975.

Selections from the Sacred Writings of the Sikhs, trans. Trilochan Singh, Jodh Singh, Kapur Singh, Harkishen Singh and Khushwant Singh, London, 1960.

Sources on the Life and Teachings of Guru Nanak, ed. Ganda Singh, Patiala, 1969.

Sri Guru-Granth Sahib, trans. Gopal Singh, 4 vols., Delhi, 1962.

Sri Guru Granth Sahib, trans. Manmohan Singh, 8 vols., Amritsar, 1962–69.

Sri Guru Tegh Bahadur Sahib: life history, sacred hymns and teachings, trans. Harbans Singh Doabia, Amritsar, 1975.

Thus Spake the Tenth Master, trans. Gopal Singh, Patiala, 1978.

Thus Spoke Guru Nanak, trans. Jogendra Singh, Amritsar, 2nd ed., 1967.

The Unique Drama, trans. Sant Singh Sekhon, Chandigarh, 1968.

OTHER WORKS

Barrier, N. G., The Sikhs and their Literature, Delhi, 1970

Bhai Vir Singh: life, times and works, ed. Gurbachan Singh Talib and Attar Singh, Chandigarh, 1973.

Cole, W. O., and Piara Singh Sambhi, The Sikhs: their religious beliefs and practices, London, 1978.

— Sikhism and its Indian Context 1469–1708, London, 1984.

— The Guru in Sikhism, London, 1982.

Fauja Singh, Guru Amar Das: life and teachings, New Delhi, 1979.

Fauja Singh and Gurbachan Singh Talib, Guru Tegh Bahadur: martyr and teacher, Patiala, 1975.

Ganda Singh, The Sikhs and their Religion, Redwood City, Cal., 1974.

Gobind Singh Mansukhani, Guru Ramdas: his life, work and philosophy, New Delhi, 1979.

Grewal, J. S., From Guru Nanak to Maharaja Ranjit Singh, Amritsar, 1972.

— Guru Nanak in History, Chandigarh, 1969.

Grewal, J. S., and Bal, S. S., Guru Gobind Singh, Chandigarh, 1967.

Harbans, Singh, Guru Gobind Singh, Chandigarh, 1966.

— Guru Nanak and the Origins of the Sikh Faith, Bombay, 1969.

Harbans Singh Doabia, Life Story of Siri Satguru Gobind Singh Ji Maharaj and some of his hymns, Amritsar, 1974.

Jogendra Singh, Sikh Ceremonies, Bombay, 1941, Chandigarh, 1968.

Johar, S. S., Handbook on Sikhism, Delhi, 1977.

— The Sikh Gurus and their Shrines, Delhi, 1976.

Juergensmeyer, M., and Barrier, N. G. (ed.), Sikh Studies: comparative perspectives on a changing tradition, Berkeley, 1979.

Kapur Singh, Parasharprasna, or the Baisakhi of Guru Gobind Singh, Jullundur, 1959.

Khushwant Singh, A History of the Sikhs, 2 vols., Princeton, N.J., 1963 and 1966.

Loehlin, C. H., The Granth of Guru Gobind Singh and the Khalsa Brotherhood, Lucknow, 1971.

— The Sikhs and their Scriptures, Lucknow, 1958.

Macauliffe, M. A., The Sikh Religion, 6 vols., Oxford, 1909, Delhi, 1963. (This work contains extensive translations from the Sikh scriptures.)

McLeod, W. H., Early Sikh Tradition: a study of the janam-sakhis, Oxford, 1980.

— The Evolution of the Sikh Community, Delhi, 1975, Oxford, 1976.

— Guru Nanak and the Sikh Religion, Oxford, 1968, Delhi, 1976.

Teja Singh, Sikhism: its ideals and institutions, Calcutta, 1951.

Thomas, T., Sikhism: the voice of the Guru, Milton Keynes, 1978.

Webster, John C. B., The Nirankari Sikhs, Delhi, 1979.

GLOSSARY

Ādi: first, orginal.

Akāl Purakh: the 'Timeless One', God.

akhaṇḍ pāṭh: continuous non-stop reading of the entire Adi Granth.

amrit: nectar, the water of immortality; sanctified water.

amrit-dhārī: one who has 'taken amrit', an initiated member of the Khalsa; cf. *sahaj-dhārī* (*q.v.*)

amrit-sanskār: the Khalsa rite of initiation.

anand: joy.

avatār: a 'descent', incarnation of a deity, usually Vishnu.

Bābā: 'Father', a term of respect applied to holy men.

bānī: speech; the utterances of the Gurus and bhagats (*q.v.*) recorded in the sacred scriptures; cf. *gurbānī* (*q.v.*)

bhagat: a devotee; in Sikh usage a composer of sacred songs (other than the Gurus) whose works appear in the Adi Granth.

Bhāī: 'Brother', a title applied to Sikhs of acknowledged learning or piety.

bhog: 'pleasure'; the conclusion of a complete reading of the Adi Granth.

Brahma: the Creator, first in the Hindu triad.

charan-āmrit: baptism with water in which the guru's toe has been dipped.

chaupāī: quatrain.

Chhīmbar: the calico-printer caste.

devī: goddess.

dharam (dharma): the appropriate moral and religious obligations attached to any particular status in Hindu society, religious belief and obligation.

dharamsālā: in early Sikh usage, a room or building used for devotional singing and prayer, later known as a gurdwara (*q.v.*).

dhotī: a cloth worn round the waist, passing between the legs and tucked in behind. Sikhs do not wear the dhotī; cf. *kachh* (*q.v.*).

dohārā: 'twofold'; a metre in Punjabi poetry.

faqīr: 'poor man'; Muslim renunciant; loosely used to designate Sufis and also non-Muslim renunciants.

gaddī: 'throne'; temporal or spiritual authority.

ghazal: ode; love poem or love song.

gopī: milkmaid; female companion of Krishna.

granth: book.

granthī: professional reader of the Sikh scriptures; custodian of a gurdwara (*q.v.*).

gurbānī: 'the Guru's utterances', the contents of the Sikh scriptures; cf. *bānī* (*q.v.*).

gur-bilās: hagiographic treatment of the lives of the Gurus emphasising their heroic qualities and sense of destiny.

gurduārā: Sikh temple.

Gur-mantra: a mantra of particular significance bestowed by a guru on his disciples.

Gurmat: the Sikh religion; Sikh doctrine.

Gurmukhī: the script used for writing Punjabi.

Gursikh: a Sikh of the Guru; a loyal Sikh.

haṭha-yoga: 'yoga of force', a variety of yoga requiring physical postures and processes of extreme difficulty.

haumai: self; self-centredness.

hukam: command; the divine order of the universe.

hukam-nāmā: a decree; a list of instructions.

Indra: the Vedic god of the firmament, chief of the gods.

janam-sākhī: hagiographic narrative, especially of the life of Guru Nanak.

jap: devout repetition of a mantra, divine name, passage from scripture, etc.

Jhīnvar: the potter and water-carrier caste.

kabitt: a poetic metre.

kachh, kachhahirā: a pair of shorts (mandatory attire for all members of the Khalsa).

Kaliyuga: the fourth and last of the cosmic ages (*yuga, q.v.*); the age of degeneracy.

kanghā: the comb which members of the Khalsa are required to wear in their *kes* (*q.v.*).

karā: the steel bangle which members of the Khalsa are required to wear.

karāh prasād: sacramental food dispensed in gurdwaras.

karorī: a high-ranking revenue collector of the Mughal period.

kathā: oral commentary on sacred scriptures; narrating of pious anecdotes; homily.

kes; uncut hair

kes-dhārī: one who keeps his hair uncut.

Khatrī: a mercantile caste, particularly important in the Punjab.

kirpān: sword or dagger (mandatory for members of the Khalsa).

kīrtan: the singing of devotional songs.

Kshatriya: the warrior division of the classical fourfold caste hierarchy.

lāvān: the reverent circumambulation of a sacred scripture or fire.

maryādā: custom, approved conduct.

masand: a regional supervisor. The Gurus delegated pastoral and tithe-collecting responsibilities to masands. During the course of the seventeenth century they became increasingly independent and were eventually disowned by Guru Gobind Singh.

māyā: (in Vedant) cosmic illusion; (in Sikh usage) the corruptible and corrupting world, with all its snares, presented to man as permanent and incorruptible and so masquerading as ultimate truth.

mūl mantra: Mool Mantra, the Basic Credal Statement with which the Adi Granth begins.

Nāī: the barber caste.

nām: the divine Name. See pp. 39–41.

nām japaṇ: repeating names of God, sacred texts, passages from scripture, etc.

nām simaraṇ: repeating passages from scripture, etc.; meditating on the divine Name.

namāz: Muslim prayer, especially the prescribed daily prayers.

Nāth: lit. 'Master'. A yogic sect of considerable influence in the Punjab prior to and during the time of the early Sikh Gurus. Its members, who are also known as Kanphat yogis, practised *haṭha-yoga* (*q.v.*) in order to obtain immortality.

Nirankār: the 'Formless One', God.

nishan (nisān): symbol, flag, standard.

nit-nem: the 'Daily Rule', portions of scripture appointed for daily recitation.

panth: lit. 'path'; system of religious belief and practice. Spelt with a capital P it designates the Sikh community. Its pronunciation is very close to the English word 'punt'.

panthic (panthik): concerning the Panth (*q.v.*).

patit: 'fallen'; an apostate Sikh, one who having accepted initiation into the Khalsa subsequently violates the Rahit (*q.v.*) in some important respect (especially by cutting hair or smoking).

paurī: stanza.

pīr: the head of a Sufi order; a Sufi saint.

pothī: volume, tome.

pūjā: Hindu worship.

pundit (paṇḍit): an erudite person; a mode of address used for Brahmans.

qāzī: a Muslim judge, administrator of Islamic law.

rāga: a series of five or more notes on which a melody is based.

rāgī: a musician employed to sing in a gurdwara (*q.v.*).

Rahit: the Khalsa code of conduct.

rahit-nāmā: a manual of the Rahit (*q.v.*).

sabhā: society.

sādhu: renunciant.

sahaj: the condition of ultimate, inexpressible beatitude; the ultimate state of mystical union.

sahaj-dhārī: a Sikh who neither accepts initiation into the Khalsa nor observes the full Rahit (*q.v.*).

sākhī: section of a janam-sakhi (*q.v.*).

sangat: assembly, religious congregation.

Satgurū: the 'True Guru', the supreme Guru.

satsang: the fellowship of true believers, congregation.

savayyā: a musical measure.

shabad (śabad): (1) the divine Word; (2) a hymn from the Adi Granth.

shalok (ślok): couplet or stanza.

Shiv, Shiva (Siva): the Destroyer, third in the Hindu triad.

shradh (śrādh): rite commemorating deceased forbear.

Shudra: the fourth section of the classical fourfold caste hierarchy.

Siddh: eighty-four exalted personages believed to have attained immortality through the practice of yoga and to be dwelling deep in the Himalayas. The term is commonly confused with Nath (*q.v.*).

simaraṇ: nām simaraṇ (q.v.).

takht: 'throne'; one of the Panth's centres of temporal authority. See p. 104.

tīrath: a place of pilgrimage for Hindus.

Vāhigurū: God.

Vaish(ya): the third section of the classical fourfold caste hierarchy.

vār: a heroic ode of several stanzas; a song of praise. See pp. 105–6.

Vishnu: the Sustainer, second in the Hindu triad.

yuga: cosmic era.

INDEX

WITHDRAWN
UNIV OF MOUNT UNION LIBRARY